COOK HEALTHY
Cook Quick

COOK HEALTHY
Cook Quick

Oxmoor House®

Library of Congress Catalog Card Number: 94-67753
ISBN: 0-8487-1424-5

Manufactured in the United States of America
First Printing 1994

∿

Editor-in-Chief: Nancy J. Fitzpatrick
Senior Foods Editor: Katherine M. Eakin
Senior Editor, Editorial Services: Olivia Kindig Wells
Art Director: James Boone

Cook Healthy, Cook Quick

Editor: Cathy A. Wesler, R.D.
Assistant Editor: Kathryn L. Matuszak, R.D.
Copy Editor: Cecilia C. Robinson
Editorial Assistants: Keri Bradford, Rebecca Meng Sommers
Contributing Writer: Nao Hauser
Indexer: Holly Ensor

Director, Test Kitchens: Kathleen Royal
Assistant Director, Test Kitchens: Gayle Hays Sadler
Test Kitchen Home Economists: Susan Hall Bellows,
Christina A. Crawford, Iris Crawley, Michele B. Fuller,
Elizabeth Luckett, Angie N. Sinclair, Jan A. Smith
Recipe Developers: Julie Fisher; Caroline A. Grant, M.S., R.D.;
Debby Maugans; Susan McIntosh, M.S., R.D.

Senior Photographer: Jim Bathie
Photographer: Ralph Anderson
Senior Photo Stylist: Kay E. Clarke
Photo Stylist: Virginia R. Cravens
Designer: Carol Middleton
Publishing Systems Administrator: Rick Tucker
Director of Production and Distribution: Phillip Lee
Production Manager: Gail H. Morris
Associate Production Manager: Theresa L. Beste
Production Assistant: Marianne Jordan

∿

Cover: *Chicken Reuben Rolls (page 145)*
Page 1: *Ambrosia Parfaits (page 99)*
Page 2: *Marinated Beef Kabobs (page 134)*
Back cover: *Peach Trifle (page 100), Creole Red Snapper (page 158),*
Fresh Tomato Spaghetti (page 127), Italian Pasta and Bean
Soup (page 32), Black Bean Empanaditas (page 53)

∿

CONTENTS

Delicious Food—Healthy and Quick   7

Quick Family Meals   13

Quick Entertaining Meals   31

Appetizers and Beverages   45

Breads   63

Desserts   81

Meatless Main Dishes   113

Meats, Poultry, and Seafood   131

Salads and Salad Dressings   163

Side Dishes   187

Soups and Sandwiches   215

Index   235

Acknowledgments and Credits   240

page 159

page 32

page 188

page 106

page 228

Foods editors
Cathy Wesler
(left) and
Kate Matuszak
make final changes
to the recipe for
Spicy Skillet
Steaks (page 135).

DELICIOUS FOOD—HEALTHY & QUICK

Delicious. Healthy. Fast. Now there's a combination you can appreciate when it comes to getting dinner on the table. And if that's your aim, then this is the cookbook for you. Browse through the recipes and you'll find that they were developed specifically to satisfy your need for great-tasting recipes that can be prepared quickly. So take a look at how our recipes are uniquely designed for speed. You'll find:

■ **A photograph with every recipe.**

■ **Easy recipes.** Hands-on preparation takes no longer than 30 minutes. And preparation and cooking times and, when appropriate, marinating and chilling times are included for easy menu planning.

■ **Short ingredient lists and simple cooking directions.**

■ **Ingredients grouped according to the cooking step.** Procedures are clear and simple to follow; your eye won't jump back and forth while your hands are busy.

■ **Low-fat convenience products are used.** These help to short-cut cooking and keep recipes healthy and savory.

■ **Easy-to-read nutritional analysis provided for each serving.**

USING NUTRIENT DATA

We've incorporated guidelines of good nutrition, too. In each nutrient analysis, we include calories, grams of fat, saturated fat, carbohydrate, fiber, and protein, along with milligrams of cholesterol and sodium.

The nutrient figures for meats are based on meat trimmed of fat and skinned before cooking. When a range for any ingredient is given, the nutrient data reflects the lesser amount. And only the amounts of alcohol and marinade that remain in the food after cooking are calculated. For fruits and vegetables, the nutrients are figured on unpeeled versions, unless specified otherwise.

All of the menus and nearly every recipe have less than 30 percent of the calories from fat. The few exceptions actually contain only a few grams of fat, but the fat percentages calculate higher.

CUT FAT, NOT FLAVOR

"This is just delicious!" is what you'll hear when you serve these recipes. You may be surprised at how we've cut the fat and calories without eliminating flavor. But our home economists and registered dietitians who tasted every recipe can attest to it. Many couldn't wait for the book to be printed so they could use it in their own busy lives!

We'll let you in on a couple of our favorites. The biggest hit was Jamaican Chili (page 115) at 266 calories and only 2.5 grams of fat. And it was a treat to know that we could bite into a Butterscotch Brownie (page 87) at just 115 calories and a mere 3.3 grams of fat.

No one will ever know how quick and easy it was for you to prepare these mouth-watering, healthy recipes. We hope you'll agree!

A WELL-ORGANIZED KITCHEN

Arrange equipment, utensils, and food for easy access and quick cooking.

TO STORE EQUIPMENT AND UTENSILS:

KEEP IT HANDY...

■ Use decorative jars to store the following items near the cooktop: wooden spoons; metal spatulas; plastic scrapers; whisks; a ladle; tongs; a baster and brush; long-handled cooking spoons and forks; a can opener; cutting tools, including peelers, kitchen scissors, a hand grater, and a garlic press; and measuring tools, including a 6-inch plastic ruler.

■ Keep awkwardly shaped equipment, such as a collapsible steamer basket, in a drawer with pot lids, and mount others—an electric hand-held mixer and similar items—on the wall.

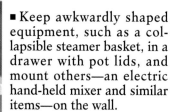

■ Keep all small measuring items together: toss the spoons into a 2-cup glass measure, or organize with plastic drawer dividers.

■ Store knives on a magnetic rack above the counter or in a block on the counter.

■ Leave often used items such as a food processor, a kitchen timer, or a blender out on the counter. Less frequently used items can be stored out of sight but within easy reach.

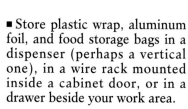

■ Store plastic wrap, aluminum foil, and food storage bags in a dispenser (perhaps a vertical one), in a wire rack mounted inside a cabinet door, or in a drawer beside your work area.

■ Hang pot holders next to both the stove and the microwave oven.

KEEP IT NEAT...

■ Mount a coffee maker, paper towel holder, and other compact equipment under the cabinets to save space and clutter.

■ Hang your most often used skillets and saucepans on the wall, a pegboard, or hanging hooks within easy reach. If you can't hang pot lids, put them all in one drawer, or stand them in a wire dish drainer in an under-the-counter cabinet along with baking sheets and pans, cake and pie pans, muffin pans, and cooling racks.

■ Store dishes on sturdy plastic-coated shelf-stackers that provide space underneath to stack smaller plates, bowls, or cups.

■ Canisters for flour and sugar save counter space. Place a dry measuring cup in each canister to use as a handy scoop.

THROW IT OUT...

■ Get rid of storage containers without lids, pot lids with no matching pots, and any pan or utensil so flimsy that you can't use it.

■ Get rid of damaged or broken equipment or utensils and any item you haven't used in the last two years.

To Store Food:

IN THE PANTRY . . .

- Keep as many labels as possible in plain sight for at-a-glance inventory.

- Consider hanging wire racks inside cabinet doors to hold spices and other small items. Or use plastic turntables and expandable shelves, which are especially useful for storing spices, flavorings, condiments, and other ingredients in small containers.

- Group similar staples by function; for example, store baking supplies in one place.

- Rotate older items to the front to use first. Although canned goods and other shelf-stable items will keep at least six months, they do begin to deteriorate after that, especially if the temperature in the pantry rises above 70 degrees.

IN THE REFRIGERATOR . . .

- Keep a pad of paper with a pencil held to the door with kitchen magnets, and list ingredients that need replenishing. (Do the same for the freezer and pantry, too.)

- Maintain an orderly refrigerator. It saves time and cuts down on food waste. Keep most often used items up front and in the door racks. Take stock every few weeks, and throw out what you don't use.

- For safety's sake, be sure to store meat, poultry, and fish in the coldest part of the refrigerator—either in the designated meat drawer or close to the cooling/freezing element.

- Store vegetables whole, unpeeled, and uncut to keep them fresh longer.

- Store washed and torn salad greens in the salad spinner, or wrap them loosely in paper towels and place them in an open plastic bag.

- You can keep homemade salad dressing in the refrigerator at least a couple of days, and commercially bottled dressing up to several months.

- Refrigerate all other leftover prepared food—either homemade or canned, such as broth or tomato sauce—no longer than two or three days; if it won't be consumed in that time, freeze it.

IN THE FREEZER . . .

- Label and date everything. Then rotate packages toward the front or the top of the freezer according to date.

- Keep a running inventory of your freezer contents for efficient meal planning.

- Always store food in small quantities. Cut up chicken, steaks, or chops, and wrap each piece individually before storing in the freezer. Then any number of pieces can be removed with ease.

- Shape ground beef into patties or balls and wrap individually before freezing. There is no need to thaw them before cooking.

- If the freezer is kept at 0 degrees or colder, you can keep prepared foods and ground beef up to two months, chicken and turkey parts three months, and commercially frozen fruits and vegetables a year.

- You cut storage time in half if the freezer temperature is a mere 10 degrees warmer, so use a freezer thermometer.

- Chop and freeze ½-cup quantities of onions, peppers, and parsley in zip-top freezer bags. Shred and freeze cheese in zip-top freezer bags.

STREAMLINED SHOPPING

Here's how to keep your kitchen stocked for cooking healthy in a hurry.

MAKE ONE SHOPPING TRIP LAST A WEEK:

■ **Plan weekly menus to include your family's favorite recipes.** Begin by taking inventory of your pantry, refrigerator, and freezer, and then plan meals around what you have on hand, including leftovers. Fill in the "holes" with new recipes.

SHOPPING LIST

skimmed milk
plain yogurt
egg substitute
Island bread
honey
chicken breasts, broad
dried apricots
apples
frozen broccoli
black bean
cooking spray
apple juice
green chilis
balsamic vinegar
Dijon mustard

■ **Write out a list as you plan menus,** before shopping, so you won't be missing any ingredients when you begin cooking. Try to stick with the shopping list to avoid impulse buying.

■ **Always check dates** to be sure you're buying the freshest packages—those with the latest dates.

■ **For convenience, use frozen vegetables,** such as asparagus spears, broccoli, green beans, and sliced carrots, instead of fresh.

VEGETABLE STORAGE TIME

Food	Storage Time
Leaf lettuce Spinach	Two days
Asparagus Green beans	Three days
Broccoli Cauliflower Mushrooms Red pepper Snow peas	Four days
Corn Green peppers Summer squash Zucchini	Five days
Cabbage Carrots Iceberg lettuce Turnips	One week
Acorn and other winter squash Potatoes Onions Sweet potatoes	Two weeks

SHOP WISELY:

■ **Buy ingredients in closest-to-usable form.** Choose such items as

    skinned, boned chicken breasts
    shredded cheese
    a jar of minced garlic
    bags of prewashed spinach and cole slaw mix
    packaged carrot sticks

The same logic should lead you straight to your supermarket's salad bar, where you may be able to buy broccoli flowerets ready to steam or stir-fry, greens ready for tossing, melons cut up for dessert, and other shortcut produce.

■ **Learn your supermarket layout** so that you won't have to backtrack for something you forgot.

■ **Buy only as much as you can use.** It's not a bargain if you use a small amount and throw the rest away.

■ **Check unit pricing.** Consider the cost per serving or per unit cost of the different sizes of a product. Buy in bulk only if it's a bargain and you have the space to store it.

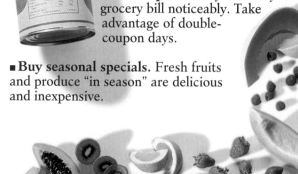

LOW SODIUM WHITE VINEGAR
READ PRODUCT LABEL
YOU PAY
89.0¢ 89¢

■ **Read labels** to compare nutrition information and grades of the product.

■ **Use coupons**—they can cut your grocery bill noticeably. Take advantage of double-coupon days.

■ **Buy seasonal specials.** Fresh fruits and produce "in season" are delicious and inexpensive.

STAPLE INGREDIENTS CHECKLIST

IN THE PANTRY:
These ingredients will keep six months to one year.

BAKING SUPPLIES

Biscuit and baking mix, fat-free
Baking powder
Baking soda
Chocolate, semisweet mini-morsels
Cocoa, unsweetened
Cornstarch
Flours: all-purpose
    cake
    whole wheat
Milk: nonfat dry milk powder
    canned evaporated skimmed milk
Oats, quick-cooking
Oils: vegetable
    olive
Sugar: granulated
    powdered
    light brown
Sweeteners: honey
    light-colored corn syrup
Vegetable cooking spray: plain
    buttered flavored
    olive oil-flavored

FRUITS AND VEGETABLES

Dried fruit: apricots
    apples
    prunes
    raisins
Fruits, canned, in light syrup or in
  juice: apricot halves
    whole berry cranberry sauce
    mandarin oranges
    sliced peaches
    pear halves
    crushed pineapple
    unsweetened applesauce
Juices, unsweetened: apple
    grape
Tomato products, no-salt-added:
    whole tomatoes
    sauce
    paste
    juice
    low-fat pasta sauce
Tomatoes, sun-dried
Vegetables, canned: green chiles
    ripe olives
    pimientos
    pumpkin
    roasted red pepper in water
    water chestnuts

GRAINS, LEGUMES, AND PASTAS

Beans, canned, no-salt-added if
  available: black
    black-eyed peas
    garbanzos (chick peas)
    kidney
    navy
    pinto
    red
Bulgar
Couscous
Lentils, dried
Pasta, dry: spaghetti
    fettuccine (plain or spinach)
    elbow macaroni
    egg noodles
Rice: long-grain white and brown
    instant white and brown

CONDIMENTS AND SEASONINGS

Italian dressing, oil-free
Jams, no-sugar-added: apple jelly
    orange marmalade
    raspberry spread
Mayonnaise, light or nonfat
Mustard: prepared
    Dijon
    honey
Seasoning sauces: hot sauce
    reduced-calorie catsup
    no-salt-added salsa
    low-sodium soy sauce
    low-sodium Worcestershire sauce
Vinegars: white
    balsamic
    cider

MISCELLANEOUS

Bouillon granules: beef-flavor
    chicken-flavor
Broth, canned: low-sodium beef
    low-sodium chicken
    vegetable
Crackers, fat-free
Garlic-in-a-jar
Gelatin, unflavored
Graham crackers
Peanut butter, reduced-fat
Tuna, canned in water

IN THE REFRIGERATOR:
These items will keep
at least a week, but check freshness
dates before purchasing.

Seasonings, for convenience:
    fresh jalapeño chiles
    gingerroot, cut into 1/2-inch pieces
Eggs
Nonfat buttermilk
Reduced-fat Cheddar and
    other semi-firm cheeses
Light process cream cheese product
Grated Parmesan cheese
Lite ricotta cheese
Nonfat sour cream alternative
Plain nonfat yogurt
Stick margarine

IN THE FREEZER:
These items can be frozen
two months to one year if kept at
0 degrees or colder.

Frozen egg substitute
Juice concentrates: orange
    lemonade
    grape
Phyllo pastry
Vanilla nonfat frozen yogurt
Fruits, unsweetened: blueberries
    peaches
    raspberries
    strawberries
Vegetables: asparagus
    green beans
    broccoli
    carrots
    whole kernel corn
    lima beans
    chopped onions
    English peas
    snow pea pods
    chopped peppers
    spinach
Breads: French loaves
    hamburger buns
    corn and flour tortillas
Frozen cooked salad shrimp
Skinned, boned chicken breast halves

SPEEDY ACTION

Maximize time and minimize cleanup to cook healthy *and* cook quick.

COOK QUICK

○ Use two sets of measuring cups so you can measure consecutive ingredients without washing or wiping out the measure repeatedly.

○ Measure dry ingredients before moist ones to minimize clean-up. Before measuring honey and other sticky ingredients, rinse the measure with cold water first; then the honey will slide right out.

○ Chop an ingredient only once, even if it's called for in more than one step. For example, if you need one tablespoon of chopped parsley in a meat mixture and another in a sauce, it can be cut for both steps at the same time.

○ Buy the best-quality knives you can afford, since they will probably last a lifetime. Keep your knives sharp. Cutting is much quicker with a sharp blade.

○ Use two cutting boards to hold separately chopped ingredients without your having to transfer them.

○ Use a food processor to chop, slice, or shred several ingredients together or consecutively without washing the workbowl if they will later be combined. The mini-chopper is good for small quantities of fresh herbs or garlic and other frequently used ingredients to refrigerate or freeze for later use.

○ When baking or roasting, remember to preheat the oven before you assemble the recipe; if you forget, it will take the oven about 20 minutes to reach the specified temperature.

○ Use a microwave for thawing foods quickly or for shortcuts such as softening or melting margarine.

○ Use nonstick skillets, saucepans, and baking pans, which require less oil for cooking and are easy to clean.

○ Chop canned tomatoes right in the can with kitchen scissors, and use a pizza cutter for cutting dough and bread into small pieces.

CLEAN UP FAST!

■ Clean up as you go along. This saves time and makes the work easier.

■ When broiling, put foil in the bottom of the broiler pan and grease the broiler grid to prevent sticking.

■ Wipe greasy knives with a paper towel before washing for quicker cleaning.

■ If you happen to burn or scorch food in a pan, sprinkle the burned area liberally with baking soda, and then add just enough water to moisten it. Let it stand for several hours; the burned portion should lift right out of the pan.

■ Rub a cut lemon or lime half on your cutting board, and then wash in soapy water to get rid of onion, garlic, or fish odors.

BASIC EQUIPMENT CHECKLIST FOR QUICK COOKING

2 dishwasher-safe cutting boards

2 sets of dry and liquid measuring cups

2 sets of measuring spoons

Broiler pan, broiler pan rack

Colander

Fat separator

Food processor/mini-chopper

Good quality chef's, paring, and slicing knives

Hand mixer

Meat thermometer (instant read)

Nonstick skillets, saucepans, and baking pans

Pizza cutter, vegetable peelers, kitchen scissors

Steam basket or steamer

Wire grilling basket

Wok

QUICK
FAMILY MEALS

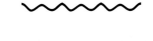

page 18

page 22

page 28

Lunch on the Bayou
Cajun-Spiced Chicken   14
Spicy Bow Ties   15
Vanilla Pudding   15

Cool Summer Lunch
Grilled Pork and Rice Salad   16
Oat Bran Muffins   17
Apricot-Pear Crisp   17

Down-Home Delicious
Molasses-Sauced Chicken   18
Creamy Garlic Potatoes   19
Fancy Peas   19

A Family Affair
Grouper Fingers with Lemon-Pepper Mayonnaise   20
Savory Rice   21
Green Beans in Tomato Sauce   21

Vegetarian Cuisine
Caribbean Rice and Beans   22
Mustard-Glazed Broiled Tomatoes   23
Tropical Cooler   23

Sunday Night Supper
Penne Pasta with Tomato Cream   24
Spinach Salad with Creamy Italian Dressing   25
Bananas Foster   25

Festive Family Supper
Ground Beef and Noodle Bake   26
Mixed Green Salad with Dijon Dressing   27
Hot Fudge Sundae   27

Kids in Charge
Sloppy Joes   28
Sweet Potato Sticks   29
Chocolate Cupcakes   29
Creamy Raspberry Frost   30
Creamy Orange Frost   30
Creamy Strawberry Frost   30

Lunch on the Bayou

Total calories per serving: 626
Calories from fat: 15%

Cajun-Spiced Chicken

Spicy Bow Ties

Commercial French rolls
(1 each)

Vanilla Pudding

*Lunch on the table
in 50 minutes*

Cajun-Spiced Chicken

½ teaspoon dried Italian seasoning
½ teaspoon paprika
½ teaspoon ground red pepper
¼ teaspoon onion powder
¼ teaspoon garlic powder
¼ teaspoon ground white pepper
¼ teaspoon freshly ground black pepper

4 (4-ounce) skinned, boned chicken breast halves

2 teaspoons olive oil

1 Combine first 7 ingredients in a heavy-duty, zip-top plastic bag. Place one chicken breast half in bag; seal bag, and shake until chicken is well coated. Remove chicken, and repeat procedure with remaining chicken.

2 Heat olive oil in a large nonstick skillet over medium heat until hot. Add chicken, and cook 3 to 4 minutes on each side or until lightly browned. Yield: 4 servings.

Nutritional content per serving: Calories 149
Fat 3.8g (Sat Fat 0.7g) Carbohydrate 0.9g Fiber 0.2g
Protein 26.4g Cholesterol 66mg Sodium 74mg

Spicy Bow Ties

Vegetable cooking spray
1 teaspoon vegetable oil
1 small sweet red pepper, seeded and chopped
½ cup frozen English peas, thawed
2 green onions, cut into 1-inch pieces

⅔ cup nonfat sour cream alternative
2 tablespoons skim milk
⅛ to ¼ teaspoon ground red pepper
⅛ teaspoon chili powder
2 to 4 drops of hot sauce
1 clove garlic, crushed

4 ounces bow tie pasta, uncooked

1 Coat a large nonstick skillet with cooking spray; add oil. Place over medium-high heat until hot. Add sweet red pepper and peas; sauté 2 to 3 minutes or until vegetables are crisp-tender. Add green onions, and sauté 30 seconds or until onions are barely limp. Remove from heat, and keep warm.

2 Combine sour cream and next 5 ingredients in a small bowl; stir well. Set aside.

3 Cook pasta according to package directions, omitting salt and fat; drain well. Place pasta in a serving bowl. Add vegetable mixture and sour cream mixture; toss gently. Serve immediately. Yield: 4 (¾-cup) servings.

Nutritional content per serving: Calories 176
Fat 2.0g (Sat Fat 0.2g) Carbohydrate 28.9g Fiber 1.1g
Protein 8.1g Cholesterol 0mg Sodium 62mg

Vanilla Pudding

½ cup sugar
2½ tablespoons cornstarch
⅛ teaspoon salt
2 cups skim milk
1 egg, lightly beaten

1 tablespoon reduced-calorie stick margarine
2 teaspoons vanilla extract

Edible snapdragons (optional)

1 Combine first 3 ingredients in a heavy saucepan. Combine milk and egg; stir well. Add to dry ingredients. Cook over medium heat, stirring constantly, until pudding mixture comes to a boil.

2 Remove pudding mixture from heat; stir in margarine and vanilla. Pour mixture into 4 (6-ounce) custard cups. Cover with plastic wrap, gently pressing directly on pudding. Chill at least 45 minutes. Garnish with snapdragons, if desired. Yield: 4 (½-cup) servings.

Nutritional content per serving: Calories 201
Fat 3.3g (Sat Fat 0.8g) Carbohydrate 36.4g Fiber 0g
Protein 5.8g Cholesterol 58mg Sodium 182mg

Meal Plan for Lunch on the Bayou:

■ Make Vanilla Pudding; chill.
■ Prepare Spicy Bow Ties through step 2. Begin step 3.
■ While pasta is cooking, prepare Cajun-Spiced Chicken. Toss cooked pasta with reserved vegetable mixture and sour cream mixture.
■ Cut commercial French rolls into ¼-inch-thick slices. Spray tops with butter-flavored vegetable cooking spray. Broil until crisp and lightly browned.

Cool Summer Lunch

Total calories per serving: 518
Calories from fat: 29%

Grilled Pork and Rice Salad

Oat Bran Muffins

Apricot-Pear Crisp

*Lunch on the table
in 60 minutes*

Grilled Pork and Rice Salad

3 (4-ounce) lean boneless center-cut loin pork
    chops (½ inch thick)

2 tablespoons low-sodium soy sauce
1 tablespoon grated fresh gingerroot
½ teaspoon ground cloves
2 large cloves garlic, crushed

    Vegetable cooking spray

2½ cups cooked instant long-grain rice (cooked
    without salt or fat)
1 cup diced purple plums
¾ cup diced sweet yellow pepper
¼ cup chopped green onions

2½ tablespoons lime juice
2 tablespoons low-sodium soy sauce
1 tablespoon olive oil
1 tablespoon honey

1 head Bibb lettuce

1 Trim fat from pork.

2 Combine 2 tablespoons soy sauce and next 3 ingredients; stir well. Brush mixture evenly over both sides of pork chops. Cover and chill 30 minutes.

3 Coat grill rack with cooking spray; place rack on grill over medium-hot coals (350° to 400°). Place pork on rack; grill, uncovered, 3 to 4 minutes on each side. Let pork cool slightly; cut into ½-inch pieces.

4 Combine pork, rice, and next 3 ingredients in a large bowl; toss well. Combine lime juice and next 3 ingredients. Drizzle over pork mixture, and toss gently. Cover and chill until ready to serve.

5 Spoon salad evenly onto individual lettuce-lined salad plates. Yield: 6 (1-cup) servings.

Nutritional content per serving: Calories 198
Fat 8.0g (Sat Fat 2.2g) Carbohydrate 19g Fiber 1.2g
Protein 11.7g Cholesterol 34mg Sodium 290mg

Oat Bran Muffins

1¼ cups oat bran hot cereal, uncooked
2 tablespoons firmly packed brown sugar
½ teaspoon baking powder
⅛ teaspoon salt

¼ cup plus 2 tablespoons skim milk
¼ cup frozen egg substitute, thawed
2 tablespoons honey
1 teaspoon vegetable oil

Vegetable cooking spray

1 Combine first 4 ingredients in a large bowl; make a well in center of mixture.

2 Combine milk and next 3 ingredients; add to dry mixture, stirring just until dry ingredients are moistened.

3 Spoon into muffin pans coated with cooking spray, filling three-fourths full. Bake at 425° for 15 minutes or until golden. Yield: 6 muffins.

Nutritional content per muffin: Calories 117
Fat 2.3g (Sat Fat 0.2g) Carbohydrate 22.4g Fiber 2.7g
Protein 5.5g Cholesterol 0mg Sodium 72mg

Apricot-Pear Crisp

1 (29-ounce) can pear halves in light syrup, drained
1 (16-ounce) can apricot halves in juice, drained
2 tablespoons golden raisins
Vegetable cooking spray

½ cup quick-cooking oats, uncooked
¼ cup all-purpose flour
¼ cup firmly packed brown sugar
⅛ teaspoon ground allspice
3 tablespoons margarine

1 Coarsely chop pear and apricot halves. Combine chopped fruit and raisins; spoon into an 8-inch square baking dish coated with cooking spray.

2 Combine oats and next 3 ingredients; cut in margarine with a pastry blender until mixture resembles coarse meal. Sprinkle oat mixture over fruit. Bake at 375° for 30 minutes or until golden. Yield: 6 servings.

Nutritional content per serving: Calories 203
Fat 6.3g (Sat Fat 1.2g) Carbohydrate 36.9g Fiber 3.0g
Protein 2.2g Cholesterol 0mg Sodium 76mg

Meal Plan for Cool Summer Lunch:

- Cook rice and complete steps 1 and 2 for Grilled Pork and Rice Salad.
- Make Oat Bran Muffins.
- Turn oven to 375°. Prepare Apricot-Pear Crisp. While crisp is baking, chop plums, pepper, and onions for pork salad.
- Complete steps 3, 4, and 5 for pork salad.

Down-Home Delicious

Total calories per serving: 482
Calories from fat: 24%

Molasses-Sauced Chicken
Creamy Garlic Potatoes
Fancy Peas

Dinner on the table
in 55 minutes

Molasses-Sauced Chicken

¼ **cup chopped green onions**
¼ **cup low-sodium soy sauce**
¼ **cup Burgundy or other dry red wine**
2½ **tablespoons molasses**
1 **tablespoon vegetable oil**
½ **teaspoon ground cumin**
½ **teaspoon ground red pepper**

6 **(6-ounce) skinned chicken breast halves**

1 Combine first 7 ingredients in a small bowl; stir well.

2 Place chicken in a shallow baking dish. Pour wine mixture over chicken. Bake, uncovered, at 400° for 40 to 45 minutes or until chicken is done, basting frequently with wine mixture. Yield: 6 servings.

Nutritional content per serving: Calories 221
Fat 6.0g (Sat Fat 1.5g) Carbohydrate 6.3g Fiber 0.2g
Protein 32.4g Cholesterol 88mg Sodium 341mg

Creamy Garlic Potatoes

4 medium baking potatoes (about 1¾ pounds),
   peeled and cut into 1-inch pieces

½ cup evaporated skimmed milk
2 tablespoons margarine, softened
¼ teaspoon salt
⅛ teaspoon ground white pepper
2 cloves garlic, minced

   Fresh chives (optional)

1 Place potato in a large saucepan; add water to cover. Bring to a boil; cover, reduce heat, and simmer 20 minutes or until potato is tender. Drain.

2 Mash potato; add milk and next 4 ingredients. Beat at medium speed of an electric mixer 2 minutes or until smooth.

3 Transfer potato mixture to a serving bowl. Garnish with chives, if desired. Yield: 6 (¾-cup) servings.

Nutritional content per serving: Calories 157
Fat 4.0g (Sat Fat 0.8g) Carbohydrate 26.6g Fiber 2.1g
Protein 4.4g Cholesterol 1mg Sodium 175mg

Fancy Peas

2 (10-ounce) packages frozen English peas

   Vegetable cooking spray
2 tablespoons reduced-calorie stick margarine
¾ cup finely chopped onion
¼ cup finely chopped green pepper
1 (2-ounce) jar diced pimiento, drained
2 tablespoons minced fresh parsley
1 bay leaf

½ teaspoon white vinegar
¼ teaspoon salt
⅛ teaspoon ground nutmeg

1 Cook peas according to package directions, omitting salt and fat; drain.

2 Coat a heavy skillet with cooking spray; add margarine. Place over medium-high heat until margarine melts. Add onion and green pepper, and sauté until tender. Add pimiento, parsley, and bay leaf, stirring well.

3 Stir in peas, vinegar, salt, and nutmeg; cook, uncovered, over medium-high heat, stirring constantly, until thoroughly heated. Remove and discard bay leaf. Yield: 6 (½-cup) servings.

Nutritional content per serving: Calories 104
Fat 3.0g (Sat Fat 0.4g) Carbohydrate 15.1g Fiber 4.7g
Protein 5.3g Cholesterol 0mg Sodium 242mg

Meal Plan for Down-Home Delicious:

■ Make Molasses-Sauced Chicken.
■ While chicken is baking, make Creamy Garlic Potatoes.
■ While potatoes are cooking, make Fancy Peas.

A Family Affair

Total calories per serving: 354
Calories from fat: 14%

Grouper Fingers with
Lemon-Pepper Mayonnaise
Savory Rice
Green Beans in
Tomato Sauce

*Dinner on the table
in 55 minutes*

Grouper Fingers with Lemon-Pepper Mayonnaise

Lemon-Pepper Mayonnaise

1½ **pounds grouper fillets**
¼ **cup nonfat mayonnaise**
1 **tablespoon water**
¾ **teaspoon grated lemon rind**
1 **tablespoon lemon juice**

¾ **cup soft whole wheat breadcrumbs, toasted**
1 **teaspoon coarsely ground pepper**
¾ **teaspoon garlic powder**
  Vegetable cooking spray

  Lemon crowns (optional)
  Fresh parsley sprigs (optional)

1 Prepare Lemon-Pepper Mayonnaise.

2 Cut fillets diagonally into 1-inch-wide strips. Combine ¼ cup mayonnaise and next 3 ingredients; stir well. Brush both sides of strips with mayonnaise mixture.

3 Combine breadcrumbs, pepper, and garlic powder. Dredge strips in breadcrumb mixture. Place on a baking sheet coated with cooking spray.

4 Bake at 425° for 25 minutes or until golden and fish flakes easily when tested with a fork.

5 Using a small sharp knife, make continuous V-shaped cuts into the center and around the middle of a lemon, if desired. Gently twist halves apart. Spoon 1 tablespoon of Lemon-Pepper Mayonnaise into each lemon crown, and top each with a parsley sprig. Yield: 6 servings.

Lemon-Pepper Mayonnaise

¼ **cup plus 2 tablespoons nonfat mayonnaise**
2 **teaspoons skim milk**
1 **teaspoon grated lemon rind**
1 **teaspoon lemon juice**
¾ **teaspoon coarsely ground pepper**
¼ **teaspoon garlic powder**

1 Combine all ingredients in a bowl; stir well. Cover; chill thoroughly. Yield: ¼ cup plus 2 tablespoons.

Nutritional content per serving: Calories 147
Fat 1.5g (Sat Fat 0.3g) Carbohydrate 9.6g Fiber 0.4g
Protein 22.9g Cholesterol 42mg Sodium 416mg

Savory Rice

½ teaspoon salt
½ teaspoon paprika
½ teaspoon dried Italian seasoning
¼ teaspoon ground red pepper
¼ teaspoon freshly ground black pepper

    Vegetable cooking spray
1 tablespoon reduced-calorie stick margarine
⅔ cup chopped onion
⅔ cup chopped celery
⅔ cup chopped green pepper
1 clove garlic, minced

1 cup long-grain rice, uncooked
2 cups canned no-salt-added chicken broth,
    undiluted

1 Combine first 5 ingredients in a small bowl; stir well, and set aside.

2 Coat a large saucepan with cooking spray; add margarine. Place over medium-high heat until margarine melts. Add onion and next 3 ingredients; sauté until vegetables are crisp-tender.

3 Stir in rice; sauté until rice is lightly browned. Stir in seasoning mixture and chicken broth. Bring to a boil; cover, reduce heat, and simmer 20 to 25 minutes or until rice is tender and liquid is absorbed. Yield: 6 (½-cup) servings.

Nutritional content per serving: Calories 148
Fat 2.3g (Sat Fat 0.4g) Carbohydrate 27.8g Fiber 1.1g
Protein 3.3g Cholesterol 0mg Sodium 273mg

Green Beans in Tomato Sauce

2 teaspoons olive oil
1 cup chopped onion
1 large clove garlic, minced

2 (10-ounce) packages frozen green beans
1 (8-ounce) can no-salt-added tomato sauce
¼ cup water
⅛ teaspoon salt

    Dash of freshly ground pepper
    Dash of ground cinnamon

1 Heat oil in a large nonstick skillet over medium-high heat until hot. Add onion and garlic, and sauté until onion is tender.

2 Add beans and next 3 ingredients. Bring to a boil; reduce heat, and simmer, uncovered, 8 to 10 minutes or until beans are tender, stirring occasionally.

3 Add pepper and cinnamon; stir well. Yield: 6 (½-cup) servings.

Nutritional content per serving: Calories 59
Fat 1.7g (Sat Fat 0.3g) Carbohydrate 10.3g Fiber 3.1g
Protein 1.9g Cholesterol 0mg Sodium 67mg

Meal Plan for A Family Affair:

■ Make Lemon-Pepper Mayonnaise; chill.
■ Make Grouper Fingers.
■ While Grouper Fingers are baking, make Savory Rice; keep warm.
■ Make Green Beans in Tomato Sauce.

Vegetarian Cuisine

Total calories per serving: 580
Calories from fat: 10%

Caribbean Rice and Beans

Mustard-Glazed
Broiled Tomatoes

Commercial dinner rolls
(1 each)

Tropical Cooler

**Dinner on the table
in 42 minutes**

Caribbean Rice and Beans

6 (¼-inch-thick) slices fresh or canned pineapple
   Vegetable cooking spray
3 tablespoons brown sugar, divided

1 teaspoon lime juice

2 teaspoons olive oil
¾ cup chopped green pepper
2 cloves garlic, minced
2 (15-ounce) cans black beans, drained
1 (2-ounce) jar diced pimiento, drained
2 tablespoons white vinegar
2 teaspoons peeled, grated gingerroot
1 teaspoon hot sauce

3 cups cooked long-grain instant brown rice
   (cooked without salt or fat)
¼ cup minced fresh cilantro

1 Coat both sides of pineapple slices with cooking spray. Rub 2 tablespoons sugar evenly on both sides of pineapple slices. Place pineapple on rack of a broiler pan coated with cooking spray. Broil 5½ inches from heat (with electric oven door partially opened) 4 minutes. Turn pineapple; broil an additional 2 minutes or until lightly browned.

2 Combine remaining 1 tablespoon brown sugar and lime juice. Brush sugar mixture on pineapple. Cut each slice into 3 pieces; set aside.

3 Coat a large nonstick skillet with cooking spray; add oil. Place over medium-high heat until hot. Add green pepper and garlic; sauté until pepper is tender. Stir in beans and next 4 ingredients; cook 2 minutes or until thoroughly heated, stirring frequently.

4 Add rice and cilantro, stirring well. Spoon rice mixture evenly onto individual serving plates. Arrange pineapple around rice mixture. Yield: 6 servings.

Nutritional content per serving: Calories 315
Fat 4.1g (Sat Fat 0.6g) Carbohydrate 62.1g Fiber 7.3g
Protein 10.8g Cholesterol 0mg Sodium 248mg

Mustard-Glazed Broiled Tomatoes

3 medium tomatoes (about 1 pound)
  Vegetable cooking spray

2½ tablespoons coarse-grained mustard
2½ teaspoons brown sugar
1½ teaspoons minced fresh parsley

1 Cut tomatoes in half crosswise. Place tomato halves, cut side up, on rack of a broiler pan coated with cooking spray.

2 Combine mustard and brown sugar; stir well. Spread mustard mixture evenly over cut sides of tomato halves. Broil 5½ inches from heat (with electric oven door partially open) 4 minutes or until lightly browned and bubbly. Sprinkle evenly with parsley. Yield: 6 servings.

Nutritional content per serving: Calories 34
Fat 0.7g (Sat Fat 0.1g) Carbohydrate 6.9g Fiber 0.9g
Protein 0.9g Cholesterol 0mg Sodium 92mg

Tropical Cooler

4¼ cups pineapple-orange juice, chilled
¼ cup plus 2 tablespoons frozen lemonade
    concentrate, thawed and undiluted
1½ cups ginger ale

  Lemon slices (optional)
  Lemon mint sprigs (optional)

1 Combine pineapple-orange juice and lemonade in a large pitcher; gently stir in ginger ale just before serving.

2 If desired, garnish with lemon slices and lemon mint sprigs. Yield: 6 (1-cup) servings.

Nutritional content per serving: Calories 148
Fat 0.2g (Sat Fat 0g) Carbohydrate 37.8g Fiber 0.1g
Protein 0.4g Cholesterol 0mg Sodium 4mg

Meal Plan for Vegetarian Cuisine:

- Cook rice for Caribbean Rice and Beans.
- Make rice and beans; keep warm.
- Make Mustard-Glazed Broiled Tomatoes; keep warm.
- Make Tropical Cooler.

Sunday Night Supper

Total calories per serving: 463
Calories from fat: 8%

Penne Pasta with
Tomato Cream

Spinach Salad with
Creamy Italian Dressing

Bananas Foster

*Supper on the table
in 52 minutes*

Penne Pasta with Tomato Cream

6 ounces penne pasta, uncooked

Vegetable cooking spray
4 ounces Canadian bacon, chopped
¾ cup chopped sweet red pepper
¼ cup chopped onion
1 clove garlic, minced

1 (14½-ounce) can no-salt-added whole peeled
    tomatoes, undrained and chopped
1 teaspoon sugar
½ teaspoon dried basil
¼ teaspoon freshly ground pepper
¼ teaspoon salt

2 teaspoons all-purpose flour
¼ cup evaporated skimmed milk

Fresh basil sprig (optional)

1 Cook pasta according to package directions, omitting salt and fat; drain and set aside.

2 Coat a large nonstick skillet with cooking spray; place over medium-high heat until hot. Add Canadian bacon and next 3 ingredients, and sauté until vegetables are tender. Add tomato and next 4 ingredients. Bring mixture to a boil. Cover, reduce heat, and simmer 10 minutes.

3 Combine flour and milk; stir well. Add flour mixture to tomato mixture, and cook over medium heat, stirring constantly, until slightly thickened.

4 Add pasta, stirring well. Cook over medium heat 2 to 3 minutes or until thoroughly heated. Transfer mixture to a serving bowl. Garnish with a basil sprig, if desired. Yield: 4 (1¼-cup) servings.

Nutritional content per serving: Calories 257
Fat 3.1g (Sat Fat 0.8g) Carbohydrate 43.4g Fiber 2.2g
Protein 13.9g Cholesterol 15mg Sodium 582mg

Spinach Salad with Creamy Italian Dressing

½ cup sun-dried tomato
1 cup hot water

½ medium-size cucumber

3 cups torn fresh spinach
½ small purple onion, sliced and separated into rings
½ cup sliced fresh mushrooms

    Creamy Italian Dressing

1 Combine tomato and water in a small bowl; cover and let stand 15 minutes. Drain; coarsely chop tomato, and set aside.

2 Holding cucumber in one hand, run a citrus stripper or vegetable peeler lengthwise down the sides of cucumber to create strips about every ½ inch, if desired. Thinly slice cucumber.

3 Combine tomato, cucumber, spinach, onion, and mushrooms; toss gently. Arrange salad evenly on individual salad plates. Drizzle Creamy Italian Dressing evenly over salads. Yield: 4 (1-cup) servings.

Creamy Italian Dressing

    3 tablespoons nonfat mayonnaise
    2 tablespoons skim milk
    1 tablespoon white wine vinegar
    1 teaspoon grated Parmesan cheese
½ teaspoon sugar
¼ teaspoon dried basil
⅛ teaspoon Italian seasoning
    1 clove garlic, crushed

1 Combine all ingredients in a small bowl; stir well with a wire wisk. Yield: ⅓ cup.

Nutritional content per serving: Calories 50
Fat 0.5g (Sat Fat 0.2g) Carbohydrate 10.3g Fiber 2.5g
Protein 2.6g Cholesterol 0mg Sodium 322mg

Bananas Foster

½ cup unsweetened apple juice
⅛ teaspoon apple pie spice
2 medium-size ripe firm bananas, peeled and split lengthwise

1¼ teaspoons cornstarch
1 tablespoon rum
⅛ teaspoon maple flavoring
⅛ teaspoon butter flavoring

2 cups vanilla nonfat frozen yogurt

1 Combine apple juice and apple pie spice in a large skillet. Add bananas to juice mixture; cook over medium heat 2 minutes or just until bananas are heated, basting often with juice.

2 Combine cornstarch, rum, and flavorings; add to banana mixture. Cook, stirring constantly, 1 minute or until slightly thickened. Scoop ½ cup frozen yogurt into each individual bowl. Top yogurt evenly with banana mixture. Yield: 4 servings.

Nutritional content per serving: Calories 156
Fat 0.3g (Sat Fat 0.1g) Carbohydrate 36.6g Fiber 1.8g
Protein 4.1g Cholesterol 0mg Sodium 63mg

Meal Plan for Sunday Night Supper:

- Make Spinach Salad with Creamy Italian Dressing.
- Make Penne Pasta with Tomato Cream; keep warm.
- Complete step 1 of Bananas Foster.
- Just before serving, drizzle dressing over salads, and then complete step 2 of dessert.

Festive Family Supper

Total calories per serving: 541
Calories from fat: 22%

Ground Beef and
Noodle Bake

Mixed Green Salad with
Dijon Dressing

Hot Fudge Sundae

***Supper on the table
in 57 minutes***

Ground Beef and Noodle Bake

6 ounces medium egg noodles, uncooked

1 pound ground round
1 cup sliced fresh mushrooms
⅓ cup chopped onion
2 cloves garlic, minced

2 (8-ounce) cans no-salt-added tomato sauce
½ teaspoon freshly ground pepper
¼ teaspoon salt

1 (12-ounce) carton 1% low-fat cottage cheese
1 (8-ounce) carton nonfat sour cream alternative
⅓ cup chopped green onions
2 tablespoons grated Parmesan cheese
1 tablespoon poppy seeds

¾ cup (3 ounces) shredded reduced-fat sharp
      Cheddar cheese, divided
      Vegetable cooking spray

1 Cook noodles according to package directions, omitting salt and fat. Drain and set aside.

2 Cook ground round and next 3 ingredients in a large nonstick skillet over medium heat until meat is browned, stirring until it crumbles. Drain and pat dry with paper towels. Wipe drippings from skillet with a paper towel. Return meat mixture to skillet. Add tomato sauce, pepper, and salt.

3 Combine cottage cheese and next 4 ingredients in a large bowl. Stir in meat mixture, noodles, and ⅓ cup Cheddar cheese.

4 Coat a 2-quart casserole with cooking spray. Place noodle mixture in dish. Cover and bake at 350° for 20 minutes. Uncover; sprinkle with remaining cheese. Bake, uncovered, an additional 5 minutes. Yield: 8 servings.

Nutritional content per serving: Calories 288
Fat 7.8g (Sat Fat 3.2g) Carbohydrate 25.8g Fiber 2.0g
Protein 27.2g Cholesterol 65mg Sodium 400mg

Mixed Green Salad with Dijon Dressing

4 cups torn red leaf lettuce
4 cups torn Bibb lettuce
2 large tomatoes, cut into wedges
1 large green pepper, seeded and cut into rings
6 green onions, cut into 1-inch pieces
½ cup (2 ounces) finely shredded nonfat
    mozzarella cheese

    Dijon Dressing

1 Combine first 6 ingredients, and toss gently. Add Dijon Dressing to salad mixture; toss gently to coat. Yield: 8 (1-cup) servings.

Dijon Dressing

¼ cup nonfat mayonnaise
2 tablespoons water
1 tablespoon Dijon mustard
1 tablespoon honey
1 tablespoon cider vinegar
1½ teaspoons vegetable oil
⅛ teaspoon cayenne pepper
1 clove garlic, crushed

1 Combine all ingredients in a small bowl. Whisk vigorously until blended. Yield: ½ cup plus 2 tablespoons.

Nutritional content per serving: Calories 60
Fat 1.4g (Sat Fat 0.2g) Carbohydrate 9.7g Fiber 1.7g
Protein 3.5g Cholesterol 1mg Sodium 211mg

Hot Fudge Sundae

½ cup sugar
¼ cup unsweetened cocoa
1 tablespoon cornstarch
2 teaspoons instant coffee granules
½ cup plus 2 tablespoons evaporated skimmed
    milk

2 teaspoons margarine
½ teaspoon vanilla extract

4 cups low-fat vanilla ice cream
2 small bananas, sliced
2 teaspoons coarsely chopped pecans

1 Combine first 4 ingredients in a medium saucepan. Gradually stir in milk. Bring to a boil over medium heat, stirring constantly, until thickened. Remove from heat.

2 Add margarine and vanilla, stirring until margarine melts.

3 To serve, scoop ½ cup low-fat vanilla ice cream into each individual bowl. Top ice cream evenly with hot fudge sauce, banana slices, and pecans. Yield: 8 servings.

Nutritional content per serving: Calories 193
Fat 4.3g (Sat Fat 2.0g) Carbohydrate 34.8g Fiber 0.4g
Protein 5.0g Cholesterol 10mg Sodium 90mg

Meal Plan for Festive Family Supper:

■ Make Ground Beef and Noodle Bake.
■ Make Mixed Green Salad with Dijon Dressing.
■ Complete steps 1 and 2 of Hot Fudge Sundae.
■ Toss salad with dressing.
■ Just before serving, complete step 3 of sundae.

Kids in Charge

Total calories per serving: 757
Calories from fat: 19%

Sloppy Joes
Sweet Potato Sticks
Chocolate Cupcakes
Creamy Raspberry Frost

*Lunch on the table
in 57 minutes*

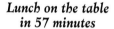

Sloppy Joes

Vegetable cooking spray
1½ pounds ground round
1 cup chopped onion
½ cup chopped green pepper

1 cup catsup
1 (8-ounce) can no-salt-added tomato sauce
1½ tablespoons low-sodium Worcestershire sauce
1½ tablespoons lemon juice
1½ tablespoons prepared mustard
1 tablespoon dark brown sugar
¼ teaspoon garlic powder
¼ teaspoon pepper

8 reduced-calorie whole wheat hamburger buns

1 Coat a large nonstick skillet with cooking spray. Place over medium-high heat until hot. Add ground round, onion, and green pepper. Cook until beef is browned, stirring until it crumbles. Drain and pat dry with paper towels. Wipe drippings from skillet with a paper towel.

2 Return meat mixture to skillet. Add catsup and next 7 ingredients; stir well. Cook, uncovered, over medium heat 10 minutes or until thoroughly heated and slightly thickened, stirring frequently.

3 Spoon meat mixture evenly over bottom halves of buns. Top with remaining bun halves. Yield: 8 servings.

Nutritional content per serving: Calories 272
Fat 6.7g (Sat Fat 2.2g) Carbohydrate 30.0g Fiber 2.9g
Protein 22.1g Cholesterol 54mg Sodium 673mg

Sweet Potato Sticks

4 medium-size sweet potatoes (about 2 pounds),
   peeled

1 tablespoon vegetable oil
⅓ cup grated Parmesan cheese
   Vegetable cooking spray

1 Cut potatoes lengthwise into ½-inch-thick slices. Cut slices into ¼-inch-wide strips. Place potato strips in a large bowl.

2 Drizzle oil over potato strips; toss well. Sprinkle with cheese, and toss well. Arrange potato strips in a single layer on baking sheets coated with cooking spray.

3 Bake at 400° for 35 to 40 minutes or until potato strips are crisp and lightly browned, stirring every 10 minutes. Yield: 8 servings.

Nutritional content per serving: Calories 139
Fat 3.1g (Sat Fat 0.9g) Carbohydrate 25.1g Fiber 3.1g
Protein 3.1g Cholesterol 3mg Sodium 75mg

Chocolate Cupcakes

1½ cups all-purpose flour
  1 teaspoon baking soda
  ½ teaspoon salt
  ½ cup sugar
  ¼ cup unsweetened cocoa

  ½ cup unsweetened orange juice
  ⅓ cup water
  3 tablespoons vegetable oil
  1 tablespoon white vinegar
  1 teaspoon vanilla extract
  ⅓ cup semisweet chocolate mini-morsels

  1 tablespoon powdered sugar

1 Combine first 5 ingredients in a bowl; make a well in center of mixture.

2 Combine juice and next 4 ingredients; add to dry ingredients, stirring just until dry ingredients are moistened. Fold in chocolate mini-morsels.

3 Spoon into foil- or paper-lined muffin pans, filling two-thirds full. Bake at 375° for 15 minutes or until a wooden pick inserted in center comes out clean. Remove from pans immediately; cool on a wire rack. Sprinkle with powdered sugar. Yield: 10 cupcakes.

Nutritional content per cupcake: Calories 177
Fat 5.6g (Sat Fat 1.5g) Carbohydrate 29.3g Fiber 0.6g
Protein 2.8g Cholesterol 0mg Sodium 245mg

(menu continues on next page)

Creamy Raspberry Frost

2 (10-ounce) packages frozen raspberries in light
   syrup
2 (12-ounce) cans evaporated skimmed milk,
   chilled
½ cup sifted powdered sugar
8 ice cubes

1 Combine half of all ingredients in container of an electric blender; cover and process until smooth. Repeat procedure with remaining half of ingredients. Serve immediately. Yield: 8 (1-cup) servings.

Nutritional content per serving: Calories 169
Fat 0.3g (Sat Fat 0.1g) Carbohydrate 36g Fiber 5g
Protein 6.9g Cholesterol 3mg Sodium 99mg

Variations:

Creamy Orange Frost: Omit sugar, and substitute 1 (12-ounce) container frozen orange juice for raspberries. Yield: 6 (1-cup) servings.

Nutritional content per serving: Calories 179
Fat 0.3g (Sat Fat 0.2g) Carbohydrate 35g Fiber 0.5g
Protein 9.9g Cholesterol 5mg Sodium 132mg

Creamy Strawberry Frost: Substitute 2 (10-ounce) packages strawberries in light syrup for raspberries. Yield: 8 (1-cup) servings.

Nutritional content per serving: Calories 151
Fat 0.3g (Sat Fat 0.1g) Carbohydrate 32g Fiber 0.4g
Protein 6.8g Cholesterol 3mg Sodium 99mg

Meal Plan for Kids in Charge:

- Make Chocolate Cupcakes. Turn oven to 400°.
- Make Sweet Potato Sticks; keep warm.
- Complete steps 1 and 2 of Sloppy Joes; keep warm.
- Make Creamy Raspberry Frost. Just before serving, complete step 3 of Sloppy Joes.

QUICK
ENTERTAINING MEALS

〰〰〰

page 38

page 40

page 42

Rustic Italian Lunch
Italian Pasta and Bean Soup   32
Sage and Cheese Biscuits   33
Amaretto Velvet Frosty   33

Seafood in a Snap
Deviled Crab   34
Vegetable Stir-Fry   35
Wild Rice Salad   35

French Fare
Grilled Amberjack au Poivre   36
Tangy Carrot-Jicama Salad   37
Peaches en Papillote with Raspberry Sauce   37

Indian Curry Feast
Sweet Curry Chicken   38
Green Onion Rice   39
Spiked Cranberry-Apple Cider   39

Sunset Supper
Turkey Jalepeño   40
Seasoned Browned Rice with Mushrooms   41
Snow Pea Stir-Fry   41

Tropical Dinner
Calypso Beef Tenderloin Steaks   42
Basil Scalloped Potatoes   43
Coconut Baby Carrots   43
Lemon-Sauced Cakes   44

Rustic Italian Lunch

Total calories per serving: 506
Calories from fat: 15%

Italian Pasta and Bean Soup
Sage and Cheese Biscuits
Amaretto Velvet Frosty

*Lunch on the table
in 45 minutes*

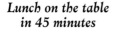

Italian Pasta and Bean Soup

Vegetable cooking spray
1 tablespoon olive oil
1 cup chopped onion
1 cup sliced carrot
½ cup chopped green pepper
2 cloves garlic, crushed

2 (13¾-ounce) cans no-salt-added beef broth
1 (28-ounce) can crushed tomatoes
1 (15-ounce) can white kidney beans or cannellini beans, rinsed and drained
1 (15-ounce) can red kidney beans, rinsed and drained
1½ teaspoons dried Italian seasoning
½ teaspoon salt
½ teaspoon liquid red pepper seasoning
¼ teaspoon pepper

6 ounces ditalini pasta

½ cup freshly grated Parmesan cheese

1 Coat a Dutch oven with cooking spray; add oil and place over medium-high heat. Add onion and next 3 ingredients; sauté until vegetables are crisp-tender.

2 Add beef broth and next 7 ingredients; bring to a boil. Reduce heat to low; cover and simmer 20 minutes, stirring occasionally.

3 Add pasta to vegetable mixture. Cover and cook 10 to 15 minutes or until pasta is tender. Ladle soup into individual bowls; top each serving with 1 tablespoon cheese. Yield: 8 (1¼-cup) servings.

Nutritional content per serving: Calories 232
Fat 4.5g (Sat Fat 1.5g) Carbohydrate 36.2g Fiber 4.2g
Protein 10.8g Cholesterol 5mg Sodium 497mg

Sage and Cheese Biscuits

1 cup all-purpose flour
1½ teaspoons baking powder
¼ teaspoon salt
1 teaspoon ground sage
½ teaspoon sugar
⅛ teaspoon freshly ground pepper
2 tablespoons margarine

¼ cup plus 2 tablespoons evaporated skimmed milk
2 tablespoons (½ ounce) shredded reduced-fat Monterey Jack cheese

1½ teaspoons all-purpose flour

1 Combine first 6 ingredients in a large bowl; cut in margarine with a pastry blender until mixture resembles coarse meal.

2 Add milk and cheese, stirring just until dry ingredients are moistened.

3 Sprinkle 1½ teaspoons flour evenly over work surface. Turn dough out onto floured surface, and knead 10 to 12 times. Roll dough to ½-inch thickness; cut into rounds using a 2-inch biscuit cutter.

4 Place rounds on an ungreased baking sheet. Bake at 450° for 8 to 10 minutes or until biscuits are golden. Yield: 8 biscuits.

Nutritional content per biscuit: Calories 99
Fat 3.4g (Sat Fat 0.8g) Carbohydrate 14.1g Fiber 0.5g
Protein 3.0g Cholesterol 2mg Sodium 130mg

Amaretto Velvet Frosty

2 cups skim milk
¼ cup instant nonfat dry milk powder
¾ cup amaretto
3 cups vanilla nonfat yogurt
¼ teaspoon vanilla extract
⅛ teaspoon almond extract

Ice cubes

1 tablespoon chopped almonds, toasted and divided

1 Combine skim milk and nonfat dry milk powder, stirring well. Add amaretto and next 3 ingredients. Place half of milk mixture in container of an electric blender.

2 Gradually add enough ice cubes to bring mixture to a 4-cup level; cover and process until smooth. Pour mixture into a large pitcher. Repeat procedure with remaining half of milk mixture. Stir well. Sprinkle each serving evenly with almonds. Serve immediately. Yield: 8 (1-cup) servings.

Nutritional content per serving: Calories 175
Fat 0.7g (Sat Fat 0.2) Carbohydrate 25.3g Fiber 0.1g
Protein 6.2g Cholesterol 2mg Sodium 97mg

Meal Plan for Rustic Italian Lunch:

■ Complete steps 1 and 2 of Italian Pasta and Bean Soup.
■ Make Sage and Cheese Biscuits; keep warm.
■ Add pasta in step 3 of soup.
■ While pasta cooks, make Amaretto Velvet Frosty.
■ Sprinkle cheese over soup.

Seafood in a Snap

Total calories per serving: 441
Calories from fat: 14%

Deviled Crab
Vegetable Stir-Fry
Wild Rice Salad
Commercial hard rolls
(1 each)

*Dinner on the table
in 50 minutes*

Deviled Crab

Vegetable cooking spray
1 teaspoon reduced-calorie stick margarine
1 cup chopped celery
½ cup finely chopped onion

1 pound fresh crabmeat, drained and flaked
1 cup diced whole wheat bread
¼ cup frozen egg substitute, thawed
3 tablespoons chopped fresh parsley
2 tablespoons dry sherry
1 teaspoon dried thyme
½ teaspoon pepper

Fresh thyme sprigs (optional)

1 Coat a large nonstick skillet with cooking spray; add margarine. Place over medium-high heat until margarine melts. Add celery and onion; sauté until tender.

2 Remove mixture from heat; stir in crabmeat and next 6 ingredients.

3 Spoon crabmeat mixture evenly into 6 baking shells or 6 (6-ounce) ovenproof ramekins coated with cooking spray. Place on a baking sheet. Bake at 350° for 20 to 25 minutes or until golden. Garnish with thyme sprigs, if desired. Yield: 6 servings.

Nutritional content per serving: Calories 122
Fat 2.4g (Sat Fat 0.2g) Carbohydrate 7.6g Fiber 1.2g
Protein 17.3g Cholesterol 74mg Sodium 295mg

Vegetable Stir-Fry

Vegetable cooking spray
1 teaspoon peanut oil
3 carrots, scraped and sliced diagonally
1 medium-size green pepper, seeded and cut into 1-inch pieces
1 medium-size sweet red pepper, seeded and cut into 1-inch pieces

3 green onions, cut into 1-inch pieces
1 (15-ounce) can baby corn on the cob, drained
1 (6-ounce) package frozen snow pea pods, thawed and drained

¼ cup low-sodium soy sauce
1 teaspoon chicken-flavored bouillon granules
¾ teaspoon cornstarch
¼ teaspoon ground ginger

1 Coat a wok with cooking spray; drizzle oil around top of wok, coating sides. Heat at medium (350°) until hot. Add carrot, and stir-fry 2 minutes. Add peppers; stir-fry 3 to 4 minutes or until crisp-tender. Remove vegetables from wok; set vegetables aside, and keep warm.

2 Add green onions, corn, and snow peas to wok; stir-fry 2 minutes or until crisp-tender. Return carrot and peppers to wok.

3 Combine soy sauce and remaining ingredients; stir well. Add soy sauce mixture to vegetables; stir-fry 3 minutes or until thickened. Yield: 6 (¾-cup) servings.

Nutritional content per serving: Calories 62
Fat 1.6g (Sat Fat 0.3g) Carbohydrate 9.9g Fiber 2.6g
Protein 2.6g Cholesterol 3mg Sodium 396mg

Wild Rice Salad

⅔ cup instant wild rice, uncooked
⅓ cup instant long-grain rice, uncooked

½ cup chopped celery
⅓ cup minced fresh chives
⅓ cup chopped sweet red pepper
⅓ cup reduced-calorie Italian dressing
2 teaspoons vinegar

2 tablespoons slivered almonds, toasted
6 leaves Bibb lettuce (optional)

1 Cook wild rice and white rice according to package directions, omitting salt and fat. Set aside, and let cool.

2 Combine rices, celery, chives, and red pepper. Combine dressing and vinegar; add to rice mixture, and toss well. Cover and chill.

3 To serve, stir in almonds, and spoon over lettuce-lined salad plates, if desired. Yield: 6 (½-cup) servings.

Nutritional content per serving: Calories 101
Fat 1.2g (Sat Fat 0.2g) Carbohydrate 19.7g Fiber 1.5g
Protein 3.6g Cholesterol 0mg Sodium 200mg

Meal Plan for Seafood in a Snap:

■ Make Wild Rice Salad, and chill.
■ Make Deviled Crab.
■ While crab is baking, make Vegetable Stir-Fry.

French Fare

Total calories per serving: 252
Calories from fat: 15%

Grilled Amberjack
au Poivre

Tangy Carrot-Jicama Salad

Peaches en Papillote with
Raspberry Sauce

*Dinner on the table
in 60 minutes*

Grilled Amberjack au Poivre

6 (4-ounce) amberjack steaks
⅓ cup lemon juice
⅓ cup red wine vinegar
1 tablespoon sugar
1 teaspoon minced thyme
⅛ teaspoon salt
3 cloves garlic, minced

3 tablespoons cracked pepper

Vegetable cooking spray
Fresh thyme sprigs (optional)

1 Place amberjack in a shallow dish. Combine lemon juice and next 5 ingredients in a small bowl; stir well. Pour over fish, turning to coat. Cover and marinate in the refrigerator 30 minutes, turning occasionally.

2 Remove fish from marinade, discarding marinade. Sprinkle pepper evenly over both sides of fish, pressing pepper into fish.

3 Coat grill rack with cooking spray. Place on grill over medium coals (300° to 350°). Place fish on rack; grill, covered, 4 to 6 minutes on each side or until fish flakes easily when tested with a fork. (Do not overcook or the fish will be dry.) Transfer fish to individual serving plates. Garnish with thyme sprigs, if desired. Yield: 6 servings.

Nutritional content per serving: Calories 134
Fat 2.4g (Sat Fat 0.6g) Carbohydrate 6.3g Fiber 0.8g
Protein 21.4g Cholesterol 47mg Sodium 126mg

Tangy Carrot-Jicama Salad

½ cup orange juice
3 tablespoons white wine vinegar
1 tablespoon plus 1 teaspoon vegetable oil
¼ teaspoon salt
⅛ teaspoon freshly ground pepper

2 large carrots, cut into thin strips
½ small jicama, peeled and cut into thin strips
3 tablespoons currants

1 Whisk together first 5 ingredients in a shallow dish until well blended.

2 Add carrot, jicama, and currants; toss gently to coat. Cover and refrigerate at least 30 minutes, tossing occasionally. Serve with a slotted spoon. Yield: 6 (½-cup) servings.

Nutritional content per serving: Calories 59
Fat 1.7g (Sat Fat 0.3g) Carbohydrate 10.6g Fiber 0.9g
Protein 0.8g Cholesterol 0mg Sodium 62mg

Peaches en Papillote with Raspberry Sauce

1 (16-ounce) bag frozen sliced unsweetened peaches, thawed

Raspberry Sauce

1 Cut 6 (10-inch) squares of parchment paper; fold squares in half, creasing firmly. Trim each folded rectangle into a large heart shape.

2 Arrange 5 peach slices on a paper heart near the crease. Fold over remaining half of heart. Starting with rounded edge, pleat and crimp edges together to make a seal. Twist end tightly to seal; place on a large baking sheet. Repeat with remaining peach slices and paper hearts.

3 Bake peaches at 425° for 12 minutes or until parchment bags are puffed and lightly browned. Place bags on individual dessert plates, and cut open. Spoon warm Raspberry Sauce evenly over peaches, and serve warm. Yield: 6 servings.

Raspberry Sauce

1 cup frozen unsweetened raspberries, thawed

3 tablespoons water
1½ teaspoons cornstarch
1½ tablespoons raspberry or other fruit-flavored schnapps
2 teaspoons sugar

1 Place raspberries in container of an electric blender; cover and process until smooth. Place puree in a wire-mesh strainer; press with back of spoon against the sides of the strainer to squeeze out ½ cup puree. Discard seeds and pulp in strainer.

2 Combine raspberry puree, water, and cornstarch in a small saucepan; stir well. Add schnapps and sugar; cook over medium heat, stirring constantly, until thickened and bubbly. Serve warm. Yield: ⅔ cup.

Nutritional content per serving: Calories 59
Fat 0.2g (Sat Fat 0g) Carbohydrate 14.8g Fiber 2.7g
Protein 0.7g Cholesterol 0mg Sodium 0mg

Meal Plan for French Fare:

- Complete step 1 of Grilled Amberjack au Poivre.
- Make Tangy Carrot-Jicama Salad, and chill.
- Complete steps 1 and 2 of Peaches en Papillote with Raspberry Sauce.
- Complete steps 2 and 3 of amberjack.
- Just before serving, complete step 3 of Peaches en Papillote; while baking, make Raspberry Sauce.

Indian Curry Feast

Total calories per serving: 508
Calories from fat: 8%

Sweet Curry Chicken

Green Onion Rice

Spiked
Cranberry-Apple Cider

*Dinner on the table
in 57 minutes*

Sweet Curry Chicken

1 (20-ounce) can unsweetened pineapple tidbits
¼ cup unsweetened pineapple juice
1 tablespoon cornstarch
1¾ teaspoons curry powder
2 teaspoons honey

3 tablespoons all-purpose flour
½ teaspoon dried crushed red pepper
1½ pounds unbreaded chicken breast nuggets

Vegetable cooking spray
1 tablespoon vegetable oil

1 medium-size green pepper, seeded and cut into
¼-inch-wide strips
1 medium-size sweet yellow pepper, seeded and
cut into ¼-inch-wide strips
½ teaspoon salt

1 Drain pineapple tidbits, reserving juice. Set pineapple tidbits aside. Combine reserved pineapple juice, unsweetened pineapple juice, and next 3 ingredients in a small saucepan. Bring to a boil over medium heat, stirring constantly. Reduce heat; simmer 3 to 4 minutes or until thickened and bubbly. Set aside.

2 Place flour and crushed red pepper in a heavy-duty, zip-top plastic bag. Add chicken, and seal bag; shake until chicken is lightly coated. Shake off excess flour mixture.

3 Coat a nonstick skillet with cooking spray; add oil. Place over medium-high heat until hot. Add chicken; cook 4 minutes on each side or until chicken is lightly browned. Remove chicken from skillet. Wipe drippings from skillet with a paper towel.

4 Coat skillet with cooking spray; place over medium-high heat until hot. Add pepper strips; cook, stirring constantly, 2 to 3 minutes or until pepper is crisp-tender. Add cooked chicken, reserved pineapple tidbits, pineapple juice mixture, and salt. Cook over medium heat until thoroughly heated. Yield: 6 servings.

Nutritional content per serving: Calories 227
Fat 4.1g (Sat Fat 0.7g) Carbohydrate 27.4g Fiber 1.8g
Protein 19.8g Cholesterol 47mg Sodium 253mg

Green Onion Rice

2¾ cups cooked instant long-grain rice (cooked without salt or fat)
½ cup chopped green onions
¼ teaspoon curry powder
¼ teaspoon ground cumin
¼ teaspoon freshly ground pepper
Vegetable cooking spray

1 Place first 5 ingredients in a large skillet coated with cooking spray. Sauté over medium-high heat 3 to 5 minutes or until mixture is thoroughly heated. Yield: 6 (½-cup) servings.

Nutritional content per serving: Calories 103 Fat 0.2g (Sat Fat 0g) Carbohydrate 22.8g Fiber 0.7g Protein 2.0g Cholesterol 0mg Sodium 2mg

Spiked Cranberry-Apple Cider

4 cups cranberry-apple drink
3 tablespoons sugar
¼ cup thawed frozen lemonade concentrate, undiluted

2 (3-inch) sticks cinnamon
½ teaspoon whole cloves
¼ teaspoon whole allspice

¼ cup light rum
Lemon slices (optional)
Cloves (optional)
6 (3-inch) sticks cinnamon (optional)

1 Combine first 3 ingredients in a large saucepan.

2 Tie 2 cinnamon sticks, ½ teaspoon cloves, and allspice in a cheesecloth bag; add to cranberry-apple drink mixture. Bring to a boil; cover, reduce heat, and simmer 10 minutes.

3 Remove mixture from heat. Remove and discard spice bag. Stir in rum. If desired, garnish with lemon wedges, cloves, and cinnamon sticks. Yield: 6 (¾-cup) servings.

Nutritional content per serving: Calories 178 Fat 0.0g (Sat Fat 0g) Carbohydrate 39.9g Fiber 0g Protein 0.2g Cholesterol 0mg Sodium 4mg

Variation:

Orange Twist: For a nonalcoholic version, omit rum, and add 1½ cups orange juice to cranberry-apple drink mixture before bringing to a boil. Yield: 6 (1-cup) servings.

Nutritional content per serving: Calories 184 Fat 0.1g (Sat Fat 0.1g) Carbohydrate 46.6g Fiber 0.2g Protein 0.6g Cholesterol 0mg Sodium 4mg

Meal Plan for Indian Curry Feast:

- Make Spiked Cranberry-Apple Cider; keep warm.
- Complete steps 1 and 2 of Sweet Curry Chicken; set aside.
- Make Green Onion Rice; keep warm.
- Complete steps 3 and 4 of curry chicken.

Sunset Supper

Total calories per serving: 545
Calories from fat: 16%

Turkey Jalepeño

Seasoned Browned Rice
with Mushrooms

Snow Pea Stir-Fry

*Supper on the table
in 53 minutes*

Turkey Jalapeño

1 pound turkey breast cutlets
⅓ cup all-purpose flour
½ teaspoon freshly ground pepper

2 teaspoons vegetable oil

Vegetable cooking spray
¼ cup sliced green onions
½ teaspoon peeled, minced gingerroot

½ cup red jalapeño jelly
¼ cup unsweetened apple juice
1 tablespoon red wine vinegar
1 teaspoon low-sodium Worcestershire sauce

2 teaspoons cornstarch
1 tablespoon water
Green onion curls (optional)

1 Place cutlets between 2 sheets of heavy-duty plastic wrap, and flatten to ⅛-inch thickness, using a meat mallet or rolling pin. Combine flour and pepper; dredge turkey cutlets in flour mixture.

2 Heat oil in a large nonstick skillet over medium heat until hot. Add cutlets, and cook 3 to 4 minutes on each side or until done. Transfer to a platter, and keep warm. Wipe drippings from skillet with a paper towel.

3 Coat skillet with cooking spray; place over medium-high heat until hot. Add sliced green onions and gingerroot; sauté until tender. Add jelly and next 3 ingredients. Reduce heat, and cook until jelly melts and mixture is thoroughly heated.

4 Combine cornstarch and water; stir until smooth. Add to jelly mixture. Cook, stirring constantly, until thickened and bubbly. Spoon sauce over turkey cutlets; garnish with green onion curls, if desired. Yield: 4 servings.

Nutritional content per serving: Calories 335
Fat 5.9g (Sat Fat 1.5g) Carbohydrate 38.3g Fiber 0.7g
Protein 31.3g Cholesterol 70mg Sodium 84mg

Seasoned Browned Rice with Mushrooms

1½ teaspoons margarine
½ cup chopped onion
½ cup instant long-grain rice, uncooked
2 ounces vermicelli, uncooked and broken into
  1-inch pieces

1¼ cups water
1 (4-ounce) can sliced mushrooms, drained
1½ teaspoons chicken-flavored bouillon granules
½ teaspoon dried oregano
½ teaspoon dried thyme
⅛ teaspoon freshly ground pepper
2 tablespoons chopped fresh parsley

1 Melt margarine in a medium saucepan over medium-high heat. Add onion, and sauté until tender. Add rice and vermicelli; sauté, stirring constantly, 3 to 5 minutes or until rice and pasta are lightly browned.

2 Combine water and next 5 ingredients. Add to rice mixture, stirring well. Bring to a boil; cover, reduce heat, and simmer 10 minutes or until rice and pasta are tender and liquid is absorbed. Fluff with a fork, and stir in parsley. Yield: 4 (½-cup) servings.

Nutritional content per serving: Calories 141
Fat 2.2g (Sat Fat 0.5g) Carbohydrate 27.0g Fiber 0.9g
Protein 3.5g Cholesterol 0mg Sodium 382mg

Snow Pea Stir-Fry

Vegetable cooking spray
1 teaspoon dark sesame oil
½ cup diagonally sliced carrot

2 (6-ounce) packages frozen snow pea pods
¼ cup sliced water chestnuts
½ cup canned low-sodium chicken broth,
  undiluted

2 teaspoons low-sodium soy sauce
1 teaspoon cornstarch

1 Coat a large nonstick skillet with cooking spray; add oil. Place over medium-high heat until hot. Add carrot; sauté 2 minutes.

2 Add snow peas, water chestnuts, and broth; bring to a boil. Cover, reduce heat, and simmer 2 to 3 minutes or until vegetables are crisp-tender.

3 Combine soy sauce and cornstarch; add to vegetable mixture. Cook over medium heat, stirring constantly, until thickened. Yield: 4 (½-cup) servings.

Nutritional content per serving: Calories 69
Fat 1.7g (Sat Fat 0.2g) Carbohydrate 10.4g Fiber 2.9g
Protein 3.4g Cholesterol 0mg Sodium 100mg

Microwaving Directions: Coat a 1½-quart casserole with cooking spray; add oil. Microwave at HIGH 45 seconds or until hot. Add carrot and snow peas. Microwave at HIGH 1 minute, stirring once. Add water chestnuts and broth; cover with heavy-duty plastic wrap, and vent. Microwave at HIGH 2 to 3 minutes or until vegetables are crisp-tender. Combine soy sauce and cornstarch; add to vegetable mixture, stirring well. Cover and vent; microwave at HIGH 1 to 2 minutes or until thickened, stirring after 1 minute.

Meal Plan for Sunset Supper:

- Complete steps 1 and 2 of Turkey Jalapeño; set aside.
- Make Seasoned Browned Rice with Mushrooms; keep warm.
- Make Snow Pea Stir-Fry; keep warm.
- Complete steps 3 and 4 of Turkey Jalapeño.

Tropical Dinner

Total calories per serving: 654
Total calories from fat: 28%

Calypso Beef Tenderloin
Steaks

Basil Scalloped Potatoes

Coconut Baby Carrots

Lemon-Sauced Cakes

*Dinner on the table
in 60 minutes*

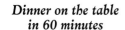

Calypso Beef Tenderloin Steaks

¾ cup canned low-sodium chicken broth,
   undiluted
½ cup unsweetened orange juice
2½ tablespoons reduced-calorie catsup
2 tablespoons brown sugar
2 tablespoons lime juice
2 tablespoons dark rum
1 teaspoon ground ginger
¼ teaspoon ground cloves
¼ teaspoon dried thyme
¼ teaspoon ground red pepper
1 large clove garlic, minced

1 (1½-pound) lean boneless beef tenderloin

Vegetable cooking spray

Lime slices (optional)
Fresh basil sprigs (optional)

1 Combine first 11 ingredients in a medium bowl; stir well with a wire whisk.

2 Trim fat from tenderloin; cut tenderloin into 6 equal steaks. Place in a large heavy-duty, zip-top plastic bag; pour marinade over steaks. Seal bag; shake well. Marinate in refrigerator 30 minutes, turning bag occasionally.

3 Remove steaks from marinade, reserving marinade. Place steaks on rack of a broiler pan coated with cooking spray. Broil 5½ inches from heat (with electric oven door partially opened) 6 to 8 minutes on each side or to desired degree of doneness, basting frequently with marinade. If desired, garnish with lime slices and basil sprigs. Yield: 6 servings.

Nutritional content per serving: Calories 233
Fat 8.7g (Sat Fat 3.3g) Carbohydrate 8.5g Fiber 0.1g
Protein 25.9g Cholesterol 75mg Sodium 71mg

Basil Scalloped Potatoes

Vegetable cooking spray
2 cloves garlic, minced

¾ cup skim milk, divided
1 tablespoon all-purpose flour

¾ cup evaporated skimmed milk
2 tablespoons chopped fresh basil
¼ teaspoon salt
¼ teaspoon dried crushed red pepper
⅛ teaspoon ground white pepper

4 cups peeled, thinly sliced baking potato
   (about 1¾ pounds)

½ cup (2 ounces) shredded Gruyère cheese
2 tablespoons freshly grated Parmesan cheese

1 Coat a large saucepan with cooking spray; place over medium-high heat until hot. Add garlic, and sauté until tender.

2 Combine ¼ cup skim milk and flour; stir with a wire whisk until smooth. Add flour mixture to garlic; cook, stirring constantly, 1 minute or until mixture thickens.

3 Gradually add remaining ½ cup skim milk, evaporated milk, and next 4 ingredients. Bring to a boil, stirring constantly. Add potato.

4 Spoon half of potato mixture into an 11- x 7- x 1½-inch baking dish coated with cooking spray. Top with half of Gruyère cheese. Repeat layers. Sprinkle with Parmesan cheese.

5 Cover and bake at 350° for 30 minutes. Uncover and bake an additional 15 minutes. Let stand 10 minutes before serving. Yield: 6 (½-cup) servings.

Nutritional content per serving: Calories 161
Fat 4.1g (Sat Fat 2.3g) Carbohydrate 21.5g Fiber 2.2g
Protein 10.4g Cholesterol 14mg Sodium 232mg

Coconut Baby Carrots

1 (16-ounce) package frozen baby carrots, thawed
2 tablespoons reduced-calorie stick margarine
2 tablespoons honey
2 tablespoons chutney
½ teaspoon mustard seeds
¼ cup unsweetened grated coconut, toasted

1 Combine first 5 ingredients in a large skillet. Cook over medium-high heat until thoroughly heated, stirring occasionally. Transfer carrot mixture to a serving platter; sprinkle with coconut. Yield: 6 (½-cup) servings.

Nutritional content per serving: Calories 105
Fat 4.2g (Sat Fat 1.7g) Carbohydrate 17.7g Fiber 2.6g
Protein 1.1g Cholesterol 0mg Sodium 76mg

(menu continues on next page)

Lemon-Sauced Cakes

¼ cup sugar
2 teaspoons cornstarch
Dash of salt
½ cup water

¾ teaspoon grated lemon rind
2½ tablespoons lemon juice
1 tablespoon margarine

8 ounces reduced-fat poundcake
6 tablespoons reduced-calorie whipped topping

1 Combine sugar, cornstarch, and salt in a 2-cup glass measure; add water, and stir until sugar dissolves.

2 Microwave at HIGH for 1 minute; stir well. Microwave at HIGH for 1 to 1½ minutes, stirring at 30-second intervals, until mixture is clear, thickened, and bubbly.

3 Stir in lemon rind, lemon juice, and margarine.

4 Cut poundcake into 6 slices; place on individual serving plates. Top each slice with 2 tablespoons lemon sauce and 1 tablespoon whipped topping. Yield: 6 servings.

Nutritional content per serving: Calories 155
Fat 3.5g (Sat Fat 0.7g) Carbohydrate 30.3g Fiber 0.5g
Protein 1.7g Cholesterol 0mg Sodium 184mg

Variation:

Lime-Sauced Cakes: Substitute ¾ teaspoon grated lime rind and 2½ tablespoons lime juice for lemon rind and juice. Yield: 6 servings.

Nutritional content per serving: Calories 155
Fat 3.5g (Sat Fat 0.7g) Carbohydrate 30.3g Fiber 0.5g
Protein 1.7g Cholesterol 0mg Sodium 184mg

Meal Plan for Tropical Dinner:

- Complete steps 1 and 2 of Calypso Beef Tenderloin Steaks.
- Complete steps 1, 2, and 3 of Lemon-Sauced Cakes; set aside.
- Make Basil Scalloped Potatoes.
- Make Coconut Baby Carrots; keep warm.
- Complete step 3 of tenderloin steaks.
- Just before serving, complete step 4 of Lemon-Sauced Cakes.

APPETIZERS & BEVERAGES

page 48

page 55

page 58

Appetizers

Creamy Pineapple Dip   46

Orange-Poppy Seed Dip   47

Artichoke and Green Chile Dip   48

Spicy Snack Mix   49

Antipasto Kabobs   50

Broiled Fruit Kabobs   51

Ground Beef and Cheese Snacks   52

Black Bean Empanaditas   53

Chicken-Chile Potato Skins   54

Miniature Chicken Tostadas   55

Banana-Chocolate Chip Pops   56

Honey-Banana Pops   56

Beverages

Creamy Vanilla Milkshake   57

Strawberry Milkshake   57

Tropical Milkshake   57

Raspberry Frozen Daiquiris   58

Strawberry Frozen Daiquiris   58

Apple-Grape Punch   59

Orange-Pineapple Slush   60

Very Berry Slush   60

Spicy Tomato Sipper   61

Zippy Red-Eye   61

Hot Cocoa Mix   62

Minted Hot Cocoa Mix   62

Mocha-Cocoa Mix   62

Creamy Pineapple Dip

Preparation Time: 5 minutes
Chilling Time: at least
25 minutes

1 cup lemon low-fat yogurt
3 tablespoons frozen pineapple juice concentrate,
   thawed and undiluted
1 tablespoon nonfat sour cream alternative

1 Combine all ingredients in a small bowl; stir well. Cover and chill at least 25 minutes.

2 Stir just before serving. Serve with assorted fresh fruit. Store remaining dip, tightly covered, in the refrigerator up to 5 days. Yield: 1¼ cups.

Nutritional content per tablespoon: Calories 22
Fat 0.1g (Sat Fat 0.1g) Carbohydrate 4.7g Fiber 0g
Protein 0.5g Cholesterol 0mg Sodium 9mg

Orange-Poppy Seed Dip

Preparation Time: 10 minutes
Chilling Time: at least
25 minutes

Use paper towels to drain yogurt quickly. The towels absorb some of the yogurt's liquid, making its consistency thicker.

~~~~~~~~~~

½ **cup vanilla low-fat yogurt**

¼ **cup light process cream cheese product, softened**

¼ **cup orange marmalade**
 1 **teaspoon poppy seeds**

 Orange curls (optional)

1 Spoon yogurt onto several layers of heavy-duty paper towels, and spread to ½-inch thickness. Cover with additional paper towels; let stand 5 minutes. Scrape yogurt into a medium bowl, using a rubber spatula.

2 Add cream cheese to yogurt. Beat at medium speed of an electric mixer until smooth.

3 Stir in marmalade and poppy seeds. Cover and chill at least 25 minutes.

4 Stir just before serving. Garnish with orange curls, if desired. Serve with assorted fresh fruit. Store remaining dip, tightly covered, in the refrigerator up to 5 days. Yield: ¾ cup.

Nutritional content per tablespoon: Calories 36
Fat 1.0g (Sat Fat 0.6g) Carbohydrate 6.1g Fiber 0g
Protein 1.0g Cholesterol 3mg Sodium 36mg

Artichoke and Green Chile Dip

Preparation Time: 15 minutes
Cooking Time: 26–27 minutes

You can chill this dip overnight. Then bake for 30 minutes; add cheese, and broil until lightly browned.

⅔ cup nonfat mayonnaise
½ cup plain low-fat yogurt

1 (14-ounce) can artichoke hearts, drained and chopped
1 (4-ounce) can chopped green chiles, drained
¼ cup plus 2 tablespoons freshly grated Parmesan cheese
¼ teaspoon garlic powder
¼ teaspoon hot sauce

Vegetable cooking spray

2 tablespoons freshly grated Parmesan cheese
Fresh green chile slices (optional)

1 Combine mayonnaise and yogurt in a medium bowl, stirring until smooth.

2 Add chopped artichoke hearts and next 4 ingredients, stirring well.

3 Spoon mixture into a 1-quart baking dish coated with cooking spray. Bake, uncovered, at 350° for 25 minutes.

4 Sprinkle with 2 tablespoons Parmesan cheese. Broil 5½ inches from heat (with electric oven door partially opened) 1½ minutes or until lightly browned. Garnish with green chile slices, if desired. Serve with whole wheat toast points, breadsticks, unsalted crackers, or Melba rounds. Yield: 2¾ cups.

Nutritional content per tablespoon: Calories 13
Fat 0.4g (Sat Fat 0.2g) Carbohydrate 1.7g Fiber 0.1g
Protein 0.7g Cholesterol 1mg Sodium 78mg

Spicy Snack Mix

Preparation Time: 10 minutes
Cooking Time: 18–20 minutes

1½ cups bite-size crispy corn cereal squares
1½ cups bite-size crispy rice cereal squares
1½ cups bite-size crispy wheat cereal squares
¾ cup small unsalted pretzels
¼ cup unsalted dry roasted peanuts

¼ cup nonfat margarine, melted
2 tablespoons low-sodium soy sauce
1½ teaspoons chili powder
½ teaspoon garlic powder
¼ teaspoon ground red pepper

1 Combine first 5 ingredients in a large heavy-duty zip-top plastic bag.

2 Combine margarine and remaining ingredients; pour over cereal mixture. Seal bag; shake well to coat.

3 Place cereal mixture in a 15- x 10- x 1-inch jellyroll pan. Bake at 300° for 18 to 20 minutes, stirring occasionally. Remove from oven; let cool completely. Store snack mix in an airtight container. Yield: 10 (½-cup) servings.

Nutritional content per serving: Calories 59
Fat 0.6g (Sat Fat 0.1g) Carbohydrate 11.6g Fiber 0.6g
Protein 1.3g Cholesterol 0mg Sodium 223mg

Antipasto Kabobs

Preparation Time: 15 minutes
Marinating Time: 30 minutes

Commercial reduced-
calorie Italian dressing may
be used instead
of the seasoned marinade
for an even quicker
version of this recipe.

1 medium carrot, scraped

1 medium-size yellow squash, cut into
 ¼-inch slices
1 small green pepper, seeded and cut into
 1-inch pieces
8 cherry tomatoes
8 ripe olives
8 small whole fresh mushrooms

¼ cup white wine vinegar
¼ cup water
1 tablespoon olive oil
1 teaspoon dried Italian seasoning
⅛ teaspoon garlic powder
⅛ teaspoon pepper

4 ounces reduced-fat Monterey Jack cheese, cubed

1 Slice carrot with a vegetable peeler lengthwise into long thin strips. Place strips in a large shallow dish.

2 Add squash and next 4 ingredients; set aside.

3 Combine vinegar and next 5 ingredients in a glass jar; cover tightly, and shake vigorously. Pour over vegetables. Cover and marinate in refrigerator 30 minutes.

4 Thread vegetables and cheese alternately onto 8 (6-inch) wooden skewers; brush with marinade. Yield: 8 kabobs.

Nutritional content per kabob: Calories 68
Fat 3.3g (Sat Fat 1.1g) Carbohydrate 4.6g Fiber 1.3g
Protein 5.8g Cholesterol 5mg Sodium 58mg

Broiled Fruit Kabobs

Preparation Time: 20 minutes
Cooking Time: 2–4 minutes

Many supermarkets
carry fresh pineapples
that have been peeled
and cored and
are ready to be cut
into spears or chunks.

8 slices turkey bacon, halved

16 (1-inch) fresh pineapple chunks
1 large Granny Smith apple, cored and cut
   into 24 (1-inch) pieces
1 large red apple, cored and cut into 24
   (1-inch) pieces

3 tablespoons maple syrup

¼ cup firmly packed light brown sugar
⅛ teaspoon ground allspice

1 Partially cook bacon in a large nonstick skillet over medium heat. Drain and pat dry with paper towels.

2 Curl bacon around pineapple chunks; arrange alternately with apple pieces on 8 (12-inch) wooden skewers.

3 Place skewers on rack of a broiler pan, and brush fruit with maple syrup.

4 Combine brown sugar and allspice; sprinkle over fruit. Broil 5½ inches from heat (with electric oven door partially opened) 2 to 4 minutes or until bacon is crisp. Serve immediately. Yield: 8 kabobs.

Nutritional content per kabob: Calories 135
Fat 3.6g (Sat Fat 0.9g) Carbohydrate 21.9g Fiber 1.8g
Protein 3.5g Cholesterol 16mg Sodium 336mg

Ground Beef and Cheese Snacks

Preparation Time: 20 minutes
Cooking Time: 10–12 minutes

The crust is made from refrigerated bread dough that's low in both fat and cholesterol.

〜〜〜〜〜

Vegetable cooking spray
½ pound ground round
⅔ cup chopped green pepper
½ cup chopped onion
1 clove garlic, minced

¾ cup (3 ounces) shredded reduced-fat sharp Cheddar cheese
¾ cup (3 ounces) shredded part-skim mozzarella cheese
⅓ cup no-salt-added tomato sauce
¾ teaspoon dried Italian seasoning
¼ teaspoon freshly ground pepper

1 (11-ounce) package refrigerated crusty French loaf dough

1 tablespoon grated Parmesan cheese

1 Coat a large nonstick skillet with cooking spray; add ground round and next 3 ingredients. Cook over medium heat until beef is browned, stirring until it crumbles. Drain and pat dry with paper towels. Wipe drippings from skillet with a paper towel.

2 Combine meat mixture, Cheddar cheese, and next 4 ingredients; stir well.

3 Unroll dough into a large rectangle; cut into 36 (2-inch) squares. Place squares on a large baking sheet coated with cooking spray. Spoon about 1½ teaspoons meat mixture onto each dough square. Sprinkle Parmesan cheese evenly over squares.

4 Bake at 425° for 10 to 12 minutes or until crust is crisp and lightly browned. Serve warm. Yield: 3 dozen appetizers.

Nutritional content per appetizer: Calories 50 Fat 1.6g (Sat Fat 0.7g) Carbohydrate 4.7g Fiber 0.1g Protein 3.9g Cholesterol 8mg Sodium 79mg

Make Ahead: Prepare meat mixture as instructed in steps 1 and 2. Cool meat mixture slightly, and place in an airtight container. Refrigerate up to 24 hours. Remove meat mixture from refrigerator, and continue with step 3 as directed above.

Black Bean Empanaditas

Preparation Time: 25 minutes
Cooking Time: 15–18 minutes

Empanar is Spanish for "to bake in pastry." Empanaditas are tiny, ravioli-size pastries.

Vegetable cooking spray
3 ounces lean ground pork
2 tablespoons finely chopped onion
1½ tablespoons finely chopped sweet red pepper
1 small clove garlic, minced

⅓ cup drained canned black beans
2 tablespoons no-salt-added tomato sauce
1 tablespoon Burgundy or other dry red wine
1½ teaspoons chopped fresh cilantro
⅛ teaspoon ground cumin
⅛ teaspoon ground allspice

1 (10-ounce) package refrigerated pizza crust

1 Coat a large nonstick skillet with cooking spray; add ground pork and next 3 ingredients. Cook over medium heat until meat is browned, stirring until it crumbles. Drain and pat dry with paper towels. Wipe drippings from skillet with a paper towel.

2 Return pork mixture to skillet. Add black beans and next 5 ingredients. Cook over medium-high heat 8 to 10 minutes or until liquid is absorbed, stirring frequently. Remove from heat.

3 Roll pizza crust into a 13-inch square. Cut with a 3½-inch round biscuit cutter; place on baking sheets coated with cooking spray.

4 Place 1 tablespoon bean mixture in center of each circle. Fold dough over bean mixture to form half-circles. Seal edges of dough securely by pressing with a fork. Spray tops of empanaditas with cooking spray.

5 Bake at 375° for 15 to 18 minutes or until lightly browned. Serve warm. Yield: 1 dozen.

Nutritional content per appetizer: Calories 75
Fat 2.0g (Sat Fat 0.5g) Carbohydrate 10.5g Fiber 0.3g
Protein 3.9g Cholesterol 6mg Sodium 159mg

Make Ahead: Prepare filling mixture as instructed in steps 1 and 2. Cool filling mixture slightly, and place in an airtight container. Refrigerate up to 24 hours. Remove filling mixture from refrigerator, and continue with step 3 as directed above.

Chicken-Chile Potato Skins

Preparation Time: 25 minutes
Cooking Time: 4–6 minutes

8 (5-ounce) baking potatoes

Butter-flavored vegetable cooking spray

¼ teaspoon garlic powder
¼ teaspoon salt
¼ teaspoon ground red pepper

1 cup shredded cooked chicken
3 tablespoons chopped green chiles
1 small jalapeño pepper, seeded and minced

1 cup (4 ounces) shredded reduced-fat Monterey
    Jack cheese
Chopped fresh chives (optional)

1 Wash potatoes, and pat dry. Prick each potato several times with a fork. Arrange 4 potatoes in a circle 1 inch apart on a layer of paper towels in microwave oven. Microwave, uncovered, at HIGH 8 to 10 minutes or until potatoes are tender, turning and rearranging potatoes halfway through cooking time. Repeat procedure with remaining 4 potatoes. Let potatoes cool to touch.

2 Cut each potato in half lengthwise; scoop out pulp, leaving ¼-inch-thick shells. Reserve pulp for another use. Place potato shells on an ungreased baking sheet. Spray shells with cooking spray.

3 Combine garlic powder, salt, and red pepper; sprinkle evenly over shells.

4 Combine chicken, chiles, and jalapeño pepper; spoon evenly into shells.

5 Sprinkle with cheese. Bake at 450° for 4 to 6 minutes or until cheese melts. Garnish with chives, if desired. Yield: 16 appetizers.

Nutritional content per appetizer: Calories 82
Fat 2.1g (Sat Fat 1.0g) Carbohydrate 11.1g Fiber 0.8g
Protein 4.9g Cholesterol 10mg Sodium 98mg

Miniature Chicken Tostadas

Preparation Time: 15 minutes
Cooking Time: 11–12 minutes

For a different look, use scissors to cut each tortilla into 6 wedges.

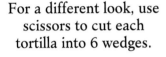

1 cup finely chopped cooked chicken breast (skinned before cooking and cooked without salt)
½ cup chopped jicama
½ cup (2 ounces) shredded reduced-fat Cheddar cheese
¼ cup nonfat mayonnaise
1 tablespoon diced pimiento, drained
1 (4-ounce) can chopped green chiles, drained

6 (6-inch) corn tortillas

1 Combine first 6 ingredients in a small bowl; stir well. Set aside.

2 Cut each tortilla into 6 circles using a 2-inch biscuit cutter. Place tortilla chips on an ungreased baking sheet. Bake at 350° for 6 minutes. Turn chips, and bake an additional 2 to 3 minutes or until golden and crisp.

3 Spread chicken mixture evenly over chips (about 1 tablespoon per chip). Broil 5½ inches from heat (with electric oven door partially opened) 3 minutes or until hot and bubbly. Serve warm. Yield: 3 dozen appetizers.

Nutritional content per appetizer: Calories 24
Fat 0.5g (Sat Fat 0.2g) Carbohydrate 2.8g Fiber 0.3g
Protein 1.9g Cholesterol 4mg Sodium 38mg

Banana-Chocolate Chip Pops

Preparation Time: 15 minutes
Freezing Time: at least
4 hours

~~

Honey-Banana Pops

Preparation Time: 5 minutes
Freezing Time: at least
4 hours

1 (8-ounce) carton coffee-flavored low-fat yogurt
1 cup 1% low-fat chocolate milk
2 small bananas, peeled and cut into chunks

3 tablespoons miniature semisweet chocolate
   morsels

8 (3-ounce) paper cups
8 wooden sticks

1 Combine first 3 ingredients in container of an electric blender or food processor; cover and process until smooth.

2 Stir in chocolate morsels. Pour mixture evenly into paper cups. Cover tops of cups with aluminum foil, and insert a stick through foil into center of each cup. Freeze at least 4 hours.

3 To serve, remove foil, and peel paper cup away from each pop. Yield: 8 pops.

Nutritional content per pop: Calories 108
Fat 3.2g (Sat Fat 1.5g) Carbohydrate 18.0g Fiber 0.8g
Protein 3.3g Cholesterol 1mg Sodium 50mg

Honey-Banana Pops

2 (8-ounce) cartons vanilla low-fat yogurt
2 medium-size ripe bananas, peeled and mashed
2 tablespoons honey
1 teaspoon vanilla extract
¼ teaspoon ground cinnamon

8 (3-ounce) paper cups
8 wooden sticks

1 Combine first 5 ingredients in container of an electric blender or food processor; cover and process just until smooth.

2 Pour mixture evenly into paper cups. Cover tops of cups with aluminum foil, and insert a stick through foil into center of each cup. Freeze at least 4 hours.

3 To serve, remove foil, and peel paper away from each pop. Yield: 8 pops.

Nutritional content per pop: Calories 91
Fat 0.8g (Sat Fat 0.5g) Carbohydrate 18.7g Fiber 0.8g
Protein 3.1g Cholesterol 3mg Sodium 38mg

Creamy Vanilla Milkshake

Preparation Time: 5 minutes

4 cups vanilla nonfat frozen yogurt
1¾ cups skim milk
½ teaspoon vanilla extract

1 Combine all ingredients in container of an electric blender or food processor; cover and process until smooth. Serve immediately. Yield: 5 (1-cup) servings.

Nutritional content per serving: Calories 162
Fat 0.1g (Sat Fat 0.1g) Carbohydrate 33.2g Fiber 0g
Protein 8.4g Cholesterol 2mg Sodium 141mg

Variations:

Strawberry Milkshake: Substitute strawberry nonfat frozen yogurt for vanilla nonfat frozen yogurt. Omit vanilla extract. Add 1½ cups fresh strawberries or 1½ cups frozen unsweetened strawberries, thawed, to ingredients in blender. Yield: 6 (1-cup) servings.

Nutritional content per serving: Calories 145
Fat 0.3g (Sat Fat 0.1g) Carbohydrate 30.1g Fiber 0.9g
Protein 7.2g Cholesterol 1mg Sodium 118mg

Tropical Milkshake: Omit vanilla extract. Add 1 (8-ounce) can unsweetened crushed pineapple, undrained; 1 cup cubed papaya; ½ cup unsweetened pineapple juice; and ½ teaspoon rum extract to ingredients in blender. Yield: 8 (1-cup) servings.

Nutritional content per serving: Calories 135
Fat 0.2g (Sat Fat 0.1g) Carbohydrate 29.1g Fiber 0.6g
Protein 5.6g Cholesterol 1mg Sodium 89mg

Raspberry Frozen Daiquiris

Preparation Time: 5 minutes

1 (10-ounce) package frozen raspberries in light
  syrup
¾ cup frozen pink lemonade concentrate, thawed
  and undiluted
¾ cup light rum
3 tablespoons powdered sugar

4 cups crushed ice

1 Combine first 4 ingredients in container of an electric blender or food processor; cover and process until combined. Add crushed ice, and process just until slushy. Serve immediately. Yield: 6 (1-cup) servings.

Nutritional content per serving: Calories 198
Fat 0.2g (Sat Fat 0g) Carbohydrate 33.4g Fiber 3.5g
Protein 0.4g Cholesterol 0mg Sodium 2mg

Variation:

Strawberry Frozen Daiquiris: Substitute 1(10-ounce) package frozen strawberries in light syrup for the raspberries. Yield: 6 (1-cup) servings.

Nutritional content per serving: Calories 186
Fat 0.2g (Sat Fat 0g) Carbohydrate 30.9g Fiber 0.4g
Protein 0.4g Cholesterol 0mg Sodium 2mg

Apple-Grape Punch

Preparation Time: 5 minutes
Chilling Time: at least
30 minutes

To make ice cubes that won't dilute your punch, freeze fruit juice in ice trays. Add frozen juice cubes to punch before serving.

1 (48-ounce) bottle unsweetened apple juice
1 (24-ounce) bottle unsweetened grape juice
1 (12-ounce) can frozen lemonade concentrate, thawed and undiluted

1 (33.8-ounce) bottle club soda, chilled

1 Combine first 3 ingredients in a large pitcher; stir well. Chill thoroughly.

2 Just before serving, stir in club soda. Yield: 15 (1-cup) servings.

Nutritional content per serving: Calories 114 Fat 0.1g (Sat Fat 0g) Carbohydrate 29.0g Fiber 0.3g Protein 0.1g Cholesterol 0mg Sodium 19mg

Orange-Pineapple Slush

Preparation Time: **5 minutes**

Whip up
a fruit slush
when you crave
thirst-quenching
refreshment.

3 cups ice cubes
1 cup freshly squeezed orange juice
½ cup pineapple juice
¼ cup freshly squeezed lemon juice
3 tablespoons sugar

1 Combine first 5 ingredients in container of an electric blender or food processor; cover and process on high speed until smooth and frothy. Serve immediately. Yield: 4 (1-cup) servings.

Nutritional content per serving: Calories 86
Fat 0.1g (Sat Fat 0.1g) Carbohydrate 21.7g Fiber 0.2g
Protein 0.6g Cholesterol 0mg Sodium 1mg

Variation:

Very Berry Slush: Substitute cranberry juice cocktail for orange juice; omit pineapple juice. Add 1 tablespoon raspberry lemonade concentrate, thawed and ½ cup water. Continue with recipe as directed. Yield: 4 (1-cup) servings.

Nutritional content per serving: Calories 86
Fat 0.0g (Sat Fat 0g) Carbohydrate 22.5g Fiber 0.0g
Protein 0.1g Cholesterol 0mg Sodium 3mg

Spicy Tomato Sipper

Preparation Time: 5 minutes
Chilling Time: at least
30 minutes

2¾ cups no-salt-added tomato juice
2 tablespoons lime juice
2 teaspoons low-sodium Worcestershire sauce
1 teaspoon prepared horseradish
½ teaspoon celery salt
¼ teaspoon hot sauce

Lime curls (optional)

1 Combine first 6 ingredients in a small pitcher; stir well. Cover and chill thoroughly. Garnish with lime curls, if desired. Yield: 3 (1-cup) servings.

Nutritional content per serving: Calories 51
Fat 0.0g (Sat Fat 0g) Carbohydrate 12.9g Fiber 0.9g
Protein 2.3g Cholesterol 0mg Sodium 390mg

Variation:

Zippy Red-Eye: Increase tomato juice to 3¼ cups and hot sauce to ½ teaspoon. Continue with recipe as directed. Just before serving, stir in ½ cup vodka. Serve over ice. Garnish with celery sticks, if desired. Yield: 4 (1-cup) servings.

Nutritional content per serving: Calories 110
Fat 0.0g (Sat Fat 0g) Carbohydrate 11.2g Fiber 0g
Protein 2.0g Cholesterol 0mg Sodium 298mg

Hot Cocoa Mix

Preparation Time: **5 minutes**

These flavored cocoa mixes can be stored up to three months in airtight containers.

1¾ cups instant nonfat dry milk powder
1 cup sifted powdered sugar
⅔ cup miniature marshmallows
½ cup unsweetened cocoa
½ teaspoon ground cinnamon

1 Combine all ingredients; stir well. Store in an airtight container. To serve, spoon 3 tablespoons cocoa mix into each individual mug. Add ¾ cup hot water; stir well. Yield: 16 (1-cup) servings.

Nutritional content per serving: Calories 95
Fat 0.5g (Sat Fat 0.3g) Carbohydrate 17.2g Fiber 0g
Protein 5.6g Cholesterol 3mg Sodium 72mg

Variations:

Minted Hot Cocoa Mix: Omit marshmallows and cinnamon, and add 4 (4½-inch) sticks of peppermint candy, crushed, to Hot Cocoa Mix. Yield: 14 (1-cup) servings.

Nutritional content per serving: Calories 105
Fat 0.5g (Sat Fat 0.3g) Carbohydrate 18.8g Fiber 0g
Protein 6.3g Cholesterol 3mg Sodium 82mg

Mocha-Cocoa Mix: Omit marshmallows, and add ¼ cup instant coffee granules to Hot Cocoa Mix. Yield: 14 (1-cup) servings.

Nutritional content per serving: Calories 105
Fat 0.6g (Sat Fat 0.3g) Carbohydrate 18.7g Fiber 0.1g
Protein 6.5g Cholesterol 3mg Sodium 82mg

BREADS

page 64

page 67

page 79

Biscuits and Breadsticks
Buttermilk Biscuits   64
Red Pepper-Rosemary Pinwheels   65
Parmesan Breadsticks   66
Cinnamon Breadsticks   66
Orange-Glazed Breadsticks   66

Pancakes and Waffles
Whole Wheat-Apple Pancakes with Apple Topping   67
Waffles with Strawberry Syrup   68
Gingerbread Waffles with Creamy Maple Topping   69

Muffins and Loaves
Blueberry Muffins   70
Miniature Blueberry Muffins   70
Overnight Bran Muffins   71
Whole Wheat-Banana Muffins   72
Whole Wheat-Banana Loaf   72
Buttermilk Corn Sticks   73
Mexican Corn Sticks   74
Chile-Cheese Cornbread   75
Triple Herb Popovers   76
Cumin Mini-Loaf   77
Cumin Muffins   77
Strawberry Bread   78
Spiced Pumpkin Bread with Pineapple Spread   79
Herbed Garlic Bread   80

Buttermilk Biscuits

Preparation Time: 10 minutes
Cooking Time: 8–10 minutes

Contrary to its
name, buttermilk
is naturally
low in fat.

1³⁄₄ **cups all-purpose flour**
   2 **teaspoons baking powder**
 ¹⁄₂ **teaspoon baking soda**
 ¹⁄₂ **teaspoon salt**
 ¹⁄₂ **teaspoon sugar**

 ²⁄₃ **cup nonfat buttermilk**
   2 **tablespoons vegetable oil**
   1 **tablespoon nonfat sour cream alternative**

   Butter-flavored vegetable cooking spray

1 Combine first 5 ingredients in a medium bowl; make a well in center of mixture.

2 Combine buttermilk, oil, and sour cream; add to dry ingredients, stirring just until moistened.

3 Turn dough out onto a lightly floured surface. Knead 5 to 6 times. Roll dough to ³⁄₄-inch thickness, and cut into rounds with a 2¹⁄₂-inch biscuit cutter. Place on an ungreased baking sheet. Spray tops lightly with cooking spray. Bake at 400° 8 to 10 minutes or until lightly browned. Yield: 1 dozen.

Nutritional content per biscuit: Calories 94
Fat 2.6g (Sat Fat 0.4g) Carbohydrate 15.1g Fiber 0.5g
Protein 2.5g Cholesterol 0mg Sodium 166mg

Red Pepper-Rosemary Pinwheels

Preparation Time: 25 minutes
Cooking Time: 15–18 minutes

Dental floss is perfect to use for cutting through the dough.

〜〜〜〜〜

Vegetable cooking spray
½ cup finely chopped sweet red pepper
¼ cup minced onion
1 clove garlic, minced
1 tablespoon fresh rosemary, minced
¼ teaspoon ground red pepper

1¼ cups all-purpose flour
1 teaspoon baking powder
¼ teaspoon salt
3 tablespoons reduced-calorie stick margarine

3 tablespoons skim milk
1 egg, lightly beaten

1 Coat a nonstick skillet with cooking spray; place over medium-high heat until hot. Add chopped red pepper, onion, and garlic; sauté until tender. Add rosemary and ground red pepper; remove from heat, and set aside.

2 Combine flour, baking powder, and salt in a medium bowl; cut in margarine with a pastry blender until mixture resembles coarse meal.

3 Combine milk and egg; add to dry ingredients, stirring just until moistened. Turn dough out onto a lightly floured surface, and knead 5 or 6 times.

4 Place dough between 2 pieces of heavy-duty plastic wrap, and roll into a 10- x 8-inch rectangle. Remove top piece of plastic wrap. Spread vegetable mixture evenly over dough. Roll up, jellyroll fashion, starting at long side. Pinch ends and seam to seal.

5 Cut roll into 10 (1-inch) slices. Place slices in muffin pans coated with cooking spray. Bake at 400° for 15 to 18 minutes or until golden. Remove from pans immediately. Yield: 10 pinwheels.

Nutritional content per pinwheel: Calories 90
Fat 3.1g (Sat Fat 0.5g) Carbohydrate 13.3g Fiber 0.7g
Protein 2.6g Cholesterol 22mg Sodium 101mg

Parmesan Breadsticks

Preparation Time: 20 minutes
Rising Time: 20–30 minutes
Cooking Time: 12 minutes

1 (16-ounce) package hot roll mix
¼ cup grated Parmesan cheese
1 cup hot water (120° to 130°)
1 egg white, lightly beaten
2 tablespoons vegetable oil
1 teaspoon dried Italian seasoning
   Butter-flavored vegetable cooking spray
2 tablespoons plus 2 teaspoons grated Parmesan
   cheese

1 Combine roll mix, yeast from packet, and ¼ cup cheese in a bowl. Add hot water and next 3 ingredients; stir until moistened. Shape dough into a ball. Turn dough out onto a lightly floured surface; knead until smooth and elastic (about 5 minutes). Cover; let rest 5 minutes.

2 Roll dough into a 16- x 12-inch rectangle on a lightly floured surface. Cut rectangle with a pastry cutter to form 16 strips. Cut 16 strips in half lengthwise to form 32 (6-inch) strips.

3 Twist each strip 5 or 6 times; place on baking sheets coated with cooking spray. Spray tops of strips with cooking spray; sprinkle each strip with ¼ teaspoon cheese.

4 Cover; let rise in a warm place (85°), free from drafts, 20 to 30 minutes, or until doubled in bulk. Bake at 375° for 12 minutes or until golden. Yield: 32 breadsticks.

Nutritional content per breadstick: Calories 63
Fat 1.2g (Sat Fat 0.4g) Carbohydrate 10.6g Fiber 0g
Protein 2.0g Cholesterol 1mg Sodium 121mg

Variations:

Cinnamon Breadsticks: Follow directions for steps 1 through 3, omitting cheese and Italian seasoning. Combine ¼ cup sugar and ¾ teaspoon ground cinnamon. Brush strips with ¼ cup reduced-calorie stick margarine, melted; sprinkle with cinnamon mixture. Let rise, and bake as directed in step 4.

Nutritional content per breadstick: Calories 71
Fat 1.8g (Sat Fat 0.2g) Carbohydrate 11.7g Fiber 0g
Protein 1.6g Cholesterol 0mg Sodium 115mg

Orange-Glazed Breadsticks: Follow directions for steps 1 through 3, omitting cheese and Italian seasoning and adding 1 tablespoon grated orange rind. Let rise, and bake as directed in step 4. Combine 1¼ cups sifted powdered sugar, 1½ tablespoons skim milk, and ¼ teaspoon orange extract. Drizzle over breadsticks.

Nutritional content per serving: Calories 77
Fat 0.9g (Sat Fat 0.2g) Carbohydrate 15.2g Fiber 0g
Protein 1.6g Cholesterol 0mg Sodium 102mg

Whole Wheat-Apple Pancakes with Apple Topping

Preparation Time: 15 minutes
Cooking Time: 12–15 minutes

½ cup all-purpose flour
½ cup whole wheat flour
1 teaspoon baking soda
⅛ teaspoon salt
1 tablespoon sugar

1 cup nonfat buttermilk
1 egg, lightly beaten
2 teaspoons vegetable oil

½ cup peeled, finely chopped apple

Vegetable cooking spray
Apple Topping

1 Combine first 5 ingredients in a medium bowl; make a well in center of mixture.

2 Combine buttermilk, egg, and oil; add to dry ingredients, stirring just until moistened. Stir in apple.

3 For each pancake, pour ¼ cup batter onto a hot griddle or skillet coated with cooking spray, spreading batter to a 4-inch circle. Cook pancakes until tops are covered with bubbles and edges look cooked; turn pancakes, and cook other side. Top pancakes evenly with Apple Topping. Yield: 10 (4-inch) pancakes.

Apple Topping

½ cup unsweetened applesauce
½ cup reduced-calorie apple jelly
½ teaspoon apple pie spice

1 Combine all ingredients in a small saucepan. Cook over low heat until jelly melts, stirring occasionally. Yield: 1 cup.

Nutritional content per pancake with topping: Calories 109 Fat 1.8g (Sat Fat 0.4g) Carbohydrate 20.7g Fiber 1.3g Protein 3.2g Cholesterol 23mg Sodium 203mg

Waffles with Strawberry Syrup

Preparation Time: 15 minutes
Cooking Time: 30 minutes

Waffles and pancakes
are excellent
sources of complex
carbohydrates.

~~~~~~~

1¾ cups all-purpose flour
1¼ teaspoons baking powder
2 tablespoons sugar

1 egg, separated
1 cup skim milk
2 tablespoons plus 2 teaspoons reduced-calorie
   stick margarine, melted

1 egg white

Vegetable cooking spray
Strawberry Syrup

1 Combine first 3 ingredients in a medium bowl; make a well in center of mixture.

2 Beat egg yolk in a small bowl; add milk and margarine, stirring well. Add liquid mixture to dry ingredients, stirring until smooth.

3 Beat 2 egg whites at high speed of an electric mixer until stiff peaks form; fold beaten egg white into batter.

4 Coat a heart-shaped waffle iron with cooking spray; allow waffle iron to preheat. For each waffle, pour ½ cup batter onto hot waffle iron, spreading batter to edges. Bake 4 to 5 minutes or until steaming stops. Repeat procedure with remaining batter. Top each waffle with 1 tablespoon Strawberry Syrup. Yield: 20 (3-inch) waffles.

Strawberry Syrup

1¼ cups unsweetened apple juice
1 cup sugar
1 cup sliced fresh strawberries
⅓ cup water

1 Combine all ingredients in a medium saucepan. Bring to a boil. Reduce heat, and simmer 30 minutes or until mixture is reduced to 1¼ cups, stirring occasionally. Serve warm or chilled. Yield: 1¼ cups.

Nutritional content per waffle with syrup: Calories 110 Fat 1.4g (Sat Fat 0.3g) Carbohydrate 22.6g Fiber 0.5g Protein 2.1g Cholesterol 11mg Sodium 28mg

Gingerbread Waffles with Creamy Maple Topping

Preparation Time: 20 minutes
Cooking Time: 8–10 minutes

2 tablespoons reduced-calorie stick margarine, softened
2 tablespoons molasses
1 egg

1 cup all-purpose flour
⅓ cup whole wheat flour
1 teaspoon baking powder
½ teaspoon baking soda
1 teaspoon ground ginger
¼ teaspoon ground cinnamon
⅛ teaspoon ground cloves

¾ cup skim milk

1 egg white

Vegetable cooking spray
Creamy Maple Topping

1 Beat margarine and molasses at medium-high speed of an electric mixer until smooth; add egg, beating well.

2 Combine all-purpose flour and next 6 ingredients, stirring well. Add flour mixture to creamed mixture alternately with milk, beginning and ending with flour mixture. Beat just until blended after each addition.

3 Beat egg white at high speed of an electric mixer until stiff peaks form. Gently fold into batter.

4 Coat an 8-inch-square waffle iron with cooking spray; allow waffle iron to preheat. Pour 2 cups batter onto hot waffle iron, spreading batter to edges. Bake 4 to 5 minutes or until steaming stops. Repeat procedure with remaining batter. Top each waffle with 1 tablespoon Creamy Maple Topping. Yield: 8 (4-inch) waffles.

Creamy Maple Topping

¼ cup lite ricotta cheese
1½ tablespoons honey
¼ cup vanilla low-fat yogurt
¼ teaspoon maple flavoring

1 Combine cheese and honey in container of an electric blender or food processor; cover and process until smooth. Transfer mixture to a small bowl. Add yogurt and flavoring; stir well. Cover and refrigerate until ready to use. Yield: ½ cup.

Nutritional content per waffle with topping: Calories 148 Fat 3.3g (Sat Fat 0.5g) Carbohydrate 25.1g Fiber 1.1g Protein 5.5g Cholesterol 30mg Sodium 146mg

Blueberry Muffins

Preparation Time: 15 minutes
Cooking Time: 20–25 minutes

Grated lemon and
orange rinds
lend citrus appeal
to this moist muffin.

~~~~~~~~~

1¾ cups all-purpose flour
2 teaspoons baking powder
¼ teaspoon salt
½ teaspoon ground allspice
1 cup fresh or frozen blueberries, thawed and
   drained

¾ cup skim milk
⅓ cup sugar
¼ cup vegetable oil
1 egg, beaten
1 teaspoon grated lemon rind
1 teaspoon grated orange rind
1 teaspoon vanilla extract

Vegetable cooking spray

1 Combine first 4 ingredients in a medium bowl; add blueberries, and toss to coat. Make a well in center of mixture.

2 Combine milk and next 6 ingredients; add to dry ingredients, stirring just until moistened.

3 Spoon batter into muffin pans coated with cooking spray, filling three-fourths full. Bake at 400° for 20 to 25 minutes or until golden. Remove from pans immediately. Yield: 1 dozen.

Nutritional content per muffin: Calories 150
Fat 5.5g (Sat Fat 1.0g) Carbohydrate 22.2g Fiber 0.9g
Protein 3.0g Cholesterol 19mg Sodium 63mg

Variation:

Miniature Blueberry Muffins:
Follow directions for steps 1 and 2. Spoon batter into miniature (1¾-inch) muffin pans coated with cooking spray, filling three-fourths full. Bake at 400° for 15 minutes or until golden. Remove from pans immediately. Yield: 3 dozen.

Nutritional content per miniature muffin: Calories 50
Fat 1.8g (Sat Fat 0.3g) Carbohydrate 7.4g Fiber 0.3g
Protein 1.0g Cholesterol 6mg Sodium 21mg

Make-Ahead Directions: Freeze muffins in a labeled airtight container up to 2 weeks. Thaw at room temperature, or microwave 1 regular or 2 miniature muffins at MEDIUM (50% power) 30 seconds or until warm.

Overnight Bran Muffins

Preparation Time: 10 minutes
Chilling Time: at least
8 hours
Cooking Time: 14–15 minutes

You can make this
muffin batter ahead of
time and store
it in the refrigerator
up to three days.

4 cups wheat bran flakes cereal with raisins
2½ cups all-purpose flour
1½ teaspoons baking soda
1 teaspoon salt
1 cup mixed dried fruit
⅔ cup sugar

2 cups nonfat buttermilk
¼ cup corn oil
2 eggs, lightly beaten

Vegetable cooking spray

1 Combine first 6 ingredients in a large bowl; make a well in center of mixture.

2 Combine buttermilk, eggs, and oil; add to dry ingredients, stirring just until moistened. Cover and chill at least 8 hours.

3 Spoon batter into muffin pans coated with cooking spray, filling about three-fourths full. Bake at 400° for 14 to 15 minutes or until golden. Remove from pans immediately. Yield: 2 dozen.

Nutritional content per muffin: Calories 156
Fat 3.3g (Sat Fat 0.6g) Carbohydrate 29.2g Fiber 1.9g
Protein 4.0g Cholesterol 19mg Sodium 288mg

Whole Wheat-Banana Muffins

Preparation Time: 10 minutes
Cooking Time: 20 minutes

These muffins are
suited for today's
fast-paced lifestyle.
Teamed with a glass of milk,
one will make
a light breakfast when you
have just minutes
to spare.

1 cup all-purpose flour
1 cup whole wheat flour
¼ cup toasted wheat germ
1 teaspoon baking powder
1 teaspoon baking soda
½ teaspoon salt

1⅓ cups mashed ripe banana (about 3 large)
½ cup plus 2 tablespoons sugar
¼ cup vegetable oil
1 egg, lightly beaten

Vegetable cooking spray

1 Combine first 6 ingredients in a large bowl; make a well in center of mixture.

2 Combine banana and next 3 ingredients; add to dry ingredients, stirring just until moistened.

3 Spoon mixture into muffin pans coated with cooking spray, filling two-thirds full. Bake at 350° for 20 minutes. Yield: 16 muffins.

Nutritional content per muffin: Calories 148
Fat 4.4g (Sat Fat 0.7g) Carbohydrate 25.6g Fiber 2.1g
Protein 2.8g Cholesterol 14mg Sodium 157mg

Variation:

Whole Wheat-Banana Loaf: Follow directions for steps 1 and 2. Spoon batter into a 9- x 5- x 3-inch loafpan coated with cooking spray. Bake at 400° for 40 to 45 minutes or until a wooden pick inserted in center comes out clean. Yield: 18 (½-inch) slices.

Nutritional content per slice: Calories 131
Fat 3.9g (Sat Fat 0.6g) Carbohydrate 22.8g Fiber 1.8g
Protein 2.5g Cholesterol 12mg Sodium 140mg

Buttermilk Corn Sticks

Preparation Time: **10 minutes**
Cooking Time: **10 minutes**

Corn stick pans come
in various shapes,
so your yield
for this recipe could vary.
Just be sure to fill your
pan two-thirds full.

⅔ cup yellow cornmeal
½ cup all-purpose flour
¾ teaspoon baking powder
½ teaspoon baking soda
¼ teaspoon salt
¼ teaspoon paprika

¾ cup nonfat buttermilk
2 tablespoons sugar
2 tablespoons vegetable oil
1 egg, lightly beaten

Vegetable cooking spray

1 Combine first 6 ingredients in a medium bowl; make a well in center of mixture.

2 Combine buttermilk and next 3 ingredients; add to dry ingredients, stirring just until moistened.

3 Place cast-iron corn stick pans coated with cooking spray in a 425° oven for 3 minutes or until hot. Remove pans from oven; spoon batter into pans, filling two-thirds full. Bake at 425° for 10 minutes or until lightly browned. Yield: 1 dozen.

Nutritional content per corn stick: Calories 88
Fat 3.0g (Sat Fat 0.6g) Carbohydrate 13.0g Fiber 0.5g
Protein 2.3g Cholesterol 19mg Sodium 124mg

Mexican Corn Sticks

Preparation Time: 10 minutes
Cooking Time: 18–20 minutes

To keep the cheese
from sticking
to the pans, coat them
lightly with cooking spray
and don't preheat
the pans before filling
with batter.

1¼ cups all-purpose flour
¾ cup yellow cornmeal
2 teaspoons baking powder
1 teaspoon baking soda
¼ teaspoon salt
Dash of ground red pepper

¾ cup nonfat buttermilk
1 (8¾-ounce) can no-salt-added cream-style corn
1 (4-ounce) can chopped green chiles, undrained
2 egg whites, lightly beaten
½ cup (2 ounces) shredded reduced-fat sharp
Cheddar cheese

Vegetable cooking spray

1 Combine first 6 ingredients in a medium bowl; make a well in center of mixture.

2 Combine buttermilk and next 3 ingredients; add to dry ingredients, stirring just until moistened. Fold in cheese.

3 Spoon batter into cactus-shaped cast-iron pans coated with cooking spray, filling two-thirds full. Bake at 425° for 18 to 20 minutes or until golden. Remove from pans immediately. Yield: 16 corn sticks.

Nutritional content per corn stick: Calories 91
Fat 1.2g (Sat Fat 0.5g) Carbohydrate 16.7g Fiber 0.9g
Protein 3.8g Cholesterol 3mg Sodium 194mg

Chile-Cheese Cornbread

Preparation Time: 10 minutes
Cooking Time: 30 minutes

1 cup yellow cornmeal
1 cup all-purpose flour
1 tablespoon plus 1 teaspoon baking powder
¼ teaspoon salt
¼ cup nonfat dry milk powder
1 tablespoon sugar

1 cup water
½ cup frozen egg substitute, thawed
2 tablespoons vegetable oil

¾ cup (3 ounces) shredded 40% less-fat Cheddar
    cheese
1 (4-ounce) can chopped green chiles, drained

Vegetable cooking spray

1 Combine first 6 ingredients in a medium bowl; make a well in center of mixture.

2 Combine water, egg substitute, and oil; add to dry ingredients, stirring just until moistened. Stir in cheese and green chiles.

3 Pour batter into an 8-inch square baking dish coated with cooking spray. Bake at 375° for 30 minutes or until golden. Yield: 16 servings.

Nutritional content per serving: Calories 107
Fat 3.0g (Sat Fat 0.9g) Carbohydrate 15.3g Fiber 0.7g
Protein 4.6g Cholesterol 4mg Sodium 125mg

Triple Herb Popovers

Preparation Time: 10 minutes
Cooking Time: 50–55 minutes

1 cup bread flour
1 cup skim milk
2 eggs, lightly beaten
2 egg whites
1 tablespoon reduced-calorie stick margarine, melted
1 teaspoon dried basil
1 teaspoon dried oregano
1 teaspoon dried thyme
½ teaspoon freshly ground pepper
¼ teaspoon salt

Vegetable cooking spray

1 Combine first 10 ingredients in a medium bowl; stir with a wire whisk until smooth.

2 Pour batter evenly into popover pan cups coated with cooking spray. Place in a cold oven.

3 Turn oven on 450°, and bake 15 minutes. Reduce heat to 350°, and bake an additional 35 to 40 minutes or until popovers are crusty and brown. Serve immediately. Yield: 6 popovers.

Nutritional content per popover: Calories 141
Fat 3.6g (Sat Fat 0.8g) Carbohydrate 19.4g Fiber 0.2g
Protein 7.5g Cholesterol 74mg Sodium 177mg

Cumin Mini-Loaf

Preparation Time: 15 minutes
Cooking Time: 40 minutes

Serve this savory
bread with
light luncheon fare
such as green
or pasta salads.

~~~~~~~~

1½ cups all-purpose flour
1 tablespoon baking powder
¼ teaspoon salt
2 tablespoons sugar
2 teaspoons ground cumin
½ teaspoon cumin seed, slightly crushed
¼ teaspoon dry mustard

⅔ cup skim milk
⅓ cup frozen egg substitute, thawed
2½ tablespoons vegetable oil
2 tablespoons picante sauce

Vegetable cooking spray

1 Combine first 7 ingredients in a medium bowl; make a well in center of mixture.

2 Combine milk and next 3 ingredients; stir well. Add to dry ingredients, stirring just until moistened.

3 Spoon batter into a 7½- x 3- x 2-inch loafpan coated with cooking spray. Bake at 350° for 40 minutes or until a wooden pick inserted in center comes out clean. Remove from pan, and let cool on a wire rack. Yield: 10 (¾-inch) slices.

Nutritional content per slice: Calories 123
Fat 3.9g (Sat Fat 0.5g) Carbohydrate 18.5g Fiber 0.6g
Protein 3.4g Cholesterol 0mg Sodium 114mg

Variation:

Cumin Muffins: Follow directions for steps 1 and 2. Spoon batter into muffin pans coated with cooking spray, filling two-thirds full. Bake at 400° for 18 to 20 minutes or until a wooden pick inserted in center comes out clean. Remove from pans immediately, and serve warm. Yield: 10 muffins.

Nutritional content per muffin: Calories 123
Fat 3.9g (Sat Fat 0.5g) Carbohydrate 18.5g Fiber 0.6g
Protein 3.4g Cholesterol 0mg Sodium 114mg

Strawberry Bread

Preparation Time: 15 minutes
Cooking Time: 53–58 minutes

Fresh strawberries keep
this bread moist,
so it needs very little oil.

2 cups sifted cake flour
1 teaspoon baking soda
¼ teaspoon salt
¾ cup sugar
1 teaspoon ground cinnamon

¼ cup skim milk
2 tablespoons vegetable oil
2 eggs, lightly beaten

1 cup chopped fresh strawberries
1 tablespoon cake flour

Vegetable cooking spray

1 Combine first 5 ingredients in a medium bowl; make a well in center of mixture.

2 Combine milk, oil, and eggs; add to dry ingredients, stirring just until moistened.

3 Dredge strawberries in 1 tablespoon flour; gently fold into batter.

4 Spoon batter into an 8½- x 4½- x 3-inch loafpan coated with cooking spray. Bake at 350° for 53 to 58 minutes. Cool in pan 5 minutes; remove from pan, and let cool completely on a wire rack. Yield: 16 (½-inch) slices.

Nutritional content per slice: Calories 117
Fat 2.5g (Sat Fat 0.5g) Carbohydrate 21.4g Fiber 0.3g
Protein 2.2g Cholesterol 28mg Sodium 126mg

Spiced Pumpkin Bread with Pineapple Spread

Preparation Time: 15 minutes
Cooking Time: 45–50 minutes

2 cups sifted cake flour
2 teaspoons baking powder
¼ teaspoon baking soda
¼ teaspoon salt
⅔ cup firmly packed brown sugar
1 teaspoon ground cinnamon
¼ teaspoon ground ginger
¼ teaspoon ground cloves

1 cup canned pumpkin
¼ cup unsweetened applesauce
3 tablespoons vegetable oil
1 teaspoon vanilla extract
2 eggs, lightly beaten

Vegetable cooking spray

Pineapple Spread

1 Combine first 8 ingredients in a medium bowl; make a well in center of mixture.

2 Combine pumpkin and next 4 ingredients; add to dry ingredients, stirring just until moistened.

3 Spoon batter into a 9- x 5- x 3-inch loafpan coated with cooking spray. Bake at 350° for 45 to 50 minutes or until a wooden pick inserted in center comes out clean. Let cool in pan 10 minutes; remove loaf from pan, and let cool completely on a wire rack. Top slices with Pineapple Spread. Yield: 18 (½-inch) slices.

Pineapple Spread

1 (8-ounce) carton light process cream cheese product, softened
1 (8-ounce) can crushed pineapple in juice, drained
1½ tablespoons honey
⅛ teaspoon ground ginger

1 Combine all ingredients in a bowl; stir well. Cover and chill at least 30 minutes. Yield: 1⅓ cups.

Nutritional content per slice with spread: Calories 150 Fat 5.2g (Sat Fat 1.9g) Carbohydrate 23.0g Fiber 0.4g Protein 3.2g Cholesterol 32mg Sodium 133mg

Herbed Garlic Bread

Preparation Time: 5 minutes
Cooking Time: 15 minutes

For the flavor of
commercial garlic bread
with a lot less fat,
buy plain French bread and
spread with our lower-fat
herb mixture.

¼ cup reduced-calorie stick margarine, softened
1½ tablespoons freshly grated Parmesan cheese
2 teaspoons minced fresh parsley
2 teaspoons minced fresh basil
¼ teaspoon garlic powder

12 (¾-inch-thick) slices French bread

1 Combine first 5 ingredients in a small bowl; stir well. Spread mixture evenly on one side of bread slices.

2 Wrap bread in aluminum foil, and bake at 400° for 15 minutes. Yield: 12 (¾-inch) slices.

Nutritional content per slice: Calories 103
Fat 3.0g (Sat Fat 0.5g) Carbohydrate 15.8g Fiber 0.7g
Protein 2.6g Cholesterol 1mg Sodium 203mg

DESSERTS

~~~~~~

page 82

page 96

page 107

Cakes
Applesauce Spice Cupcakes   82
Carrot-Raisin Snack Cake   83
Coffee Crunch Cake   84
Moist Cranberry Coffee Cake   85

Cookies
Strawberry-Oat Squares   86
Butterscotch Brownies   87
Peanut Butter Swirl Brownies   88
Lemon Soufflé Bars   89
Orange Soufflé Bars   89

Frozen Desserts
Bananas Melba   90
Blackberry Frozen Yogurt   91
Raspberry Frozen Yogurt   92
Frozen Vanilla Custard with Chocolate-Mint Sauce   93
Frozen Yogurt Pie with Raspberry-Graham Crust   94
Frozen Yogurt Pie with Strawberry-Graham Crust   94
Mandarin Phyllo Baskets   95
Frozen Peanutty Dessert   96
Frozen Rainbow Torte   97

Fruit Desserts
Champagne Fruit Compote   98
Ambrosia Parfaits   99
Peach Trifle   100

Pastries
Apple-Cinnamon Turnovers   101
Blueberry-Pineapple Cobbler   102
Peach Cobbler   103
Cheesecake Tartlets with Strawberry Glaze   104

Puddings and Soufflés
Banana Pudding   105
Double Chocolate Pudding   106
Brown Sugar Pudding   106
Fresh Strawberry Mousse   107
Warm Chocolate Soufflés with Custard Sauce   108

Sauces
Brandied Fruit Sauce   109
Praline-Pecan Sauce   110
Chunky Pineapple Sauce   111
Luscious Strawberry Sauce   112

Applesauce Spice Cupcakes

Preparation Time: 15 minutes
Cooking Time: 16–18 minutes

Applesauce replaces
much of the fat
in this recipe, producing
moist, tender cupcakes.

3 cups sifted cake flour
2½ teaspoons baking powder
1 teaspoon baking soda
½ teaspoon salt
1½ cups sugar
½ teaspoon ground ginger

½ cup frozen egg substitute, thawed
½ cup skim milk
⅓ cup vegetable oil

1½ cups cinnamon applesauce
2 teaspoons vanilla extract

3 egg whites

2 teaspoons powdered sugar
⅛ teaspoon ground cinnamon

1 Combine first 6 ingredients in a large bowl; make a well in center of mixture.

2 Combine egg substitute, milk, and oil; add to dry ingredients, stirring just until moistened. Stir in applesauce and vanilla.

3 Beat egg whites at high speed of an electric mixer until stiff peaks form. Gently fold beaten egg white into applesauce mixture.

4 Spoon batter into paper-lined muffin pans, filling each three-fourths full. Bake at 400° for 16 to 18 minutes or until a wooden pick inserted in center comes out clean. Remove from pans immediately, and let cool completely on wire racks. Combine powdered sugar and cinnamon; sift evenly over cupcakes. Yield: 2 dozen.

Nutritional content per cupcake: Calories 145
Fat 3.1g (Sat Fat 0.6g) Carbohydrate 27.2g Fiber 0.2g
Protein 2.2g Cholesterol 0mg Sodium 119mg

Carrot-Raisin Snack Cake

Preparation Time: 20 minutes
Cooking Time: 25 minutes

⅓ cup margarine, softened
½ cup firmly packed dark brown sugar
⅔ cup unsweetened applesauce
½ cup frozen egg substitute, thawed

1½ cups sifted cake flour
1½ teaspoons baking powder
¼ teaspoon salt
1 teaspoon ground cinnamon
1 cup finely shredded carrot
½ cup raisins

Vegetable cooking spray

1 tablespoon powdered sugar

1 Beat margarine at medium speed of an electric mixer until creamy; gradually add brown sugar, beating well. Add applesauce and egg substitute; beat well.

2 Combine flour and next 3 ingredients; add to margarine mixture, stirring well. Stir in carrot and raisins.

3 Pour batter into an 8-inch square pan coated with cooking spray. Bake at 350° for 25 minutes or until a wooden pick inserted in center comes out clean. Cool in pan on a wire rack. Sift powdered sugar over cooled cake. Yield: 9 servings.

Nutritional content per serving: Calories 218
Fat 7.0g (Sat Fat 1.4g) Carbohydrate 36.6g Fiber 1.0g
Protein 3.3g Cholesterol 0mg Sodium 174mg

Coffee Crunch Cake

Preparation Time: 20 minutes
Cooking Time: 35–40 minutes

1 tablespoon instant coffee granules
2 tablespoons hot water

1 cup nonfat sour cream alternative
⅓ cup frozen egg substitute, thawed
¼ cup skim milk
¼ cup vegetable oil
1 teaspoon vanilla extract

2 cups sifted cake flour
2 teaspoons baking powder
¼ teaspoon salt
1 cup sugar
1 teaspoon ground cinnamon

Vegetable cooking spray

⅓ cup chocolate-coated coffee beans, chopped

1 Combine coffee granules and water in a medium bowl, stirring until granules dissolve. Stir in sour cream and next 4 ingredients.

2 Combine flour and next 4 ingredients in a large bowl; add coffee mixture, stirring just until moistened.

3 Pour batter into a 9-inch square pan coated with cooking spray; sprinkle with coffee beans. Bake at 350° for 35 to 40 minutes or until a wooden pick inserted in center comes out clean. Yield: 12 servings.

Nutritional content per serving: Calories 199
Fat 5.1g (Sat Fat 1.1g) Carbohydrate 33.7g Fiber 0.1g
Protein 3.8g Cholesterol 0mg Sodium 76mg

Moist Cranberry Coffee Cake

Preparation Time: 25 minutes
Cooking Time: 45–50 minutes

Moist Cranberry Coffee Cake has a sweet cranberry filling and a sprinkling of allspice, brown sugar, and oats—ingredients you probably have on hand.

½ cup reduced-calorie stick margarine, softened
⅔ cup sugar
1 egg
1 teaspoon vanilla extract

1¼ cups all-purpose flour
2 teaspoons baking powder
¼ cup skim milk

2 egg whites
Vegetable cooking spray

1 cup jellied whole berry cranberry sauce
3 tablespoons sugar

2 tablespoons regular oats, uncooked
1 tablespoon brown sugar
¾ teaspoon ground allspice

1 Beat margarine at medium speed of an electric mixer until creamy; gradually add ⅔ cup sugar, beating well. Add egg and vanilla; beat well.

2 Combine flour and baking powder; add to butter mixture alternately with milk, beginning and ending with flour mixture. Mix after each addition.

3 Beat egg whites at high speed of an electric mixer until stiff peaks form. Gently fold egg whites into batter. Spoon half of batter into an 8-inch square pan coated with cooking spray.

4 Combine cranberry sauce and 3 tablespoons sugar; spoon over batter. Spoon remaining batter over cranberry mixture.

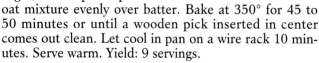

5 Combine oats, brown sugar, and allspice. Sprinkle oat mixture evenly over batter. Bake at 350° for 45 to 50 minutes or until a wooden pick inserted in center comes out clean. Let cool in pan on a wire rack 10 minutes. Serve warm. Yield: 9 servings.

Nutritional content per serving: Calories 264
Fat 7.5g (Sat Fat 0.2g) Carbohydrate 47.3g Fiber 0.8g
Protein 3.8g Cholesterol 25mg Sodium 130mg

Strawberry-Oat Squares

Preparation Time: 20 minutes
Cooking Time: 22–24 minutes
Chilling Time: 1 hour

Enjoy these cool
and creamy squares
as a light dessert
or snack.

¾ cup sifted cake flour
½ cup quick-cooking oats, uncooked
⅓ cup sifted powdered sugar
¼ cup plus 2 tablespoons margarine
    Vegetable cooking spray

1 (8-ounce) carton light process cream cheese
    product
½ cup 1% low-fat cottage cheese
¼ cup sugar
¼ teaspoon lemon extract

1 (10-ounce) package frozen strawberries in
    syrup, thawed and undrained
½ cup canned crushed pineapple in juice,
    undrained
1 tablespoon cornstarch

    Strawberry slices (optional)
    Mint sprigs (optional)

1 Combine first 3 ingredients in a medium bowl; cut in margarine with a pastry blender until mixture resembles coarse meal. Press oat mixture into bottom of an 8-inch square pan coated with cooking spray. Bake at 350° for 10 to 12 minutes or until lightly browned.

2 Position knife blade in food processor bowl; add cream cheese and next 3 ingredients. Process until smooth. Spoon over prepared crust. Set aside.

3 Combine thawed strawberries, pineapple, and cornstarch in a small saucepan; stirring until smooth. Cook over medium heat, stirring constantly, until thickened. Spoon over cheese mixture.

4 Bake at 350° for 12 minutes; cool completely. Cover and chill thoroughly. Cut into squares. If desired, garnish each square with a strawberry slice and a mint sprig. Yield: 16 squares.

Nutritional content per square: Calories 130
Fat 5.5g (Sat Fat 1.5g) Carbohydrate 17.8g Fiber 0.4g
Protein 3.4g Cholesterol 9mg Sodium 152mg

Butterscotch Brownies

Preparation Time: 15 minutes
Cooking Time: 25 minutes

¼ cup plus 2 tablespoons margarine, softened
1½ cups firmly packed dark brown sugar
½ cup frozen egg substitute, thawed
2 teaspoons vanilla extract

2 cups all-purpose flour
1 teaspoon baking powder
¼ teaspoon baking soda
½ teaspoon salt
½ cup plus 2 tablespoons butterscotch morsels

Vegetable cooking spray

1 Beat margarine at medium speed of an electric mixer until creamy; gradually add brown sugar, beating well. Add egg substitute and vanilla, beating well.

2 Combine flour and next 3 ingredients. Add to margarine mixture, beating well. Stir in butterscotch morsels.

3 Spoon mixture into a 13- x 9- x 2-inch pan coated with cooking spray. Bake at 350° for 25 minutes or until a wooden pick inserted in center comes out clean. Remove from oven, and let cool completely on a wire rack. Yield: 2½ dozen.

Nutritional content per brownie: Calories 115
Fat 3.3g (Sat Fat 0.6g) Carbohydrate 19.8g Fiber 0.2g
Protein 1.4g Cholesterol 0mg Sodium 89mg

Peanut Butter Swirl Brownies

Preparation Time: 22 minutes
Cooking Time: 25 minutes

We slimmed these
brownies down
by using reduced-calorie
margarine and 25% less-fat
peanut butter.

¼ cup plus 2 tablespoons reduced-calorie stick
    margarine, melted
1¼ cups firmly packed brown sugar
½ cup frozen egg substitute, thawed
1 teaspoon vanilla extract

1½ cups all-purpose flour
½ teaspoon baking powder
½ teaspoon salt

2 tablespoons unsweetened cocoa
¼ cup 25% less-fat creamy peanut butter

Vegetable cooking spray

1 Combine margarine and brown sugar in a medium bowl; add egg substitute. Beat at medium speed of an electric mixer until thoroughly combined. Add vanilla; beat well.

2 Combine flour, baking powder, and salt; add to sugar mixture, stirring well.

3 Divide batter in half. Stir cocoa into 1 half; stir peanut butter into other half. (Peanut butter mixture will be thick.)

4 Spoon dollops of each batter alternately into a 9-inch square pan coated with cooking spray. Cut through batters in pan with a knife to create a swirled pattern. Bake at 350° for 25 minutes or until a wooden pick inserted in center comes out clean. Remove from oven, and let cool completely on a wire rack. Yield: 16 brownies.

Nutritional content per brownie: Calories 162
Fat 4.5g (Sat Fat 0.7g) Carbohydrate 28.1g Fiber 0.4g
Protein 3.2g Cholesterol 0mg Sodium 151mg

Lemon Soufflé Bars

Preparation Time: 25 minutes
Cooking Time: 33–35 minutes

The filling for
Lemon Soufflé Bars
is free of cholesterol,
thanks to egg substitute.
For variety,
we've included an
orange-flavored version.

¼ cup margarine, softened
⅓ cup sugar
1 egg white
½ teaspoon vanilla extract

1¼ cups all-purpose flour
⅛ teaspoon salt

Vegetable cooking spray

1 (8-ounce) carton frozen egg substitute, thawed
1 cup sugar
½ cup all-purpose flour
½ teaspoon baking powder
1 tablespoon freshly grated lemon rind
⅓ cup lemon juice

2 teaspoons powdered sugar

1 Beat margarine at medium speed of an electric mixer until creamy; gradually add ⅓ cup sugar, beating well. Add egg white and vanilla, beating well.

2 Combine 1¼ cups flour and salt; add to margarine mixture, stirring well. Pat into bottom of a 13- x 9- x 2-inch baking dish coated with cooking spray. Bake at 375° for 15 minutes or until lightly browned.

3 Combine egg substitute and 1 cup sugar; beat at medium speed until blended. Combine ½ cup flour and baking powder. Add flour mixture, lemon rind, and lemon juice to egg substitute mixture; stir well. Pour over baked crust.

4 Bake at 350° for 18 to 20 minutes or until set. Let cool completely on a wire rack. Sprinkle with powdered sugar. Cut into bars. Yield: 3 dozen.

Nutritional content per bar: Calories 67
Fat 1.3g (Sat Fat 0.3g) Carbohydrate 12.6g Fiber 0.2g
Protein 1.4g Cholesterol 0mg Sodium 34mg

Variation:

Orange Soufflé Bars: Substitute 1 tablespoon freshly grated orange rind and ⅓ cup unsweetened orange juice for lemon rind and juice. Add ½ teaspoon orange extract to egg substitute mixture. Cut into shapes using cookie cutters dipped in powdered sugar, if desired. Yield: 3 dozen.

Nutritional content per bar: Calories 67
Fat 1.3g (Sat Fat 0.3g) Carbohydrate 12.5g Fiber 0.2g
Protein 1.4g Cholesterol 0mg Sodium 34mg

Bananas Melba

Preparation Time: 15 minutes
Cooking Time: 5 minutes

Bananas Melba takes
little time to prepare, yet
it looks so elegant.

1 (12-ounce) package frozen unsweetened
    raspberries, thawed

¼ cup sugar
¼ cup unsweetened orange juice
1 tablespoon cornstarch

1⅓ cups vanilla ice milk
  2 medium bananas, peeled and sliced

    Edible flowers (optional)

1 Place raspberries in container of an electric blender or food processor; cover and process 45 seconds or until smooth. Transfer to a wire-mesh strainer; press with back of spoon against the sides of the strainer to squeeze out juice. Discard seeds and pulp in strainer.

2 Combine raspberry juice, sugar, orange juice, and cornstarch in a small saucepan. Cook over medium heat, stirring constantly, until thickened. Remove from heat.

3 Set aside ¼ cup raspberry sauce. Spoon remaining raspberry sauce evenly into 4 individual dessert bowls. Scoop ⅓ cup ice milk into each bowl. Arrange banana slices evenly around ice milk. Drizzle 1 tablespoon reserved sauce over each serving. Garnish with edible flowers, if desired. Serve immediately. Yield: 4 servings.

Nutritional content per serving: Calories 204
Fat 2.5g (Sat Fat 1.3g) Carbohydrate 45.8g Fiber 5.9g
Protein 2.9g Cholesterol 6mg Sodium 38mg

Blackberry Frozen Yogurt

Preparation Time: 15 minutes
Chilling Time: at least 2 hours
Freezing Time: 25 minutes

3 cups fresh blackberries

½ cup sugar
1 tablespoon cornstarch
1 cup skim milk
¼ cup light-colored corn syrup

1 cup plain low-fat yogurt

Fresh blackberries (optional)
Fresh mint sprigs (optional)

1 Place 3 cups blackberries in container of an electric blender or food processor; cover and process 45 seconds or until smooth. Transfer to a wire-mesh strainer; press with back of spoon against the sides of the strainer to squeeze out juice. Discard seeds and pulp in strainer.

2 Combine sugar and cornstarch in a small saucepan. Add milk; bring to a boil, and cook, stirring constantly, 1 minute. Remove from heat. Stir in blackberry puree and corn syrup. Cool completely.

3 Combine blackberry mixture and yogurt in a bowl, stirring well. Cover and chill thoroughly.

4 Pour mixture into freezer can of a 2-quart hand-turned or electric freezer. Freeze according to manufacturer's instructions. Pack freezer with additional ice and rock salt, and let stand 1 hour. Scoop into individual dessert bowls. If desired, garnish with blackberries and mint sprigs. Serve immediately. Yield: 7 (½-cup) servings.

Nutritional content per serving: Calories 165
Fat 0.7g (Sat Fat 0.3g) Carbohydrate 37.8g Fiber 4.5g
Protein 3.2g Cholesterol 2mg Sodium 54mg

Raspberry Frozen Yogurt

Preparation Time: 15 minutes
Chilling Time: at least 2 hours
Freezing Time: 25 minutes

½ **cup skim milk**
2 **teaspoons cornstarch**
½ **cup light-colored corn syrup**

1 **(12-ounce) package frozen unsweetened**
  raspberries, thawed
1 **(8-ounce) carton vanilla low-fat yogurt**

  Crushed ice (optional)

1 Combine milk and cornstarch in a small saucepan; stir well. Cook over medium heat, stirring constantly, until mixture is thickened and bubbly. Remove from heat, and stir in corn syrup. Set aside.

2 Place raspberries in container of an electric blender or food processor; cover and process 45 seconds or until smooth. Transfer to a wire-mesh strainer; press with back of spoon against the sides of the strainer to squeeze out juice. Discard seeds and pulp in strainer. Add raspberry juice and yogurt to milk mixture, stirring with a wire whisk until blended. Cover and chill thoroughly.

3 Pour mixture into freezer can of a 2-quart hand-turned or electric freezer. Freeze according to manufacturer's instructions. Pack freezer with additional ice and rock salt, and let stand 1 hour. Scoop into individual dessert bowls. Place bowls on crushed ice before serving, if desired. Serve immediately. Yield: 6 (½-cup) servings.

Nutritional content per serving: Calories 143
Fat 0.7g (Sat Fat 0.3g) Carbohydrate 31.9g Fiber 3.2g
Protein 2.9g Cholesterol 2mg Sodium 69mg

Frozen Vanilla Custard with Chocolate-Mint Sauce

Preparation Time: 15 minutes
Chilling Time: at least 2 hours
Freezing Time: 25 minutes

Evaporated skimmed milk and nonfat dry milk powder replace the usual cream in this frozen custard.

2 cups skim milk, divided
1 (12-ounce) can evaporated skimmed milk
½ cup sugar
¼ cup instant nonfat dry milk powder
2 tablespoons cornstarch

2 egg yolks, lightly beaten
1 tablespoon vanilla extract

Chocolate-Mint Sauce

1 Combine 1 cup milk, evaporated milk, and next 3 ingredients in a large saucepan; stir well. Cook over medium heat, stirring constantly, until mixture comes to a boil and thickens slightly. Remove from heat.

2 Gradually stir one-fourth of hot milk mixture into egg yolks; add to remaining hot mixture, stirring constantly. Cook over low heat, stirring constantly, 1 minute. Remove from heat; stir in remaining 1 cup milk and vanilla. Cover and chill thoroughly.

3 Pour mixture into freezer can of a 2-quart hand-turned or electric freezer. Freeze according to manufacturer's instructions. Pack freezer with additional ice and rock salt, and let stand 1 hour, if desired. Scoop ½ cup frozen custard into each individual dessert bowl. Top each serving with 1½ tablespoons Chocolate-Mint Sauce. Serve immediately. Yield: 8 servings.

Chocolate-Mint Sauce

¼ cup sugar
3 tablespoons unsweetened cocoa
2 teaspoons cornstarch
¾ cup water
2 tablespoons crème de menthe
1 teaspoon vanilla extract

1 Combine first 3 ingredients in a medium saucepan. Gradually stir in water. Bring to a boil over medium heat, stirring constantly. Stir in crème de menthe and vanilla. Cook, stirring constantly, 1 minute. Serve warm. Yield: ¾ cup.

Nutritional content per serving: Calories 189
Fat 1.8g (Sat Fat 0.7g) Carbohydrate 34.5g Fiber 0g
Protein 8.0g Cholesterol 58mg Sodium 104mg

Frozen Yogurt Pie with Raspberry-Graham Crust

Preparation Time: 20 minutes
Freezing Time: at least
8½ hours

¼ **cup no-sugar-added seedless raspberry spread**
1⅔ **cups graham cracker crumbs**
　Vegetable cooking spray

2 **cups vanilla low-fat frozen yogurt, softened**

2 **cups chocolate low-fat frozen yogurt, softened**

2 **tablespoons semisweet chocolate morsels**
2 **teaspoons no-sugar-added seedless raspberry**
　spread
1 **teaspoon reduced-calorie stick margarine**

　Fresh raspberries (optional)
　Fresh mint sprigs (optional)

1 Bring ¼ cup raspberry spread to a boil in a small saucepan, stirring with a wire whisk until smooth. Stir in cracker crumbs. Firmly press crumb mixture, using wax paper, evenly into bottom and up sides of a 9-inch pieplate coated with cooking spray.

2 Spread vanilla yogurt in bottom of pie shell; freeze 30 minutes. Remove from freezer, and top vanilla yogurt with chocolate yogurt. Cover and freeze at least 8 hours.

3 Heat chocolate morsels, 2 teaspoons raspberry spread, and margarine in a small saucepan over low heat, stirring constantly, until melted. Drizzle chocolate mixture in thin lines over pie. Let pie stand at room temperature 5 minutes before slicing. If desired, garnish with raspberries and mint sprigs. Yield: 8 servings.

Nutritional content per serving: Calories 214
Fat 5.1g (Sat Fat 2.2g) Carbohydrate 40.0g Fiber 0.2g
Protein 3.9g Cholesterol 9mg Sodium 167mg

Variation:

Frozen Yogurt Pie with Strawberry-Graham Crust: Substitute no-sugar-added strawberry spread for raspberry spread. Yield: 8 servings.

Nutritional content per serving: Calories 214
Fat 5.1g (Sat Fat 2.2g) Carbohydrate 40.0g Fiber 0.2g
Protein 3.9g Cholesterol 9mg Sodium 167mg

Mandarin Phyllo Baskets

Preparation Time: 15 minutes
Cooking Time: 12 minutes

~~~~~~~~~~

2 sheets commercial frozen phyllo pastry, thawed
  Butter-flavored vegetable cooking spray
2 tablespoons sugar

½ cup unsweetened pineapple juice
1½ teaspoons sugar
1½ teaspoons cornstarch

1 (11-ounce) can mandarin oranges in light syrup,
  drained

1½ cups strawberry low-fat frozen yogurt

1 Place 1 sheet phyllo on wax paper (keep remaining phyllo covered). Lightly coat phyllo with cooking spray. Sprinkle with 1 tablespoon sugar. Layer remaining phyllo sheet on first sheet; lightly coat phyllo with cooking spray, and sprinkle with 1 tablespoon sugar.

2 Using a pizza cutter, cut stack of phyllo sheets crosswise into 4 (4¼-inch-wide) strips. Stack 1 strip on top of another strip to make 1 stack of 4 phyllo layers; repeat procedure with the remaining strips to make another stack of 4 phyllo layers.

3 Using a pizza cutter, cut 1 phyllo stack crosswise to make 3 (4½-inch) squares. Repeat procedure with remaining stack.

4 Place each phyllo square in a muffin cup coated with cooking spray, allowing edges to fan outward above top of cup. Bake at 325° for 8 to 10 minutes or until golden; remove from oven, and let cool.

5 Combine pineapple juice, 1½ teaspoons sugar, and cornstarch in a small saucepan; stir well. Cook over medium heat, stirring constantly, until thickened. Remove from heat, and let cool slightly. Stir in mandarin oranges.

6 To serve, spoon ¼ cup frozen yogurt into each phyllo basket; top yogurt evenly with mandarin orange sauce. Serve immediately. Yield: 6 servings.

Nutritional content per serving: Calories 118
Fat 1.7g (Sat Fat 0.8g) Carbohydrate 24.3g Fiber 0g
Protein 1.8g Cholesterol 4mg Sodium 48mg

Frozen Peanutty Dessert

Preparation Time: 30 minutes
Freezing Time: at least 8 hours

Nonfat frozen yogurt
flanks a luscious
peanut butter
filling in this dessert.

⅔ cup chocolate wafer cookie crumbs (about 12
    cookies)
2 tablespoons sugar
1½ tablespoons reduced-calorie stick margarine,
    melted

    Vegetable cooking spray

1½ quarts vanilla nonfat frozen yogurt, divided

⅓ cup light-colored corn syrup
⅓ cup 25% less-fat creamy peanut butter

¼ cup unsalted peanuts
1 ounce semisweet chocolate, melted

1 Combine first 3 ingredients in a bowl. Press crumb mixture over bottom of an 8- x 8- x 2-inch square pan coated with cooking spray.

2 Soften 3 cups yogurt, and spread over crumbs; freeze until firm.

3 Combine corn syrup and peanut butter in a small bowl, stirring well. Spread over yogurt layer in pan.

4 Soften remaining 3 cups yogurt, and spread over peanut butter layer. Sprinkle with peanuts, and drizzle with chocolate. Cover and freeze until firm. To serve, let stand at room temperature 5 minutes before cutting. Quickly dip base of pan in warm water to loosen crust from pan. Yield: 12 servings.

Nutritional content per serving: Calories 224
Fat 7.3g (Sat Fat 1.6g) Carbohydrate 35.6g Fiber 0.6g
Protein 7.5g Cholesterol 5mg Sodium 139mg

Frozen Rainbow Torte

Preparation Time: 30 minutes
Freezing Time: at least 8 hours

Frozen Rainbow Torte is a mouth-watering dessert made from three flavors of sherbet.

~~~~~~~~~~

1 cup gingersnap crumbs (about 30 cookies)
2 tablespoons reduced-calorie stick margarine, melted
   Vegetable cooking spray

1 quart lime sherbet, softened
1 (15¾-ounce) can crushed pineapple in juice, drained

1 quart orange sherbet, softened

1 quart raspberry sherbet, softened
1 (10-ounce) package frozen raspberries in light syrup, thawed and drained

   Fresh raspberries (optional)
   Fresh mint sprigs (optional)

1 Combine gingersnap crumbs and margarine. Press crumb mixture firmly over bottom of a 10-inch spring-form pan coated with cooking spray.

2 Combine lime sherbet and pineapple in a large bowl, stirring well; spread over crumb crust. Cover and freeze until firm.

3 Spread orange sherbet over frozen lime sherbet mixture. Cover and freeze until firm.

4 Combine raspberry sherbet and thawed raspberries in a large bowl, stirring well; spread over orange sherbet. Cover and freeze at least 8 hours.

5 To serve, quickly dip base of pan in warm water to loosen crust from pan; carefully remove sides of pan. If desired, garnish with raspberries and mint sprigs. Slice into wedges. Serve immediately. Yield: 16 servings.

Nutritional content per serving: Calories 228
Fat 3.8g (Sat Fat 1.6g) Carbohydrate 35.6g Fiber 0.6g
Protein 2.0g Cholesterol 5mg Sodium 111mg

Champagne Fruit Compote

Preparation Time: 20 minutes
Chilling Time: 25 minutes

For a nonalcoholic
version of this recipe,
substitute chilled sparkling
white grape juice
for the champagne.

¾ cup unsweetened white grape juice
1 tablespoon honey
1 teaspoon grated orange rind
4 (3-inch) sticks cinnamon

2 cups fresh strawberries, halved and divided
3 medium-size ripe nectarines, sliced
1 cup seedless green grapes
1 cup seedless red grapes
3 kiwifruit, peeled and thinly sliced

½ cup champagne, chilled

1 Combine first 4 ingredients in a small saucepan. Bring to a boil; reduce heat, and simmer 5 minutes. Remove and discard cinnamon sticks. Cover and chill thoroughly.

2 Place 1 cup strawberries in a large glass bowl. Layer nectarines and grapes over strawberries; top with remaining 1 cup strawberries and kiwifruit. Cover and chill thoroughly.

3 To serve, stir champagne into chilled grape juice mixture; pour over fruit. Yield: 12 (½-cup) servings.

Nutritional content per serving: Calories 77
Fat 0.5g (Sat Fat 0.1g) Carbohydrate 17.0g Fiber 2.5g
Protein 0.9g Cholesterol 0mg Sodium 2mg

Ambrosia Parfaits

Preparation Time: 15 minutes

1 (16-ounce) carton vanilla low-fat yogurt
¼ cup crushed pineapple in juice, drained

1 banana, peeled and cut into ¼-inch-thick slices
1 (11-ounce) can mandarin oranges in light syrup,
    drained

1 tablespoon flaked coconut, toasted
4 strawberries, sliced

1 Spoon yogurt onto several layers of heavy-duty paper towels; spread to ½-inch thickness. Cover with additional paper towels; let stand 5 minutes. Scrape yogurt into a bowl, using a rubber spatula. Add pineapple, and stir well.

2 Spoon 2 tablespoons yogurt mixture into each of 4 (6-ounce) parfait glasses; top evenly with banana slices. Spoon 2 tablespoons yogurt mixture over each banana layer; top evenly with orange segments.

3 Dollop remaining yogurt mixture evenly over orange segments; sprinkle with coconut. Top with sliced strawberries. Yield: 4 servings.

Nutritional content per serving: Calories 190
Fat 2.9g (Sat Fat 2.1g) Carbohydrate 36.4 g Fiber 1.7g
Protein 6.2g Cholesterol 6mg Sodium 87mg

Peach Trifle

Preparation Time: 25 minutes

1 (8-ounce) carton vanilla low-fat yogurt

1 (3.4-ounce) package vanilla instant pudding mix
2 cups skim milk

⅓ cup strawberry jam
1 tablespoon dry sherry

8 ounces angel food cake, cut into ¾-inch cubes
  and divided
2 cups canned sliced peaches in juice, drained and
  divided

  Fresh sliced strawberries (optional)
  Fresh mint sprigs (optional)

1 Spoon yogurt onto several layers of heavy-duty paper towels; spread to ½-inch thickness. Cover with additional paper towels; let stand 5 minutes. Scrape yogurt into a bowl, using a rubber spatula.

2 Combine pudding mix and milk, stirring with a wire whisk until blended. Stir drained yogurt into pudding mixture; set aside.

3 Combine jam and sherry, stirring with a wire whisk until blended; set aside.

4 Arrange half of cake cubes in a 2-quart trifle bowl. Spread half of pudding mixture over cake cubes. Drizzle jam mixture evenly over pudding. Arrange 1 cup of sliced peaches over jam mixture. Repeat layering procedure with remaining cake, pudding, and peaches. If desired, garnish with sliced strawberries and mint sprigs. Yield: 8 servings.

Nutritional content per serving: Calories 226
Fat 0.6g (Sat Fat 0.3g) Carbohydrate 50.6g Fiber 0.4g
Protein 5.5g Cholesterol 3mg Sodium 185mg

Apple-Cinnamon Turnovers

Preparation Time: 25 minutes
Cooking Time: 10 minutes

Each of these flaky turnovers has just a smidgen of fat because it's made with phyllo pastry instead of the traditional high-fat pastry.

½ cup chunky applesauce
1 tablespoon currants
1 teaspoon all-purpose flour
¼ teaspoon ground cinnamon
⅛ teaspoon vanilla extract

4 sheets commercial frozen phyllo pastry, thawed
Butter-flavored vegetable cooking spray
1 tablespoon plus 2 teaspoons sugar, divided

¼ teaspoon ground cinnamon

1 Combine first 5 ingredients in a small bowl; stir well.

2 Place 1 sheet of phyllo on wax paper (keep remaining phyllo covered). Lightly coat phyllo with cooking spray; sprinkle with 1 teaspoon sugar. Top with another sheet of phyllo, and lightly coat with cooking spray; sprinkle with 1 teaspoon sugar. Cut stack of phyllo lengthwise into 4 strips (each approximately 18 x 3½ inches), using a sharp knife. Repeat procedure with remaining 2 phyllo sheets and 1 teaspoon sugar.

3 Place 1 tablespoon applesauce mixture at base of 1 phyllo strip. Fold right bottom corner of phyllo over filling, making a triangle. Continue folding back and forth into a triangle to end of strip. Place triangle, seam side down, on an ungreased baking sheet. Repeat procedure with remaining 3 phyllo strips and 3 tablespoons applesauce mixture. (Keep triangles covered before baking.)

4 Combine remaining 1 teaspoon sugar and ¼ teaspoon cinnamon. Coat triangles with cooking spray; sprinkle evenly with sugar mixture. Bake at 375° for 10 minutes or until golden. Serve warm or at room temperature. Yield: 8 turnovers.

Nutritional content per turnover: Calories 65
Fat 1.3g (Sat Fat 0.2g) Carbohydrate 12.8g Fiber 0.3g
Protein 0.8g Cholesterol 0mg Sodium 48mg

Blueberry-Pineapple Cobbler

Preparation Time: 20 minutes
Cooking Time: 30–35 minutes

2 (16-ounce) packages frozen blueberries, thawed
1 (8-ounce) can crushed pineapple in juice,
    undrained
½ cup sugar
2½ tablespoons cornstarch
¼ teaspoon almond extract
    Butter-flavored vegetable cooking spray

½ cup all-purpose flour
½ teaspoon baking powder
⅛ teaspoon salt
¼ cup sugar
2 tablespoons reduced-calorie stick margarine
1 tablespoon skim milk

1 teaspoon all-purpose flour

1½ teaspoons sugar
¼ teaspoon ground cinnamon

1 Combine first 5 ingredients in a large saucepan. Bring to a boil over medium heat, stirring constantly; cook 1 minute or until thickened. Remove from heat; let cool slightly. Pour blueberry mixture into a 9-inch square baking dish coated with cooking spray. Set aside.

2 Combine ½ cup flour and next 3 ingredients in a medium bowl; cut in margarine with a pastry blender until mixture resembles coarse meal and is pale yellow (about 3½ minutes). Add milk, stirring with a fork just until dry ingredients are moistened.

3 Sprinkle 1 teaspoon flour evenly over work surface. Turn dough out onto floured surface, and knead 8 to 10 times. Roll dough to ¼-inch thickness; cut into hearts with a 2-inch heart-shaped cutter. Place hearts over blueberry mixture. Spray hearts with cooking spray.

4 Combine 1½ teaspoons sugar and cinnamon; sprinkle evenly over cobbler. Bake at 400° for 30 to 35 minutes or until hearts are golden and filling is bubbly. Yield: 9 servings.

Nutritional content per serving: Calories 184
Fat 2.4g (Sat Fat 0g) Carbohydrate 41.3g Fiber 3.6g
Protein 1.3g Cholesterol 0mg Sodium 60mg

Peach Cobbler

Preparation Time: 15 minutes
Cooking Time: 35–40 minutes

A low-fat dough
flavored with peach syrup
bakes up around
peach slices
for a healthy
peach cobbler.

~~~~~~~~~~~~

Vegetable cooking spray
¼ cup reduced-calorie stick margarine, melted

2 (16-ounce) cans sliced peaches in light syrup, undrained

¾ cup all-purpose flour
1 teaspoon baking powder
½ cup plus 2 tablespoons sugar
¼ cup skim milk

1 Coat a 9-inch square baking dish with cooking spray. Place margarine in bottom of dish. Set aside.

2 Drain peaches, reserving peaches and ½ cup liquid. Set aside.

3 Combine flour, baking powder, and sugar in a medium bowl. Add reserved ½ cup peach liquid and milk, stirring well.

4 Pour batter evenly over margarine in dish. Spoon peaches over batter. (Do not stir.) Bake at 375° for 35 to 40 minutes or until golden. Yield: 6 servings.

Nutritional content per serving: Calories 244
Fat 5.2g (Sat Fat 0.7g) Carbohydrate 50.0g Fiber 0.8g
Protein 2.5g Cholesterol 0mg Sodium 85mg

Cheesecake Tartlets with Strawberry Glaze

Preparation Time: 30 minutes
Cooking Time: 18–20 minutes
Chilling Time: 15 minutes

Butter-flavored vegetable cooking spray
²⁄₃ cup vanilla wafer crumbs (about 18 cookies)

1 (8-ounce) carton light process cream cheese
     product
½ cup sugar
1½ teaspoons all-purpose flour
¼ teaspoon almond extract
¼ teaspoon vanilla extract

2 egg whites
¼ teaspoon cream of tartar

1 cup sliced fresh strawberries
2 tablespoons sugar
⅛ teaspoon almond extract

2 teaspoons cornstarch

5 medium strawberries, halved

1 Lightly coat inside of 10 paper-lined muffin cups with cooking spray. Place wafer crumbs evenly in muffin cups; set aside.

2 Beat cream cheese at medium speed of an electric mixer until creamy; gradually add ½ cup sugar, and beat well. Add flour, ¼ teaspoon almond extract, and vanilla; beat well.

3 Beat egg whites and cream of tartar at high speed until stiff peaks form. Gently fold beaten egg white into cream cheese mixture. Spoon mixture evenly over crumbs in muffin cups. Bake at 350° for 18 to 20 minutes or until set. Let cool in muffin cups. Cover and chill.

4 Combine sliced strawberries, 2 tablespoons sugar, and ⅛ teaspoon almond extract in container of an electric blender or food processor; cover and process until smooth.

5 Combine strawberry mixture and cornstarch in a small saucepan; stir well. Bring to a boil over medium heat, and cook, stirring constantly, 1 minute. Remove from heat, and let cool. Cover and chill.

6 To serve, spoon about 1 tablespoon strawberry sauce over each tartlet. Top each with a strawberry half. Yield: 10 tartlets.

Nutritional content per tartlet: Calories 149
Fat 5.7g (Sat Fat 2.7g) Carbohydrate 21.1g Fiber 0.6g
Protein 3.6g Cholesterol 13mg Sodium 169mg

Banana Pudding

Preparation Time: 25 minutes
Cooking Time: 25 minutes

½ cup sugar
3 tablespoons cornstarch
⅛ teaspoon salt
2 cups skim milk

1 (4-ounce) carton frozen egg substitute, thawed
½ teaspoon vanilla extract
¼ teaspoon butter flavoring (optional)

28 vanilla wafers
3 medium bananas, peeled and sliced

2 egg whites
¼ teaspoon cream of tartar
3 tablespoons sugar
½ teaspoon vanilla extract

1 Combine first 3 ingredients in a medium-size heavy saucepan; gradually stir in milk. Cook over medium heat, stirring constantly, until mixture comes to a boil; cook 1 additional minute. Remove from heat.

2 Gradually stir about one-fourth of hot milk mixture into egg substitute; add to remaining hot mixture, stirring constantly. Cook over medium heat, stirring constantly, 3 minutes or until mixture thickens. Remove from heat; stir in ½ teaspoon vanilla and, if desired, butter flavoring.

3 Arrange half of vanilla wafers in bottom of a 1½-quart casserole; top with half of banana slices and half of custard. Repeat layering procedure with remaining vanilla wafers, banana slices, and custard.

4 Beat egg whites and cream of tartar at high speed of an electric mixer until foamy. Gradually add 3 tablespoons sugar, 1 tablespoon at a time, beating until stiff peaks form and sugar dissolves (2 to 4 minutes). Fold in ½ teaspoon vanilla. Spread over custard, sealing to edge of dish. Bake at 325° for 25 minutes or until golden. Yield: 8 servings.

Nutritional content per serving: Calories 220
Fat 3.4g (Sat Fat 0.7g) Carbohydrate 42.6g Fiber 1.3g
Protein 5.5g Cholesterol 1mg Sodium 160mg

Double Chocolate Pudding

Preparation Time: 8 minutes
Cooking Time: 15 minutes
Chilling Time: at least
2 hours

¼ cup plus 2 tablespoons sugar
¼ cup unsweetened cocoa
3½ tablespoons cornstarch
3 cups 1% low-fat chocolate milk

1 egg yolk, lightly beaten
1 tablespoon reduced-calorie stick margarine
¾ teaspoon vanilla extract

1 tablespoon coarsely crushed mint candy pieces

1 Combine first 3 ingredients in a large heavy saucepan. Gradually add milk, stirring constantly. Cook over medium heat, stirring constantly, until mixture comes to a boil; cook an additional minute.

2 Gradually stir one-fourth of hot mixture into egg yolk; add to remaining hot mixture. Cook over medium-low heat, stirring constantly, 3 minutes or until mixture thickens. Remove from heat; add margarine and vanilla, stirring until margarine melts.

3 Pour evenly into 6 (6-ounce) dessert dishes. Cover and chill thoroughly. Before serving, sprinkle servings evenly with crushed candy. Yield: 6 servings.

Nutritional content per serving: Calories 187
Fat 3.8g (Sat Fat 1.3g) Carbohydrate 33.0g Fiber 0.1g
Protein 5.6g Cholesterol 40mg Sodium 98mg

Variation:

Brown Sugar Pudding: Substitute dark brown sugar for sugar; omit unsweetened cocoa. Substitute 2% low-fat milk for chocolate milk; increase vanilla extract to 1 teaspoon. Omit sprinkling with crushed candy. Yield: 6 servings.

Nutritional content per serving: Calories 153
Fat 4.4g (Sat Fat 1.7g) Carbohydrate 23.8g Fiber 0g
Protein 4.5g Cholesterol 46mg Sodium 86mg

Fresh Strawberry Mousse

Preparation Time: 15 minutes
Chilling Time: at least
45 minutes

A refreshing follow-up
to a filling meal,
this skinny dessert is
also light on
preparation time.

1 envelope unflavored gelatin
½ cup skim milk
¼ cup sugar

4 cups fresh strawberries, divided
⅓ cup nonfat sour cream alternative

5 tablespoons reduced-calorie whipped topping

1 Sprinkle gelatin over milk in a small saucepan; let stand 1 minute. Cook over low heat, stirring until gelatin dissolves (about 2 minutes). Remove from heat; add sugar, stirring until sugar dissolves.

2 Reserve 5 strawberries for garnish; set aside. Place remaining strawberries in container of an electric blender or food processor; cover and process until smooth. Add gelatin mixture and sour cream; cover and process until blended.

3 Spoon strawberry mixture evenly into 5 (4-ounce) parfait glasses. Cover and chill until set. Top each parfait with 1 tablespoon whipped topping and a reserved strawberry. Yield: 5 (½-cup) servings.

Nutritional content per serving: Calories 100
Fat 0.9g (Sat Fat 0.4g) Carbohydrate 19.8 g Fiber 2.4g
Protein 3.8g Cholesterol 1mg Sodium 29mg

Warm Chocolate Soufflés with Custard Sauce

Preparation Time: 30 minutes
Cooking Time: 18 minutes

3 tablespoons sugar
1 teaspoon cornstarch
¾ cup skim milk
1 egg yolk, lightly beaten
1 teaspoon vanilla extract

Vegetable cooking spray

⅓ cup plus 1 tablespoon sugar
3 tablespoons unsweetened cocoa
2 tablespoons all-purpose flour
¾ cup evaporated skimmed milk

2 egg yolks

4 egg whites
½ teaspoon cream of tartar

1 Combine 3 tablespoons sugar and cornstarch in a small saucepan; gradually stir in ¾ cup milk. Cook over medium heat, stirring constantly, until mixture thickens. Gradually stir one-fourth of hot mixture into beaten egg yolk; add to remaining hot mixture. Reduce heat to low, and cook, stirring constantly, 1 minute. Remove from heat; stir in vanilla. Set custard sauce aside; keep warm.

2 Cut 6 pieces of aluminum foil long enough to fit around 6 (6-ounce) ramekins, allowing a 1-inch overlap; fold foil lengthwise into fifths. Lightly coat one side of foil and bottom of ramekins with cooking spray. Wrap a foil strip around outside of each ramekin, coated side against ramekin, allowing it to extend 1 inch above rim to form a collar; secure with string.

3 Combine ⅓ cup plus 1 tablespoon sugar, cocoa, and flour in a large saucepan. Gradually add evaporated milk, stirring with a wire whisk until blended. Cook over medium heat, stirring constantly, until mixture is thickened and bubbly.

4 Beat 2 egg yolks until thick and pale. Gradually stir one-fourth of hot mixture into egg yolks; add to remaining hot mixture, stirring constantly. Remove from heat.

5 Beat egg whites and cream of tartar in a large bowl at high speed of an electric mixer until stiff peaks form. Gently fold one-fourth of egg white mixture into chocolate mixture. Gently fold remaining egg white mixture into chocolate mixture. Spoon evenly into ramekins. Bake at 375° for 18 minutes or until puffed. Top soufflés evenly with custard sauce. Serve immediately. Yield: 6 servings.

Nutritional content per serving: Calories 179
Fat 3.2g (Sat Fat 1.1g) Carbohydrate 29.0g Fiber 0.1g
Protein 8.2g Cholesterol 111mg Sodium 93mg

Brandied Fruit Sauce

Preparation Time: 5 minutes
Cooking Time: 10 minutes

Fat-free pound cake
can be the foundation
for many healthy
dessert sauces.
You'll find it in
the freezer section of
the grocery store.

1 cup unsweetened apple juice
2 tablespoons honey
1 teaspoon cornstarch
1 tablespoon water

1 (16-ounce) can sliced peaches in juice, drained
1½ cups sliced ripe banana (about 2 medium)
¾ teaspoon brandy flavoring

¾ cup fresh or frozen raspberries, thawed

1 Combine apple juice and honey in a saucepan; bring to a boil, stirring constantly. Combine cornstarch and water; add to juice mixture. Cook over medium heat, stirring constantly, until slightly thickened.

2 Remove from heat; stir in peaches, banana, and brandy flavoring. Gently stir in raspberries. Serve over angel food cake, fat-free pound cake, or ice milk. Yield: 3½ cups.

Nutritional content per ¼-cup serving: Calories 48
Fat 0.1g (Sat Fat 0g) Carbohydrate 11.9g Fiber 1.2g
Protein 0.4g Cholesterol 0mg Sodium 2mg

Praline-Pecan Sauce

Preparation Time: 5 minutes
Cooking Time: 10 minutes

Evaporated skim milk
thickened with cornstarch
gives this sauce
its creamy base.

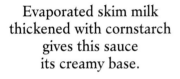

½ cup firmly packed dark brown sugar
1 tablespoon cornstarch
1 cup evaporated skim milk

¼ cup chopped pecans, toasted
1 tablespoon reduced-calorie stick margarine
2 teaspoons vanilla extract

1 Combine brown sugar and cornstarch in a medium saucepan. Gradually stir in milk. Cook over medium heat, stirring constantly, until mixture comes to a boil and thickens slightly. Remove from heat.

2 Add pecans, margarine, and vanilla, stirring until margarine melts. Serve warm over angel food cake, fat-free pound cake, or ice milk. Yield: 1½ cups plus 2 tablespoons.

Nutritional content per tablespoon: Calories 36
Fat 1.0g (Sat Fat 0.1g) Carbohydrate 5.8g Fiber 0.1g
Protein 0.8g Cholesterol 0mg Sodium 17mg

Chunky Pineapple Sauce

Preparation Time: 10 minutes
Cooking Time: 10 minutes

~~~~~~~~

2 tablespoons margarine
3 cups coarsely chopped fresh pineapple

¾ cup firmly packed brown sugar
2 tablespoons cornstarch
1⅓ cups unsweetened pineapple juice

1 tablespoon light rum (optional)

1 Heat margarine in a large skillet over medium-high heat until margarine melts. Add pineapple, and sauté 4 to 5 minutes or until tender.

2 Combine brown sugar and cornstarch in a small bowl. Gradually stir in pineapple juice. Pour over pineapple mixture. Cook over medium heat, stirring constantly, until thickened and bubbly. Remove from heat. Stir in rum, if desired. Serve over angel food cake, fat-free pound cake, or ice milk. Yield: 3½ cups.

Nutritional content per tablespoon: Calories 24
Fat 0.4g (Sat Fat 0.1g) Carbohydrate 5.1g Fiber 0.1g
Protein 0.1g Cholesterol 0mg Sodium 6mg

Luscious Strawberry Sauce

Preparation Time: 10 minutes
Cooking Time: 5 minutes
Chilling Time: 30 minutes

1 tablespoon sugar
1 tablespoon cornstarch
1 cup unsweetened orange juice
¼ teaspoon vanilla or almond extract

1½ cups sliced fresh strawberries (about 1 pint)

1 Combine sugar and cornstarch in a small saucepan. Stir in orange juice. Cook over medium heat, stirring constantly, until mixture comes to a boil and thickens. Remove from heat, and stir in extract. Let cool.

2 Combine orange juice mixture and strawberries in a bowl; stir gently. Cover and chill 30 minutes. Serve over commercial shortcakes, angel food cake, fat-free pound cake, or ice milk. Yield: 2 cups.

Nutritional content per tablespoon: Calories 8
Fat 0.0g (Sat Fat 0g) Carbohydrate 2.0g Fiber 0.2g
Protein 0.1g Cholesterol 0mg Sodium 0mg

Microwaving Directions: Combine sugar and cornstarch in a microwave-safe glass bowl. Stir in orange juice. Cover with wax paper. Microwave at HIGH 2 to 3 minutes until sauce is thickened and bubbly, stirring after each minute. Stir in extract. Let cool. Add strawberries to orange juice mixture; stir gently. Cover and chill 30 minutes.

MEATLESS MAIN DISHES

〰〰〰

page 117

page 123

page 130

Beans
Black Bean and Corn Wontons with
Pepper Cheese Sauce   114

Jamaican Chili   115

Bean Burritos   116

Bean and Vegetable Soft Tacos   117

Pastry-Wrapped Chiles Rellenos   118

Chili Vegetable Tostadas   119

Rice
Bean- and Rice-Stuffed Peppers   120

Green Chile-Rice Casserole   121

Sweet-and-Tangy Lentils and Rice   122

Sweet-and-Sour Peppers and Tofu   123

Quick Risotto Primavera   124

Pizza, Pie, and Pasta
Niçoise Pizza   125

Shepherd's Pie   126

Fresh Tomato Spaghetti   127

Vermicelli with Mushrooms and Pine Nuts   128

Fresh Pepper Pasta   129

Baked Macaroni and Cheese   130

Black Bean and Corn Wontons with Pepper Cheese Sauce

Preparation Time: 25 minutes
Cooking Time: 10 minutes

½ cup drained canned no-salt-added black beans
2 tablespoons no-salt-added commercial salsa
¼ cup frozen whole kernel corn, thawed
2½ tablespoons minced green onions
¼ teaspoon ground cumin

20 fresh or frozen wonton skins, thawed

½ (7-ounce) jar diced sweet red pepper, drained
½ cup nonfat cottage cheese
2½ tablespoons light beer
2 cloves garlic, minced
¼ cup (1 ounce) shredded fat-free mozzarella cheese
1 tablespoon grated Parmesan cheese

3 quarts water
Vegetable cooking spray
Fresh cilantro sprigs (optional)

1 Combine beans and salsa; mash with a potato masher. Stir in corn, green onions, and cumin.

2 Place bean mixture evenly in centers of 10 wonton skins. Brush edges of wonton skins with water; top with remaining 10 wonton skins. Press wonton edges together to seal, pushing out air. Trim edges with a fluted pastry wheel. Cover with a damp towel until ready to cook.

3 Combine red pepper and next 3 ingredients in container of an electric blender; cover and process until smooth, stopping once to scrape down sides. Transfer pepper mixture to a saucepan; add cheeses. Cook, stirring constantly, until cheeses melt. Remove from heat, and keep warm.

4 Bring 3 quarts water to a boil in a Dutch oven. Add filled wontons, and return water to a boil. Reduce heat, and simmer 4 to 5 minutes or until wontons are tender. Remove wontons with a slotted spoon; drain well.

5 Place wontons on a baking sheet coated with cooking spray. Broil 5½ inches from heat (with electric oven door partially opened) 3 to 4 minutes or until lightly browned.

6 Spoon pepper mixture evenly onto 2 individual serving plates. Place 5 wontons on each plate. Garnish with cilantro sprigs, if desired. Yield: 2 servings.

Nutritional content per serving: Calories 423
Fat 2.9g (Sat Fat 0.8g) Carbohydrate 71.8g Fiber 3.8g
Protein 28.3g Cholesterol 15mg Sodium 878mg

Jamaican Chili

Preparation Time: 18 minutes
Cooking Time: 20 minutes

Homemade chili in just
40 minutes?
Using canned beans
shortens both
the preparation and
cooking times.

Vegetable cooking spray
1 teaspoon olive oil
1½ cups chopped onion
2 cloves garlic, crushed
2½ cups chopped sweet yellow pepper

1 tablespoon ground cumin
1 tablespoon hot Hungarian paprika
1 tablespoon chili powder
2 teaspoons sugar
½ teaspoon salt
¼ teaspoon ground cloves

2 (14½-ounce) cans no-salt-added stewed
    tomatoes, undrained
1 (15-ounce) can kidney beans, drained
1 (15-ounce) can cannellini beans, drained
1 (15-ounce) can black beans, drained
1 cup water
2 tablespoons no-salt-added tomato paste

2 tablespoons balsamic vinegar
¼ cup plus 2 tablespoons minced fresh cilantro

1 Coat a Dutch oven with cooking spray; add olive oil. Place over medium-high heat until hot. Add onion and garlic; sauté until onion is tender. Add yellow pepper; sauté until pepper is tender. Add cumin and next 5 ingredients; sauté 1 minute.

2 Stir in tomatoes and next 5 ingredients; bring to a boil. Cover, reduce heat, and simmer 20 minutes.

3 Remove from heat; stir in vinegar. Ladle chili into individual bowls. Top each serving with 1 tablespoon cilantro. Yield: 6 (1⅔-cup) servings.

Nutritional content per serving: Calories 266
Fat 2.5g (Sat Fat 0.3g) Carbohydrate 50.0g Fiber 9.5g
Protein 14.3g Cholesterol 0mg Sodium 554mg

Bean Burritos

Preparation Time: 25 minutes
Cooking Time: 20 minutes

Vegetable cooking spray
1 cup finely chopped green onions
2 teaspoons minced garlic

2 (15-ounce) cans no-salt-added black beans,
   drained
1 (14½-ounce) can no-salt-added whole tomatoes,
   undrained and chopped
1 (½-inch-thick) slice lemon
1 tablespoon chili powder
1 teaspoon ground cumin

24 large fresh spinach leaves, washed and trimmed
8 (8-inch) flour tortillas
1½ cups crumbled feta cheese

4 cups shredded fresh spinach
1 cup chopped plum tomato

1 Coat a large nonstick skillet with cooking spray; place over medium-high heat until hot. Add green onions and garlic; sauté until tender.

2 Add black beans and next 4 ingredients; stir well. Bring to a boil; reduce heat, and simmer, uncovered, until liquid evaporates, stirring frequently. Remove and discard lemon slice. Mash beans slightly with a potato masher or wooden spoon.

3 Arrange 3 spinach leaves on each tortilla. Spoon bean mixture evenly down centers of tortillas; sprinkle evenly with cheese. Roll up tortillas, and place rolls, seam side down, in a 13- x 9- x 2-inch baking dish coated with cooking spray.

4 Cover and bake at 350° for 20 minutes or until thoroughly heated.

5 Place ½ cup shredded spinach on each individual serving plate. Top each with 1 burrito. Sprinkle 2 tablespoons chopped tomato over each serving. Yield: 8 servings.

Nutritional content per serving: Calories 275
Fat 7.7g (Sat Fat 3.7g) Carbohydrate 39.8g Fiber 6.1g
Protein 13.3g Cholesterol 19mg Sodium 433mg

Bean and Vegetable Soft Tacos

Preparation Time: 25 minutes
Cooking Time: 15 minutes

You'll never miss
the meat in these tacos.
They're filled
with marinated vegetables,
seasoned beans, and
two types of cheese.

1½ cups shredded zucchini
1½ cups shredded yellow squash
 1 cup chopped sweet red pepper
 ½ cup chopped onion

 ¼ cup red wine vinegar
 1 teaspoon vegetable oil
 ½ teaspoon ground cumin
 ¼ teaspoon salt
 ⅛ teaspoon black pepper

1½ cups drained canned black beans
 1 cup drained canned navy beans
 ¼ cup water
 ½ teaspoon chili powder
 ¼ teaspoon salt
 ¼ teaspoon garlic powder
 ¼ teaspoon dried crushed red pepper

 8 (6-inch) flour tortillas

 ½ cup (2 ounces) shredded Monterey Jack cheese
    with jalapeño pepper
 ½ cup (2 ounces) shredded 40% less-fat Cheddar
    cheese
    Fresh cilantro sprigs (optional)

1 Combine first 4 ingredients in a bowl. Combine vinegar and next 4 ingredients, stirring well with a wire whisk; pour over vegetable mixture, and toss gently. Set aside.

2 Combine black beans and next 6 ingredients in a saucepan; stir well. Bring mixture to a boil; reduce heat, and simmer, uncovered, 3 to 5 minutes or until beans are thoroughly heated and most of liquid has evaporated.

3 Wrap tortillas in aluminum foil; bake at 350° for 10 minutes or until thoroughly heated.

4 Spoon zucchini mixture evenly down centers of tortillas, using a slotted spoon. Top evenly with bean mixture; sprinkle with cheeses. Roll up tortillas; secure with wooden picks. Transfer to a serving platter, and garnish with cilantro sprigs, if desired. Yield: 8 servings.

Nutritional content per serving: Calories 267
Fat 7.1g (Sat Fat 2.7g) Carbohydrate 38.3g Fiber 4.7g
Protein 13.2g Cholesterol 10mg Sodium 598mg

Pastry-Wrapped Chiles Rellenos

Preparation Time: 30 minutes
Cooking Time: 16 minutes

For a healthy twist on traditional fried chiles rellenos, wrap the stuffed chiles in phyllo pastry and bake.

〰〰〰〰〰〰

1 cup drained canned cannellini beans, mashed
½ cup frozen whole kernel corn, thawed
¼ cup (1 ounce) shredded reduced-fat Monterey Jack cheese
2½ tablespoons minced purple onion
½ teaspoon dried basil
½ teaspoon dried oregano

4 (4-ounce) cans whole green chiles

1 (16-ounce) package commercial frozen phyllo pastry, thawed
Vegetable cooking spray

1¼ cups commercial no-salt-added salsa
½ cup plus 2 tablespoons nonfat sour cream alternative
Sliced green onions (optional)

1 Combine first 6 ingredients; stir well.

2 Drain chiles. Set 10 chiles aside; reserve remaining chiles for another use. Make a lengthwise slit down each chile. Carefully stuff bean mixture evenly into chiles; gently reshape chiles.

3 Place 1 sheet of phyllo on a damp towel (keep remaining phyllo covered). Lightly coat phyllo with cooking spray. Top with 1 sheet phyllo; lightly coat with cooking spray. Fold phyllo in half crosswise, bringing short ends together. Lightly coat with cooking spray.

4 Place 1 stuffed chile in center of phyllo, parallel with short edge and 1½ inches from bottom edge. Fold sides over chile. Roll up phyllo, jellyroll fashion, starting with short side. Place, seam side down, on an ungreased baking sheet. Lightly coat phyllo with cooking spray. Repeat procedure with remaining phyllo and stuffed chiles.

5 Bake at 400° for 16 minutes or until crisp and golden. Place 2 chiles rellenos on each serving plate; top each serving with ¼ cup salsa and 2 tablespoons sour cream. Garnish with green onions, if desired. Yield: 5 servings.

Nutritional content per serving: Calories 401
Fat 8.5g (Sat Fat 1.8g) Carbohydrate 65.9g Fiber 3.6g
Protein 13.9g Cholesterol 4mg Sodium 659mg

Chili Vegetable Tostadas

Preparation Time: 20 minutes
Cooking Time: 15 minutes

Vegetable cooking spray
2 teaspoons olive oil
2 cups coarsely chopped sweet red pepper
1 cup chopped onion
2 tablespoons seeded, minced jalapeño pepper
1 tablespoon chili powder
2 teaspoons ground cumin
½ teaspoon dried oregano

1 (16-ounce) can pinto beans, drained
1 (14½-ounce) can no-salt-added stewed
   tomatoes, undrained

1 (15½-ounce) can golden hominy, drained

8 (6-inch) corn tortillas

4 cups shredded lettuce, divided
¾ cup (3 ounces) shredded reduced-fat sharp
   Cheddar cheese, divided
½ cup nonfat sour cream alternative, divided
½ cup chopped tomato, divided
   Fresh parsley sprigs (optional)

1 Coat a large nonstick skillet with cooking spray; add olive oil. Place over medium-high heat until hot. Add red pepper and next 5 ingredients; sauté until vegetables are tender.

2 Add beans and stewed tomatoes; stir well. Reduce heat, and simmer, stirring constantly, until most of liquid is absorbed. Mash beans slightly with a potato masher or wooden spoon.

3 Add hominy, and cook until mixture is heated. Set aside, and keep warm.

4 Place tortillas on a baking sheet coated with cooking spray. Bake at 350° for 6 minutes; turn tortillas over, and bake an additional 6 minutes or until crisp.

5 Place ½ cup shredded lettuce on each individual serving plate. Top each with a tortilla. Spoon bean mixture evenly over tortillas; sprinkle each with 1½ tablespoons cheese. Top each with 1 tablespoon sour cream, and sprinkle tostadas evenly with chopped tomato. Garnish with parsley sprigs, if desired. Yield: 8 servings.

Nutritional content per serving: Calories 224
Fat 4.7g (Sat Fat 1.5g) Carbohydrate 36.3g Fiber 5.6g
Protein 10.7g Cholesterol 7mg Sodium 321mg

Bean- and Rice-Stuffed Peppers

Preparation Time: 20 minutes
Cooking Time: 30 minutes

Kids will get a kick out
of eating these "grinning"
stuffed peppers.
They'll also get lots
of vitamin C and protein.

    6 medium-size sweet red, yellow, or orange
       peppers

1½ cups cooked long-grain rice (cooked without
       salt or fat)
    ½ cup chopped onion
    1 (15-ounce) can red kidney beans, rinsed and
       drained
    1 (14½-ounce) can no-salt-added stewed
       tomatoes, undrained
    1 (4-ounce) can chopped green chiles, drained
    1 teaspoon chili powder

1½ cups (6 ounces) shredded reduced-fat sharp
       Cheddar cheese, divided

1 Cut tops off peppers, and remove seeds. Cook tops
and bottoms of peppers in boiling water 5 minutes. Drain
peppers; set aside.

2 Combine rice and next 5 ingredients in a medium
bowl; stir in 1 cup cheese. Spoon mixture evenly into
peppers, and replace pepper tops; place peppers in an
11- x 7- x 2-inch baking dish. Add hot water to dish to a
depth of ½ inch.

3 Bake, uncovered, at 350° for 25 minutes. Sprinkle
evenly with remaining ½ cup cheese; bake an additional
5 minutes or until cheese melts. Yield: 6 servings.

Nutritional content per serving: Calories 257
Fat 6.3g (Sat Fat 3.3g) Carbohydrate 36.8g Fiber 4.6g
Protein 15.4g Cholesterol 19mg Sodium 336mg

Green Chile-Rice Casserole

Preparation Time: 30 minutes
Cooking Time: 25 minutes

1 tablespoon reduced-calorie stick margarine
½ cup chopped onion

1 cup plus 2 tablespoons vegetable broth,
   undiluted
1 cup plus 2 tablespoons water
1 (4-ounce) can chopped green chiles, undrained
1 jalapeño pepper, seeded and minced
1 cup long-grain rice, uncooked

1 cup (4 ounces) shredded reduced-fat Monterey
   Jack cheese, divided
1 (8-ounce) carton nonfat sour cream alternative
1 (2-ounce) jar diced pimiento, drained
⅛ teaspoon garlic powder
   Dash of salt

   Vegetable cooking spray

   Fresno pepper slices (optional)
   Fresh cilantro sprig (optional)

1 Melt margarine in a large saucepan over medium-high heat. Add onion, and sauté until tender.

2 Add vegetable broth and next 3 ingredients. Bring to a boil; add rice, stirring well. Cover, reduce heat, and simmer 25 minutes or until rice is tender and liquid is absorbed.

3 Add ⅔ cup cheese and next 4 ingredients to rice mixture, stirring well.

4 Spoon rice mixture into a 1-quart casserole dish coated with cooking spray. Bake, uncovered, at 350° for 20 minutes. Sprinkle with remaining ⅓ cup cheese. Bake an additional 5 minutes or until cheese melts. If desired, garnish with pepper slices and a cilantro sprig. Yield: 4 (1-cup) servings.

Nutritional content per serving: Calories 335
Fat 8.1g (Sat Fat 3.3g) Carbohydrate 47.0g Fiber 1.2g
Protein 16.4g Cholesterol 19mg Sodium 566mg

Sweet-and-Tangy Lentils and Rice

Preparation Time: 15 minutes
Cooking Time: 30 minutes

Roasted red pepper, fresh cilantro, and chutney add flavor and zero fat to this meatless main dish.

〜〜〜〜〜〜

1 (7-ounce) jar roasted red pepper in water
⅓ cup minced fresh cilantro
3 tablespoons chopped ripe olives
2 teaspoons lemon juice
½ teaspoon curry powder
2 cloves garlic, crushed

3 cups water
1¾ cups dried lentils
¾ cup sliced green onions

⅓ cup commercial mango chutney
3 tablespoons honey
2 teaspoons dry mustard

3 cups cooked instant rice (cooked without salt or fat)
Fresh cilantro sprigs (optional)

1 Drain peppers, reserving liquid. Chop 3 peppers; reserve remaining peppers in liquid for another use. Combine chopped pepper, minced cilantro, and next 4 ingredients in a small bowl. Cover and set aside.

2 Combine water, lentils, and green onions in a saucepan; bring to a boil. Cover, reduce heat, and simmer 10 minutes. Stir in chutney, honey, and mustard; simmer, uncovered, 20 minutes or until lentils are tender.

3 Place ½ cup cooked rice on each individual serving plate; top evenly with lentil mixture. Spoon pepper mixture evenly over lentil mixture. Garnish with cilantro sprigs, if desired. Yield: 6 servings.

Nutritional content per serving: Calories 382
Fat 1.7g (Sat Fat 0.2g) Carbohydrate 75.4g Fiber 7.8g
Protein 18.9g Cholesterol 0mg Sodium 86mg

Sweet-and-Sour Peppers and Tofu

Preparation Time: 15 minutes
Cooking Time: 15 minutes

1 package boil-in-bag long-grain rice, uncooked

Vegetable cooking spray
2 teaspoons sesame oil
12 ounces firm tofu, drained and cut into ½-inch cubes

1 large sweet red pepper, seeded and cut into thin strips
1 large sweet yellow pepper, seeded and cut into thin strips
1 (6-ounce) package frozen snow pea pods, thawed and drained

¼ cup reduced-calorie catsup
¼ cup water
3 tablespoons brown sugar
1 tablespoon cornstarch
½ teaspoon ground ginger
½ teaspoon dried crushed red pepper
3 tablespoons rice vinegar
1 tablespoon dry sherry
2 teaspoons low-sodium soy sauce

1 Cook rice according to package directions, omitting salt and fat; set aside, and keep warm.

2 Coat a wok or large nonstick skillet with cooking spray; drizzle oil around top of wok, coating sides. Heat at medium-high (375°) until hot. Add tofu; stir-fry 3 to 4 minutes or until browned on all sides. Remove from wok; set aside, and keep warm.

3 Coat wok with cooking spray. Add pepper strips; stir-fry 2 to 3 minutes or until crisp-tender. Add snow peas; stir-fry 1 minute.

4 Combine catsup and remaining ingredients; stir well. Add to pepper mixture; stir-fry 1 to 2 minutes or until mixture is slightly thickened. Add tofu; stir-fry just until thoroughly heated. Serve over rice. Yield: 4 servings.

Nutritional content per serving: Calories 296
Fat 4.8g (Sat Fat 1.1g) Carbohydrate 45.7g Fiber 4.4g
Protein 11.5g Cholesterol 0mg Sodium 87mg

Quick Risotto Primavera

Preparation Time: 15 minutes
Microwaving Time: 33 minutes

Follow the microwave
directions carefully
to achieve a
smooth, creamy risotto.

1 (10-ounce) package frozen peas and carrots
2 tablespoons water

1 (14½-ounce) can clear vegetable broth
2 cups plus 2 tablespoons water

1 cup chopped green onions
1 teaspoon olive oil

1½ cups arborio rice, uncooked
½ teaspoon salt

½ (10-ounce) package frozen asparagus, thawed
    and cut into 1-inch pieces
1 tablespoon minced fresh dillweed
1 tablespoon minced fresh parsley
1 tablespoon minced fresh basil
1 tablespoon minced fresh thyme

¾ cup grated Asiago cheese
½ teaspoon freshly ground pepper

1 Combine peas and carrots and 2 tablespoons water in a 1-quart casserole; cover with heavy-duty plastic wrap, and vent. Microwave at HIGH 3 to 4 minutes or just until peas and carrots are tender. Drain and set aside.

2 Combine vegetable broth and 2 cups plus 2 tablespoons water in a 1½-quart casserole; microwave, uncovered, at HIGH 5 to 6 minutes or until broth simmers.

3 Combine green onions and oil in a 3-quart casserole; microwave, uncovered, at HIGH 1 minute. Stir in rice and salt; add hot broth mixture. Cover with heavy-duty plastic wrap, and vent. Microwave at HIGH 5 minutes or until mixture boils. Microwave at MEDIUM (50% power) 10 minutes; stir well. Microwave at MEDIUM LOW (30% power) 7 minutes or until rice is tender and mixture is creamy.

4 Stir in peas and carrots, asparagus, and next 4 ingredients; cover and let stand 5 minutes. Stir in cheese and pepper. Yield: 6 (1-cup) servings.

Nutritional content per serving: Calories 287
Fat 5.2g (Sat Fat 1.9g) Carbohydrate 48.9g Fiber 2.8g
Protein 10.8g Cholesterol 9.5mg Sodium 579mg

Niçoise Pizza

Preparation Time: 30 minutes
Cooking Time: 20–25 minutes

Colorful Niçoise Pizza
is piled with vegetables and
tangy goat cheese.

〜〜〜〜〜〜〜〜

Vegetable cooking spray
1 medium-size purple onion, sliced and separated
   into rings

¾ cup plus 1 tablespoon yellow cornmeal, divided
¾ cup all-purpose flour
2 teaspoons baking powder
¼ teaspoon salt

¾ cup skim milk
⅓ cup frozen egg substitute, thawed
2 teaspoons olive oil

2 (14½-ounce) cans no-salt-added stewed
   tomatoes, drained and coarsely chopped

½ cup frozen cut green beans, thawed
1 medium-size sweet red pepper, seeded and
   sliced
¼ cup shredded fresh basil
4 ounces goat cheese, crumbled

1 Coat a large nonstick skillet with cooking spray; place over medium-high heat until hot. Add onion, and sauté until tender. Set aside, and keep warm.

2 Combine ¾ cup cornmeal and next 3 ingredients in a large bowl; stir well.

3 Combine milk, egg substitute, and oil; add to dry ingredients, stirring until smooth.

4 Coat a 12-inch nonstick pizza pan with cooking spray; sprinkle with remaining 1 tablespoon cornmeal. Spread batter in pan. Sprinkle chopped tomato over batter to within 1½ inches of edge of pan.

5 Top with onion; sprinkle with green beans. Arrange red pepper over green beans; sprinkle with basil, and top with goat cheese. Bake at 400° for 20 to 25 minutes or until crust is lightly browned. Yield: 6 servings.

Nutritional content per serving: Calories 273
Fat 8.0g (Sat Fat 4.3g) Carbohydrate 39.6g Fiber 2.7g
Protein 11.4g Cholesterol 16mg Sodium 250mg

Shepherd's Pie

Preparation Time: 30 minutes
Cooking Time: 20 minutes

Our meatless version
of Shepherd's Pie uses
a delicious shortcut
for mashed potatoes—
simply cook frozen hash
browns and stir in
ricotta cheese.

3 cups frozen peas and carrots, thawed
1 cup frozen chopped onion, thawed
1 cup frozen chopped green pepper, thawed
2 teaspoons dried thyme
2 teaspoons sweet Hungarian paprika
Olive oil-flavored vegetable cooking spray

4 cups frozen hash browns, thawed

²/₃ cup lite ricotta cheese
¼ teaspoon salt

2 cups drained canned black-eyed peas
1 cup diced tomato
1 (8-ounce) can no-salt-added tomato sauce
2 teaspoons low-sodium Worcestershire sauce
¼ teaspoon salt

Sweet Hungarian paprika

1 Combine first 5 ingredients; stir well. Spoon into a 15-x 10- x 1-inch jellyroll pan coated with cooking spray; coat vegetables with cooking spray. Bake, uncovered, at 400° for 20 minutes, stirring after 10 minutes; set aside.

2 Cook hash browns in boiling water to cover 10 minutes or until tender. Drain and mash. Stir in ricotta cheese and salt; set aside.

3 Combine vegetable mixture, black-eyed peas, and next 4 ingredients, stirring well. Spoon into a 2½-quart shallow baking dish coated with cooking spray.

4 Spoon hash brown mixture in a border around edge of dish; spoon remaining hash brown mixture over center of dish. Sprinkle additional paprika over top. Bake, uncovered, at 350° for 20 minutes. Yield: 6 servings.

Nutritional content per serving: Calories 215
Fat 1.9g (Sat Fat 0.7g) Carbohydrate 40.2g Fiber 2.9g
Protein 11.4g Cholesterol 4mg Sodium 455mg

Fresh Tomato Spaghetti

Preparation Time: 20 minutes
Cooking Time: 40 minutes

Olive oil-flavored vegetable cooking spray
1¾ cups sliced fresh mushrooms
½ cup minced shallots

6 cups peeled, seeded, and chopped tomato
1½ cups no-salt-added tomato juice
1 (6-ounce) can no-salt-added tomato paste
2 tablespoons chopped fresh basil
2 teaspoons chopped fresh oregano
½ teaspoon fennel seeds
¼ teaspoon salt
1 bay leaf

12 ounces spaghetti, uncooked
Fresh oregano sprigs (optional)

1 Coat a large Dutch oven with cooking spray. Place over medium-high heat until hot. Add mushrooms and shallots; sauté until tender.

2 Add chopped tomato and next 7 ingredients, stirring well. Bring mixture to a boil; reduce heat, and simmer, uncovered, 40 minutes, stirring occasionally. Remove and discard bay leaf.

3 Cook pasta according to package directions, omitting salt and fat. Drain. Place on a serving platter, and top with tomato mixture. Garnish with oregano sprigs, if desired. Yield: 6 servings.

Nutritional content per serving: Calories 305
Fat 1.9g (Sat Fat 0.2g) Carbohydrate 63.6g Fiber 5.0g
Protein 11.5g Cholesterol 0mg Sodium 141mg

Vermicelli with Mushrooms and Pine Nuts

Preparation Time: 20 minutes
Cooking Time: 15 minutes

2 teaspoons margarine
2½ cups sliced fresh mushrooms
½ cup chopped onion

2 tablespoons all-purpose flour
1 cup evaporated skimmed milk

½ cup frozen English peas, thawed
¼ cup sliced green onions

1 (8-ounce) package vermicelli, uncooked

¼ cup freshly grated Parmesan cheese
2 tablespoons pine nuts, toasted
Freshly ground pepper (optional)

1 Melt margarine in a large nonstick skillet over medium heat. Add mushrooms and chopped onion; sauté until tender.

2 Add flour; cook, stirring constantly, 1 minute. Gradually add milk, stirring constantly. Cook, stirring constantly, until thickened and bubbly.

3 Add peas and green onions; cook over medium-low heat, stirring constantly, 1 minute or until thoroughly heated.

4 Cook vermicelli according to package directions, omitting salt and fat; drain.

5 Combine vermicelli, mushroom mixture, cheese, pine nuts, and pepper, if desired, in a serving bowl; toss gently. Serve immediately. Yield: 4 (1½-cup) servings.

Nutritional content per serving: Calories 375
Fat 6.8g (Sat Fat 2.1g) Carbohydrate 60.2g Fiber 2.9g
Protein 18.2g Cholesterol 7mg Sodium 242mg

Microwaving Directions: Place margarine and chopped onion in a 2-quart microwave-safe bowl. Cover with wax paper. Microwave at HIGH 2 minutes, stirring after 1 minute. Add mushrooms; cover with wax paper. Microwave at HIGH 2 minutes. Add flour, stirring well. Gradually stir in milk. Microwave at HIGH 3 to 4 minutes or until sauce is thickened and bubbly, stirring every minute. Add peas and green onions. Microwave at HIGH 1 minute or until thoroughly heated. Continue with recipe as directed in step 4.

Fresh Pepper Pasta

Preparation Time: 15 minutes
Cooking Time: 35 minutes

Use fresh herbs and
vegetables to heighten the
eye-appeal and flavor
of pasta dishes.

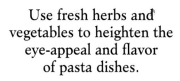

4 medium-size sweet red peppers (about 1½
    pounds), seeded and chopped
2 tablespoons Chablis or other dry white wine

¾ cup drained canned navy beans
½ cup thinly sliced green onions
¼ cup plus 2 tablespoons shredded fresh basil
    leaves
1 tablespoon minced fresh oregano
1 tablespoon chopped ripe olives

6 ounces rotini pasta, uncooked

¼ cup plus 2 tablespoons (1½ ounces) shredded
    Asiago cheese
1 tablespoon pine nuts, toasted
    Fresh basil sprigs (optional)

1 Combine red pepper and wine in a saucepan; bring to
a boil. Cover, reduce heat, and simmer 3 minutes.

2 Stir in beans and next 4 ingredients; bring to a boil.
Cover, reduce heat, and simmer 10 minutes. Uncover
and simmer 20 minutes, stirring occasionally.

3 Cook pasta according to package directions, omitting
salt and fat. Drain well.

4 Place pasta on individual serving plates. Top evenly
with pepper mixture, cheese, and pine nuts. Garnish with
basil sprigs, if desired. Yield: 3 (2-cup) servings.

Nutritional content per serving: Calories 378
Fat 7.6g (Sat Fat 2.5g) Carbohydrate 63.0g Fiber 6.3g
Protein 17.0g Cholesterol 7mg Sodium 392mg

Baked Macaroni and Cheese

Preparation Time: 20 minutes
Cooking Time: 30 minutes

We kept all
the creaminess in good
old macaroni and cheese
but cut the fat
by using skim milk and
reduced-fat cheeses.

3 tablespoons reduced-calorie stick margarine
¼ cup plus 2 tablespoons all-purpose flour
¾ teaspoon dry mustard
⅛ teaspoon ground red pepper
3 cups skim milk, divided

1¼ cups (5 ounces) shredded reduced-fat sharp
    Cheddar cheese, divided
¼ cup (1 ounce) shredded reduced-fat Swiss
    cheese
½ teaspoon salt
⅛ teaspoon black pepper

5 cups cooked large elbow macaroni (cooked
    without salt or fat)

1 Melt margarine in a large, heavy saucepan over low heat. Combine flour, dry mustard, red pepper, and 1 cup milk; stir until smooth. Add to margarine; cook, stirring constantly with a wire whisk, 1 minute.

2 Gradually add remaining 2 cups milk; stir well. Cook over medium heat, stirring constantly, 10 minutes or until slightly thickened and bubbly; remove from heat.

3 Add ¾ cup Cheddar cheese and next 3 ingredients, stirring until cheese melts.

4 Stir in macaroni; spoon into 6 (1-cup) ramekins or a 2-quart casserole. Sprinkle with remaining ½ cup Cheddar cheese. Cover and bake at 350° for 30 minutes. Let stand, covered, 5 minutes before serving. Yield: 6 (1-cup) servings.

Nutritional content per serving: Calories 346
Fat 10.1g (Sat Fat 3.9g) Carbohydrate 44.7g Fiber 2.0g
Protein 18.9g Cholesterol 21mg Sodium 494mg

MEATS, POULTRY & SEAFOOD

page 133

page 150

page 154

Beef
Greek Meatballs over Rice   132
Broiled Flank Steak   133
Marinated Beef Kabobs   134
Spicy Skillet Steaks   135

Veal
Veal Cordon Bleu   136
Veal Steaks with Caper Sauce   137

Lamb
Lamb and Spinach Pilaf   138
Lamb Steaks with Jalapeño-Apricot Sauce   139

Pork
Honey-Sesame Grilled Pork Tenderloin   140
Mustard-Honey Glazed Ham Kabobs   141

Poultry
Smoked Chicken, Pasta, and Sun-Dried Tomatoes   142
Chicken and Snow Pea Stir-Fry   143
Chicken in Tomato-Vegetable Sauce   144

Chicken Reuben Rolls   145
Citrus-Ginger Chicken   146
Greek-Seasoned Chicken with Orzo   147
Crispy Herbed Chicken   148
Herbed Chicken with
Sour Cream-Wine Sauce   149
Cornish Hens with
Raspberry-Currant Glaze   150
Turkey Romano   151
Turkey Stroganoff   152
Red Beans and Rice   153

Fish and Shellfish
Baked Catfish Fillets   154
Garlic Flounder   155
Spicy Grilled Grouper   156
Sesame-Baked Orange Roughy   157
Creole Red Snapper   158
Sweet-and-Sour Tuna Steaks   159
Creamy Lobster with Angel Hair Pasta   160
Scallops in Tarragon Sauce   161
Lime-Marinated Shrimp Kabobs   162

Greek Meatballs over Rice

Preparation Time: 20 minutes
Cooking Time: 18–20 minutes

1 pound ground round
½ cup soft whole wheat breadcrumbs
2 tablespoons finely chopped onion
2 tablespoons skim milk
1 tablespoon chopped fresh parsley
1 teaspoon minced fresh mint
1 teaspoon Worcestershire sauce
¼ teaspoon salt
¼ teaspoon pepper
1 egg white
1 clove garlic, minced

Vegetable cooking spray

2 (8-ounce) cans no-salt-added tomato sauce
2 tablespoons chopped fresh parsley
1 teaspoon dried oregano
¼ teaspoon sugar
¼ teaspoon pepper

3 cups cooked instant rice (cooked without salt or fat)

1 Combine first 11 ingredients in a medium bowl; stir well. Shape mixture into 30 (1¼-inch) meatballs.

2 Place meatballs on rack of a broiler pan coated with cooking spray. Broil 5½ inches from heat (with electric oven door partially opened) 8 to 10 minutes or until browned, turning after 6 minutes. Drain and pat dry with paper towels.

3 Combine tomato sauce and next 4 ingredients in a large skillet; bring to a boil. Add meatballs; cover, reduce heat, and simmer 10 minutes or until thoroughly heated. Serve over rice. Yield: 6 servings.

Nutritional content per serving: Calories 295
Fat 9.7g (Sat Fat 3.7g) Carbohydrate 32.3g Fiber 2.0g
Protein 19.4g Cholesterol 47mg Sodium 300mg

Broiled Flank Steak

Preparation Time: 15 minutes
Marinating Time: 30 minutes
Cooking Time: 10 minutes

Marinate this recipe overnight, if desired, to ensure an even more tender steak.

~~~~~~~~~~~~~~~

1 (1-pound) lean flank steak

3 tablespoons red wine vinegar
1½ tablespoons low-sodium soy sauce
2 teaspoons dry mustard
1 teaspoon chili powder
2 teaspoons honey
¼ teaspoon pepper
1 clove garlic, crushed

¼ cup plain nonfat yogurt
2 teaspoons Dijon mustard

Vegetable cooking spray

1 Trim fat from steak. Score steak diagonally across the grain in a diamond design at 1-inch intervals on both sides. Place steak in a heavyduty, zip-top plastic bag. Combine vinegar and next 6 ingredients; pour evenly over meat. Seal  bag, and shake until steak is well coated. Marinate in refrigerator 30 minutes, turning bag occasionally.

2 Combine yogurt and mustard in a small bowl; cover and chill 30 minutes.

3 Remove steak from marinade, reserving 2 tablespoons marinade. Place steak on rack of a broiler pan coated with cooking spray. Broil 5½ inches from heat (with electric oven door partially opened) 5 minutes on each side or to desired degree of doneness, basting frequently with reserved marinade. Slice steak diagonally across grain into ¼-inch-thick slices. Serve with mustard mixture. Yield: 4 servings.

Nutritional content per serving: Calories 229
Fat 13.2g (Sat Fat 5.5g) Carbohydrate 3.2g Fiber 0.1g
Protein 22.6g Cholesterol 60mg Sodium 195mg

Marinated Beef Kabobs

Preparation Time: 23 minutes
Marinating Time: 4–8 hours
Cooking Time: 12 minutes

To help tenderize
the beef
in these kabobs,
marinate the steak
and baste frequently
during grilling.

1 pound top round steak

½ cup red wine vinegar
¼ cup water
¼ cup low-sodium soy sauce
1½ teaspoons sugar
½ teaspoon dried thyme
¼ teaspoon freshly ground pepper
1 clove garlic, crushed

8 medium-size fresh mushrooms
1 large yellow squash, cut into ½-inch pieces
1 medium-size green pepper, seeded and cut
     into 1-inch pieces
     Vegetable cooking spray

8 cherry tomatoes

1 Trim fat from steak; cut steak into 1½-inch pieces. Place steak in a heavy-duty, zip-top plastic bag. Combine vinegar and next 6 ingredients in a small bowl; stir well. Pour over steak; seal bag, and shake until steak is well coated. Marinate in refrigerator 4 to 8 hours, turning bag occasionally.

2 Remove steak from marinade; reserve marinade. Thread steak, mushrooms, squash, and green pepper alternately on 4 (15-inch) skewers. Coat vegetables with cooking spray.

3 Coat grill rack with cooking spray; place on grill over medium-hot coals (350° to 400°). Place kabobs on rack; grill, covered, 6 minutes on each side or to desired degree of doneness, basting frequently with marinade. Add tomatoes to skewers during last 1 minute of cooking. Yield: 4 servings.

Nutritional content per serving: Calories 198
Fat 6.2g (Sat Fat 2.0g) Carbohydrate 5.9g Fiber 1.5g
Protein 29.0g Cholesterol 73mg Sodium 179mg

Broiling Directions: Follow directions for steps 1 and 2. Place kabobs on rack of a broiler pan coated with cooking spray; broil 5½ inches from heat (with electric oven door partially opened) 6 minutes on each side or to desired degree of doneness. Add tomatoes to skewers during last 1 minute of cooking.

Spicy Skillet Steaks

Preparation Time: 10 minutes
Cooking Time: 18–20 minutes

2 tablespoons cornmeal
¼ teaspoon garlic powder
¼ teaspoon ground cumin
¼ teaspoon dried whole oregano
⅛ teaspoon salt
⅛ teaspoon onion powder
⅛ teaspoon ground red pepper
4 (4-ounce) lean cubed sirloin steaks

Vegetable cooking spray

¼ cup plus 2 tablespoons no-salt-added tomato
sauce
1 (4-ounce) can chopped green chiles, drained

1 large ripe tomato, cut into 16 wedges

1 Combine first 7 ingredients; stir well. Dredge steaks in cornmeal mixture.

2 Coat a large nonstick skillet with cooking spray; place over medium heat until hot. Add steaks, and cook 5 minutes on each side or until browned.

3 Remove steaks from skillet. Drain and pat dry with paper towels. Wipe drippings from skillet with a paper towel.

4 Combine tomato sauce and chiles in skillet, stirring well; bring to a boil. Return steaks to skillet. Cover, reduce heat, and simmer 6 minutes or until steaks are tender. Add tomato wedges; cover and simmer 2 minutes or until thoroughly heated. Yield: 4 servings.

Nutritional content per serving: Calories 219
Fat 6.9g (Sat Fat 2.6g) Carbohydrate 9.5g Fiber 1.6g
Protein 28.6g Cholesterol 80mg Sodium 250mg

Veal
Cordon Bleu

Preparation Time: 25 minutes
Cooking Time: 20 minutes

Strips of lean ham
and low-fat cheese
are sandwiched
between lean cutlets
and then baked
until golden in this
lightened recipe.

8 veal cutlets (about 1 pound)
½ teaspoon freshly ground pepper

2 (¾-ounce) slices low-fat Swiss cheese
1 (1-ounce) slice lean cooked ham

2 tablespoons all-purpose flour
¼ cup plus 2 tablespoons frozen egg substitute,
    thawed
½ cup fine, dry breadcrumbs

Vegetable cooking spray
1 tablespoon reduced-calorie stick margarine

Fresh parsley sprigs (optional)
Lemon slices (optional)

1 Place cutlets between 2 sheets of wax paper, and flatten to ⅛-inch thickness, using a meat mallet or rolling pin. Sprinkle 4 cutlets with pepper.

2 Cut each cheese slice in half; place 1 half-slice in center of each of 4 peppered cutlets. Cut ham slice into 4 pieces; place evenly on top of cheese slices. Place remaining 4 cutlets over ham; gently pound edges to seal.

3 Dredge sealed cutlets in flour, shaking off excess. Dip cutlets in egg substitute. Dredge in breadcrumbs.

4 Coat a large nonstick skillet with cooking spray; add margarine. Place over medium-high heat until margarine melts. Add cutlets; cook 2 minutes on each side or until lightly browned. Place cutlets in an 11- x 7- x 2-inch baking dish coated with cooking spray.

5 Bake, uncovered, at 375° for 20 minutes. Transfer cutlets to a warm serving platter. If desired, garnish with parsley sprigs and lemon slices. Yield: 4 servings.

Nutritional content per serving: Calories 245
Fat 6.9g (Sat Fat 1.9g) Carbohydrate 13.1g Fiber 0.7g
Protein 31.1g Cholesterol 99mg Sodium 473mg

Veal Steaks with Caper Sauce

Preparation Time: **15 minutes**
Cooking Time: **30 minutes**

These veal steaks
are topped with
a piquant caper sauce.
Pair them with
a simple dish such
as rice pilaf.

2 tablespoons all-purpose flour
¼ teaspoon pepper
4 (4-ounce) boneless veal loin steaks
    (1 inch thick)
  Vegetable cooking spray
1 teaspoon olive oil

½ cup canned no-salt-added beef broth, undiluted
1½ tablespoons capers
2 teaspoons Dijon mustard

½ cup nonfat sour cream alternative

  Chopped fresh parsley (optional)

1 Combine flour and pepper; dredge veal steaks in flour mixture. Coat a large nonstick skillet with cooking spray; add oil. Place over medium-high heat until hot. Add veal, and cook 2 minutes on each side or until browned. Remove from skillet. Drain and pat dry with paper towels. Wipe drippings from skillet with a paper towel. Return veal to skillet.

2 Combine beef broth, capers, and mustard; pour over veal. Bring to a boil; cover, reduce heat, and simmer 25 minutes or until veal is tender. Transfer veal to a serving platter, and keep warm.

3 Bring broth mixture to a boil; cook, uncovered, over medium heat 5 minutes or until mixture is reduced by about half. Remove from heat; add sour cream, stirring with a wire whisk. Spoon evenly over veal. Garnish with parsley, if desired. Yield: 4 servings.

Nutritional content per serving: Calories 186
Fat 5.5g (Sat Fat 1.3g) Carbohydrate 5.4g Fiber 0.1g
Protein 25.7g Cholesterol 91mg Sodium 438mg

Lamb and Spinach Pilaf

Preparation Time: 20 minutes
Cooking Time: 15 minutes

This recipe makes the most of Indian spices and has no added fat.

~~~~~~~~~~~~~~~~~

2 cups canned no-salt-added beef broth, undiluted
1 cup bulgur (cracked wheat), uncooked
¼ teaspoon salt

1 pound lean ground lamb

1 cup chopped onion
½ cup raisins
½ cup water
2 tablespoons lemon juice
½ teaspoon ground cinnamon
¼ teaspoon salt
¼ teaspoon pepper
¼ teaspoon ground nutmeg

1 (10-ounce) package fresh washed and trimmed spinach, chopped

1 Bring broth to a boil in a medium saucepan; add bulgur and ¼ teaspoon salt. Cover, reduce heat, and simmer 15 minutes or until bulgur is tender and liquid is absorbed. Set aside, and keep warm.

2 Cook lamb in a large Dutch oven over medium heat until browned, stirring until it crumbles. Drain and pat dry with paper towels. Wipe drippings from Dutch oven with a paper towel.

3 Return lamb to Dutch oven; add onion and next 7 ingredients. Bring to a boil; cover, reduce heat, and simmer 7 minutes. Add spinach; cover and simmer an additional 3 minutes or until spinach wilts.

4 Divide bulgur mixture evenly among 6 individual serving plates. Top each serving with ⅔ cup lamb mixture. Serve immediately. Yield: 6 servings.

Nutritional content per serving: Calories 269
Fat 6.1g (Sat Fat 2.1g) Carbohydrate 32.7g Fiber 7.4g
Protein 22.1g Cholesterol 54mg Sodium 289mg

Lamb Steaks with Jalapeño-Apricot Sauce

Preparation Time: 20 minutes
Cooking Time: 10 minutes

8 (5-ounce) lean lamb sirloin steaks (¾ inch thick)

½ cup no-sugar-added apricot spread
2 tablespoons unsweetened orange juice

Vegetable cooking spray

Jalapeño-Apricot Sauce

1 Trim fat from steaks; set aside.

2 Combine apricot spread and orange juice in a small saucepan; cook over medium-low heat until spread melts, stirring occasionally.

3 Coat grill rack with cooking spray; place on grill over medium-hot coals (350° to 400°). Place steaks on rack, and grill, uncovered, 5 minutes on each side or to desired degree of doneness, basting occasionally with apricot spread mixture. Serve with Jalapeño-Apricot Sauce. Yield: 8 servings.

Jalapeño-Apricot Sauce

1 (16-ounce) can apricot halves in juice, undrained

1 tablespoon white wine vinegar
2 teaspoons cornstarch

2 tablespoons thinly sliced canned jalapeño peppers, seeded

1 Drain apricots, reserving juice; quarter apricot halves, and set aside.

2 Combine reserved apricot juice, vinegar, and cornstarch in a small saucepan. Bring to a boil; reduce heat, and simmer, stirring constantly, 1 minute or until thickened. Remove from heat. Stir in apricots and jalapeño pepper. Yield: 1¾ cups.

Nutritional content per serving: Calories 241
Fat 8.0g (Sat Fat 2.8g) Carbohydrate 16.6g Fiber 0.3g
Protein 24.5g Cholesterol 78mg Sodium 100mg

Honey-Sesame Grilled Pork Tenderloin

Preparation Time: 18 minutes
Marinating Time: at least
2 hours
Cooking Time: 25–30 minutes

Serve this pork
tenderloin with
Snow Peas,
Red Pepper, and
Pineapple (page 208).

2 (¾-pound) pork tenderloins

½ cup light beer
3 tablespoons sesame seeds
3 tablespoons honey
2 tablespoons Dijon mustard
½ teaspoon cracked pepper
2 cloves garlic, crushed

Vegetable cooking spray

Fresh rosemary sprigs (optional)

1 Trim fat from pork. Place pork in a large heavy-duty, zip-top plastic bag. Combine beer and next 5 ingredients, stirring well. Pour over tenderloins; seal bag, and shake until pork is well coated. Marinate in refrigerator at least 2 hours, turning bag occasionally.

2 Remove pork from marinade, reserving marinade. Coat grill rack with cooking spray; place on grill over medium-hot coals (350° to 400°). Place pork on rack; grill, covered, 25 to 30 minutes or until meat thermometer inserted into thickest part of tenderloin registers 160°, turning and basting occasionally with reserved marinade. Let stand 10 minutes. Slice diagonally across grain into thin slices. Garnish with rosemary sprigs, if desired. Yield: 6 servings.

Nutritional content per serving: Calories 218
Fat 6.9g (Sat Fat 1.8g) Carbohydrate 11.3g Fiber 0.3g
Protein 26.8g Cholesterol 83mg Sodium 211mg

Mustard-Honey Glazed Ham Kabobs

Preparation Time: 30 minutes
Cooking Time: 6–7 minutes

To shorten the preparation time, use fresh pineapple cubes from your grocer's salad bar.

¼ cup honey
¼ cup bourbon
3 tablespoons Dijon mustard
1 teaspoon peeled, minced gingerroot
1 clove garlic, minced

32 snow pea pods (about 6 ounces), trimmed

1 small fresh pineapple, peeled and cored
2 medium-size sweet red peppers, seeded and cut into 32 (1-inch) pieces
¾ pound lean, low-salt cooked ham, cut into 24 (1-inch) cubes

Vegetable cooking spray

2 cups cooked long-grain rice (cooked without salt or fat)

1 Combine first 5 ingredients in a small bowl; stir well, and set aside.

2 Arrange snow peas in a vegetable steamer over boiling water. Cover and steam 2 to 3 minutes or until crisp-tender. Place in ice water until cool; drain.

3 Cut pineapple into 32 (1-inch) cubes, reserving remaining pineapple for another use. Wrap 1 snow pea around each pineapple cube. Thread 4 pineapple cubes, 4 red pepper pieces, and 3 ham cubes alternately onto each of 8 (12-inch) skewers.

4 Place kabobs on rack of a broiler pan coated with cooking spray. Brush kabobs with mustard mixture. Broil 5½ inches from heat (with electric oven door partially opened) 3 minutes. Turn and baste with remaining mustard mixture; broil an additional 3 to 4 minutes or until kabobs are thoroughly heated.

5 Place rice on a large serving platter. Arrange kabobs over rice. Serve warm. Yield: 4 servings.

Nutritional content per serving: Calories 406
Fat 5.9g (Sat Fat 2.9g) Carbohydrate 62.4g Fiber 4.0g
Protein 19.5g Cholesterol 42mg Sodium 998mg

Grilling Directions: Follow directions for steps 1 through 3. Coat grill rack with cooking spray; place rack on grill over medium-hot coals (350° to 400°). Brush kabobs with mustard mixture. Place kabobs on rack; grill, uncovered, 3 minutes. Turn kabobs, and baste with remaining mustard mixture. Grill an additional 3 to 4 minutes or until kabobs are thoroughly heated. Continue with step 5 as directed above.

Smoked Chicken, Pasta, and Sun-Dried Tomatoes

Preparation Time: 25 minutes
Cooking Time: 20 minutes

Look for smoked chicken breast in the deli department of larger supermarkets and specialty grocery stores.

2 (10½-ounce) cans low-sodium chicken broth
2 cups water
6 ounces penne pasta

¾ cup sun-dried tomatoes
1½ cups boiling water

Olive oil-flavored vegetable cooking spray
1 cup chopped green pepper
½ cup chopped onion
1 clove garlic, minced

1 tablespoon margarine
1½ tablespoons all-purpose flour
1 cup skim milk

8 ounces smoked chicken breast, cubed
2 tablespoons chopped fresh basil
⅓ cup grated Parmesan cheese

1 Bring chicken broth and 2 cups water to a boil in a large saucepan; add pasta, and cook 10 to 12 minutes or until tender. Drain and set aside.

2 Place sun-dried tomatoes in a shallow dish. Pour boiling water over tomatoes, and let stand 10 minutes. Drain tomatoes, and chop.

3 Coat a nonstick skillet with cooking spray. Place over medium-high heat until hot. Add chopped tomato, green pepper, onion, and garlic; sauté until vegetables are tender. Set aside, and keep warm.

4 Melt margarine in a large saucepan over low heat. Add flour, and cook, stirring constantly with a wire whisk, 1 minute. Gradually add milk, stirring constantly. Cook, stirring constantly, until thickened and bubbly.

5 Add pasta, tomato mixture, chicken, and basil, stirring well. Cook until thoroughly heated, stirring frequently. Transfer to a serving bowl; sprinkle evenly with Parmesan cheese. Yield: 6 servings.

Nutritional content per serving: Calories 244
Fat 5.9g (Sat Fat 1.9g) Carbohydrate 32.6g Fiber 1.4g
Protein 16.1g Cholesterol 22mg Sodium 766mg

Chicken and Snow Pea Stir-Fry

Preparation Time: 20 minutes
Cooking Time: 11 minutes

6 ounces fresh snow pea pods

Vegetable cooking spray
2 teaspoons vegetable oil, divided
4 (4-ounce) skinned, boned chicken breast halves,
   cut into thin strips
1 clove garlic, minced

¾ cup julienne-cut sweet red pepper (about 1
   medium)
¾ cup julienne-cut sweet yellow pepper (about 1
   medium)

1 cup canned low-sodium chicken broth,
   undiluted
¼ cup low-sodium soy sauce
1 tablespoon plus 1 teaspoon cornstarch
3 tablespoons dry sherry
1 teaspoon peeled, grated gingerroot

¼ cup sesame seeds, toasted

3 cups cooked long-grain rice (cooked without
   salt or fat)

1 Wash snow peas; trim ends, and remove strings. Set aside.

2 Coat a wok or large nonstick skillet with cooking spray; drizzle 1 teaspoon oil around top of wok, coating sides. Heat at medium-high (375°) until hot. Add chicken and garlic; stir-fry 4 minutes or until chicken is lightly browned. Remove from wok, and drain well on paper towels. Wipe drippings from wok with a paper towel.

3 Drizzle remaining 1 teaspoon oil around top of wok. Add peppers to wok; stir-fry 2 minutes or until crisp-tender. Add snow peas and water; stir-fry 2 minutes. Remove vegetable mixture from wok, and keep warm.

4 Combine broth and next 4 ingredients; stir well. Add chicken, broth mixture, and sesame seeds to wok; stir-fry 3 minutes or until mixture is thickened and bubbly. Stir in vegetable mixture. Serve over rice. Yield: 4 servings.

Nutritional content per serving: Calories 388
Fat 8.3g (Sat Fat 1.3g) Carbohydrate 46.3g Fiber 3.0g
Protein 26.7g Cholesterol 49mg Sodium 472mg

Chicken in Tomato-Vegetable Sauce

Preparation Time: 16 minutes
Cooking Time: 20 minutes

While this hearty dish
simmers, fix a
salad and heat bread
to round
out the meal.

1 tablespoon olive oil
1 cup sliced leeks
2 cloves garlic, minced
4 (4-ounce) skinned, boned chicken breast halves,
cut diagonally into thin strips
1 teaspoon dried basil
1 teaspoon dried oregano

1 (14½-ounce) can no-salt-added whole tomatoes,
undrained and chopped
1 medium zucchini, sliced
½ cup canned low-sodium chicken broth,
undiluted
¼ cup Chablis or other dry white wine
¼ teaspoon salt

¼ cup no-salt-added tomato paste

4 cups cooked long-grain rice (cooked without
salt or fat)
2 tablespoons freshly grated Parmesan cheese
Fresh basil sprigs (optional)

1 Heat oil in a large nonstick skillet over medium-high heat until hot. Add leeks and garlic; sauté 3 minutes or until tender. Add chicken, and sauté 7 minutes or until chicken is done. Stir in basil and oregano. Remove chicken from skillet; set aside, and keep warm.

2 Add tomato and next 4 ingredients to skillet; bring to a boil. Stir in tomato paste; cover, reduce heat, and simmer 10 minutes.

3 Add chicken, and cook until thoroughly heated. Serve over rice. Sprinkle evenly with Parmesan cheese. Garnish with basil sprigs, if desired. Yield: 4 servings.

Nutritional content per serving: Calories 449
Fat 7.1g (Sat Fat 2.0g) Carbohydrate 61.1g Fiber 1.6g
Protein 33.7g Cholesterol 66mg Sodium 365mg

Chicken Reuben Rolls

Preparation Time: 20 minutes
Cooking Time: 25–30 minutes

6 (4-ounce) skinned, boned chicken breast halves
6 (¼-ounce) thin slices cooked corned beef
2 tablespoons spicy brown mustard
½ cup sauerkraut, drained

¼ teaspoon paprika

Caraway Cheese Sauce
Fresh thyme sprigs (optional)

1 Place chicken between 2 sheets of heavy-duty plastic wrap, and flatten to ⅛-inch thickness, using a meat mallet or rolling pin. Place 1 slice of corned beef on each chicken breast half. Spread evenly with mustard. Top evenly with sauerkraut.

2 Fold in sides of each chicken breast; roll up, and secure with wooden picks. Place chicken, seam side down, in an 11- x 7- x 2-inch baking dish. Sprinkle with paprika.

3 Cover and bake at 350° for 15 minutes. Uncover; bake an additional 10 to 15 minutes or until chicken is done.

4 To serve, remove wooden picks from chicken; slice each chicken roll into 6 rounds, and spoon Caraway Cheese Sauce evenly over chicken. Garnish with thyme sprigs, if desired. Yield: 6 servings.

Caraway Cheese Sauce

2 tablespoons all-purpose flour
¾ cup skim milk

½ teaspoon chicken-flavored bouillon granules
¼ teaspoon caraway seeds
⅛ teaspoon freshly ground pepper

½ cup (2 ounces) shredded reduced-fat Swiss cheese

1 Place flour in a medium saucepan; gradually stir in milk until well blended.

2 Add bouillon granules, caraway seeds, and pepper; stir well. Cook over medium heat, stirring constantly, until mixture is slightly thickened.

3 Add cheese, stirring constantly until cheese melts and mixture thickens. Yield: ¾ cup plus 2 tablespoons.

Nutritional content per serving: Calories 189
Fat 3.9g (Sat Fat 1.4g) Carbohydrate 4.9g Fiber 0.3g
Protein 32.5g Cholesterol 76mg Sodium 413mg

Citrus-Ginger Chicken

Preparation Time: 18 minutes
Cooking Time: 20 minutes

If you don't have
a citrus zester, a
paring knife or
vegetable peeler will
do the trick.

¼ cup low-sugar orange marmalade
1 tablespoon honey mustard
¾ teaspoon ground ginger
⅛ teaspoon ground red pepper

4 (4-ounce) skinned chicken breast halves

Vegetable cooking spray

2 cups cooked couscous (cooked without salt
    and fat)
Orange Sauce
Orange zest (optional)

1 Combine first 4 ingredients in a small bowl, stirring with a wire whisk to blend. Brush half of mixture over chicken. Reserve remaining half.

2 Coat a grill rack with cooking spray; place on grill over medium-hot coals (350° to 400°). Place chicken on rack; grill, covered, 10 minutes on each side or until chicken is done, basting occasionally with reserved marmalade mixture.

3 Place couscous on a serving platter. Arrange chicken over couscous; drizzle Orange Sauce over chicken. Sprinkle with orange zest, if desired. Yield: 4 servings.

Orange Sauce

¼ cup reduced-calorie stick margarine, melted
½ teaspoon grated orange rind
¼ teaspoon ground ginger

1 Combine all ingredients, stirring well. Yield: ¼ cup.

Nutritional content per serving: Calories 298
Fat 8.9g (Sat Fat 1.4g) Carbohydrate 24.1g Fiber 0.4g
Protein 29.9g Cholesterol 66mg Sodium 224mg

Greek-Seasoned Chicken with Orzo

Preparation Time: 10 minutes
Marinating Time: 30 minutes
Cooking Time: 20 minutes

Orzo is a
tiny rice-shaped pasta
that expands
to three
times its volume
when cooked.

¼ cup fresh lemon juice
3 tablespoons water
1 teaspoon olive oil
½ teaspoon dried oregano
½ teaspoon Greek-style seasoning
¼ teaspoon pepper
2 cloves garlic, crushed

4 (6-ounce) skinned chicken breast halves

1 cup orzo, uncooked
¼ cup sliced ripe olives
1½ tablespoons chopped fresh chives
1 tablespoon reduced-calorie stick margarine, melted
¾ teaspoon Greek-style seasoning

Vegetable cooking spray
Fresh oregano sprigs (optional)

1 Combine first 7 ingredients in a large heavy-duty, zip-top plastic bag; add chicken. Seal bag, and shake until chicken is well coated. Marinate in refrigerator 30 minutes, turning bag occasionally.

2 Cook orzo according to package directions, omitting salt and fat; drain. Combine cooked orzo, olives, and next 3 ingredients, tossing gently. Set aside, and keep warm.

3 Remove chicken from marinade, reserving marinade. Coat grill rack with cooking spray; place on grill over medium-hot coals (350° to 400°). Place chicken on rack; grill, covered, 10 minutes on each side or until chicken is done, basting occasionally with marinade. Serve chicken over orzo mixture. Garnish with oregano sprigs, if desired. Yield: 4 servings.

Nutritional content per serving: Calories 420
Fat 9.0g (Sat Fat 1.9g) Carbohydrate 38.6g Fiber 1.6g
Protein 43.9g Cholesterol 102mg Sodium 476mg

Crispy Herbed Chicken

Preparation Time: **20 minutes**
Cooking Time: **40–45 minutes**

This winning
replacement for
fried chicken is healthier
and eliminates
messy frying.

1¼ cups soft whole wheat breadcrumbs
1½ tablespoons minced fresh parsley
1½ teaspoons grated lemon rind
  1 tablespoon chopped fresh basil
  ½ teaspoon salt
  ½ teaspoon pepper

  3 tablespoons nonfat buttermilk
  ¾ teaspoon lemon juice
  6 (6-ounce) skinned chicken breast halves

    Vegetable cooking spray

    Lemon slices (optional)
    Fresh parsley sprigs (optional)

1 Combine first 6 ingredients in a large heavy-duty, zip-top plastic bag; seal bag, and shake well.

2 Combine buttermilk and lemon juice; brush both sides of chicken with buttermilk mixture. Place chicken in bag; seal bag, and shake until chicken is well coated.

3 Place chicken on a rack in a roasting pan coated with cooking spray. Sprinkle any remaining breadcrumb mixture over chicken.

4 Bake, uncovered, at 400° for 40 to 45 minutes or until chicken is tender. If desired, garnish with lemon slices and parsley sprigs. Yield: 6 servings.

Nutritional content per serving: Calories 167
Fat 2.0g (Sat Fat 0.5g) Carbohydrate 6.5g Fiber 0.5g
Protein 29.5g Cholesterol 71mg Sodium 345mg

Herbed Chicken with Sour Cream-Wine Sauce

Preparation Time: **10 minutes**
Cooking Time: **35 minutes**

Put away the salt for this recipe—
the chicken is seasoned with herbs.

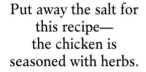

½ teaspoon dried oregano
½ teaspoon dried thyme
¼ teaspoon dried basil
⅛ teaspoon freshly ground pepper
4 (8-ounce) chicken leg quarters, skinned
    Vegetable cooking spray

⅓ cup Chablis or other dry white wine
⅓ cup canned low-sodium chicken broth,
    undiluted
⅔ cup sliced fresh mushrooms
¼ cup shredded carrot

2 tablespoons all-purpose flour
2 tablespoons water
2 tablespoons nonfat sour cream alternative
    Fresh oregano sprigs (optional)
    Fresh thyme sprigs (optional)

1 Combine first 4 ingredients; sprinkle evenly over chicken. Coat a large nonstick skillet with cooking spray; place over medium heat until hot. Add chicken; cook 2 minutes on each side or until browned.

2 Add wine and chicken broth to chicken; cover, reduce heat, and simmer 20 minutes. Add mushrooms and carrot; cover and simmer 10 minutes.

3 Transfer chicken to a serving platter; set aside, and keep warm. Combine flour and water, stirring well. Add to broth mixture in skillet; cook over medium heat, stirring constantly, until thickened. Stir in sour cream. Spoon sauce evenly over chicken. If desired, garnish with oregano and thyme sprigs. Yield: 4 servings.

Nutritional content per serving: Calories 203
Fat 6.2g (Sat Fat 1.5g) Carbohydrate 5.7g Fiber 0.5g
Protein 28.9g Cholesterol 108mg Sodium 133mg

Cornish Hens with Raspberry-Currant Glaze

Preparation Time: 15 minutes
Cooking Time: 25–30 minutes

~~~~~~~~~~

1 tablespoon sugar
2 teaspoons cornstarch
1 teaspoon coarsely ground pepper
½ cup water
⅓ cup raspberry vinegar

½ cup red currant jelly
1 tablespoon chopped fresh cilantro

Vegetable cooking spray
2 (1-pound) Cornish hens, skinned

1 Combine first 3 ingredients in a small saucepan. Stir in water and vinegar. Bring to a boil, stirring constantly; cook over medium heat, stirring constantly, until mixture is thickened.

2 Add jelly; cook just until jelly melts, stirring frequently. Stir in chopped cilantro. Remove from heat, and let cool slightly to thicken. Reserve ⅓ cup glaze.

3 Split each hen in half lengthwise with an electric knife. Coat grill rack with cooking spray; place rack on grill over medium coals (300° to 350°). Place hens on rack; grill 25 to 30 minutes or until meat thermometer inserted into breast registers 180°, turning and basting frequently with ⅔ cup glaze. Serve reserved ⅓ cup glaze with hens. Yield: 4 servings.

Nutritional content per serving: Calories 302
Fat 7.0g (Sat Fat 1.9g) Carbohydrate 32.3g Fiber 0.4g
Protein 27.5g Cholesterol 84mg Sodium 96mg

Baking Directions: Follow directions for steps 1 and 2. Place hens, cut side down, on rack of a broiler pan lined with aluminum foil. Bake at 350° for 45 minutes or until hens are done, basting frequently with ⅔ cup glaze. Shield wing tips with aluminum foil during last 15 minutes of baking, if necessary. Serve reserved ⅓ cup glaze with hens.

Turkey Romano

Preparation Time: 25 minutes
Cooking Time: 15 minutes

1 pound turkey breast cutlets, cut into 8 pieces
⅓ cup all-purpose flour
½ teaspoon freshly ground pepper

1 tablespoon vegetable oil, divided

Vegetable cooking spray
1 teaspoon reduced-calorie stick margarine
⅓ cup sliced fresh mushrooms
1 tablespoon sliced green onions

¾ cup skim milk, divided
1 tablespoon all-purpose flour
2 tablespoons grated Romano cheese
1 teaspoon lemon juice
⅛ teaspoon salt
⅛ teaspoon freshly ground pepper

⅛ teaspoon paprika
½ cup sliced green onions

1 Place cutlets between 2 sheets of heavy-duty plastic wrap, and flatten to ¼-inch thickness, using a meat mallet or rolling pin. Combine flour and ½ teaspoon pepper; dredge cutlets in flour mixture.

2 Heat 1½ teaspoons oil in a large nonstick skillet over medium-high heat until hot. Add half of cutlets, and cook 3 to 4 minutes on each side or until browned. Drain on paper towels. Repeat procedure with remaining 1½ teaspoons oil and remaining cutlets.

3 Coat a medium saucepan with cooking spray; add margarine. Place over medium-high heat until margarine melts. Add mushrooms and 1 tablespoon green onions; sauté until tender.

4 Combine 1 tablespoon milk and flour; stir until smooth. Add remaining milk to vegetable mixture. Stir in flour mixture. Cook over medium heat, stirring constantly, until slightly thickened. Add cheese and next 3 ingredients; stir well.

5 Transfer cutlets to a serving platter. Spoon cheese mixture evenly over cutlets, and sprinkle with paprika. Top evenly with ½ cup sliced green onions. Yield: 4 servings.

Nutritional content per serving: Calories 278
Fat 8.7g (Sat Fat 2.3g) Carbohydrate 13.7g Fiber 0.9g
Protein 34.5g Cholesterol 74mg Sodium 217mg

Turkey Stroganoff

Preparation Time: 15 minutes
Cooking Time: 20 minutes

8 ounces medium egg noodles, uncooked
1 tablespoon chopped fresh parsley
⅛ teaspoon salt

Vegetable cooking spray
1 pound freshly ground raw turkey
½ cup chopped onion
1½ cups sliced fresh mushrooms

⅓ cup Chablis or other dry white wine
⅛ teaspoon salt
⅛ teaspoon ground nutmeg
⅛ teaspoon freshly ground pepper

1 cup 1% low-fat cottage cheese
½ cup nonfat sour cream alternative
1 tablespoon lemon juice

Hungarian paprika (optional)

1 Cook noodles according to package directions, omitting salt and fat. Drain; toss gently with chopped parsley and ⅛ teaspoon salt. Set aside, and keep warm.

2 Coat a large nonstick skillet with cooking spray; place over medium heat until hot. Add turkey and onion; cook until turkey is browned, stirring until it crumbles. Add mushrooms; cook 2 to 3 minutes or until mushrooms are tender. Drain and pat dry with paper towels. Wipe drippings from skillet with a paper towel.

3 Return mixture to skillet; add wine and next 3 ingredients. Cook over low heat 10 minutes or until most of the liquid evaporates, stirring occasionally. Remove from heat.

4 Combine cottage cheese, sour cream, and lemon juice in container of an electric blender; cover and process until smooth, stopping once to scrape down sides.

5 Stir cheese mixture into turkey mixture; cook over low heat, stirring constantly, just until thoroughly heated. Spoon noodles onto a serving platter; top evenly with turkey mixture. Sprinkle with paprika, if desired. Yield: 4 servings.

Nutritional content per serving: Calories 440
Fat 6.5g (Sat Fat 2.0g) Carbohydrate 47.0g Fiber 2.0g
Protein 42.4g Cholesterol 130mg Sodium 491mg

Red Beans and Rice

Preparation Time: **10 minutes**
Cooking Time: **20 minutes**

Made with turkey, low-fat smoked sausage has less fat and cholesterol than regular smoked sausage.

Vegetable cooking spray
6 ounces low-fat smoked sausage, thinly sliced
1 cup chopped onion
¾ cup chopped green pepper
1 clove garlic, minced

3 (16-ounce) cans red beans, drained
1 (14½-ounce) can no-salt-added stewed tomatoes, undrained and chopped
1½ cups water
1 (6-ounce) can no-salt-added tomato paste
¼ teaspoon dried oregano
¼ teaspoon dried thyme
¼ teaspoon hot sauce
1 bay leaf

4 cups cooked long-grain rice (cooked without salt or fat)
Fresh thyme sprigs (optional)

1 Coat a Dutch oven with cooking spray. Place over medium-high heat until hot. Add sausage and next 3 ingredients; sauté until tender.

2 Add beans and next 7 ingredients; bring to a boil. Cover, reduce heat, and simmer 20 minutes or until thoroughly heated. Remove and discard bay leaf. Serve over rice. Garnish with thyme sprigs, if desired. Yield: 8 servings.

Nutritional content per serving: Calories 310
Fat 1.2g (Sat Fat 0.3g) Carbohydrate 59.2g Fiber 5.7g
Protein 15.9g Cholesterol 9mg Sodium 448mg

Baked Catfish Fillets

Preparation Time: 15 minutes
Cooking Time: 25–30 minutes

The pepper relish
adds a splash of color and
flavor to baked fish
fillets, and it's a cinch
to prepare.

Tricolored Pepper Relish

6 (4-ounce) farm-raised catfish fillets
 Vegetable cooking spray

2 tablespoons reduced-calorie stick margarine,
   melted
1 tablespoon lemon juice
¼ teaspoon ground ginger
¼ teaspoon curry powder
¼ teaspoon dried crushed red pepper

1 Prepare Tricolored Pepper Relish.

2 Place catfish fillets
on rack of a broiler pan
coated with cooking
spray.

3 Combine margarine
and next 4 ingredients;
stir well. Brush fillets
with margarine mixture.

4 Bake at 400° for 25 to 30 minutes or until fish flakes
easily when tested with a fork. Transfer fillets to a serving
platter. Top fillets evenly with Tricolored Pepper Relish.
Yield: 6 servings.

Tricolored Pepper Relish

½ cup pineapple tidbits in juice, drained
½ cup chopped sweet red pepper
⅓ cup chopped green pepper
⅓ cup chopped sweet yellow or orange pepper
1 tablespoon cider vinegar
1 tablespoon unsweetened pineapple juice
1 teaspoon sugar
1 teaspoon peeled, minced gingerroot
⅛ to ¼ teaspoon dried crushed red pepper

1 Combine all ingredients in a small bowl; stir well. Cover and chill at least 30 minutes. Yield: 1½ cups.

Nutritional content per serving: Calories 146
Fat 6.5g (Sat Fat 1.2g) Carbohydrate 5.6g Fiber 0.5g
Protein 16.5g Cholesterol 51mg Sodium 94mg

Garlic Flounder

Preparation Time: 10 minutes
Marinating Time: 30 minutes
Cooking Time: 8–10 minutes

6 (4-ounce) flounder fillets
¼ cup low-sodium soy sauce
2 tablespoons minced garlic
1½ tablespoons lemon juice
2 teaspoons sugar

1 tablespoon mixed peppercorns, crushed

Vegetable cooking spray
Fresh parsley sprigs (optional)

1 Place fillets in a shallow baking dish. Combine soy sauce and next 3 ingredients; pour over flounder. Cover and marinate in refrigerator 30 minutes.

2 Remove fillets from marinade; discard marinade. Sprinkle fillets evenly with peppercorns, pressing firmly so pepper adheres to fillets.

3 Place fillets on rack of a broiler pan coated with cooking spray. Broil 5½ inches from heat (with electric oven door partially opened) 8 to 10 minutes or until fish flakes easily when tested with a fork. Transfer to a serving platter, and garnish with parsley sprigs, if desired. Yield: 6 servings.

Nutritional content per serving: Calories 114
Fat 1.5g (Sat Fat 0.3g) Carbohydrate 2.0g Fiber 0.3g
Protein 21.6g Cholesterol 60mg Sodium 223mg

Spicy Grilled Grouper

Preparation Time: 10 minutes
Marinating Time: 30 minutes
Cooking Time: 20 minutes

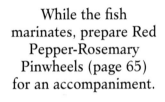

While the fish marinates, prepare Red Pepper-Rosemary Pinwheels (page 65) for an accompaniment.

1½ **pounds grouper fillets**
¼ **cup lemon juice**
1½ **teaspoons chili powder**
¼ **teaspoon ground cumin**
¼ **teaspoon paprika**
1 **clove garlic, minced**
   Dash of ground red pepper

   Vegetable cooking spray

   Fresh parsley sprigs (optional)
   Lemon wedges dipped in chili powder (optional)

1 Cut fillets into 6 equal pieces. Place fish in a shallow baking dish. Combine lemon juice and next 5 ingredients, stirring well; pour over fillets. Cover and marinate in refrigerator 30 minutes.

2 Remove fish from marinade, reserving marinade. Coat grill rack with cooking spray; place on grill over medium-hot coals (350° to 400°). Coat a wire grilling basket with cooking spray. Place fish in basket, and grill 10 minutes on each side or until fish flakes easily when tested with a fork, basting frequently with reserved marinade. Transfer fish to a serving platter. If desired, garnish with parsley sprigs and lemon wedges. Yield: 6 servings.

Nutritional content per serving: Calories 124
Fat 1.5g (Sat Fat 0.3g) Carbohydrate 1.5g Fiber 0.3g
Protein 24.8g Cholesterol 47mg Sodium 59mg

Sesame-Baked Orange Roughy

Preparation Time: 15 minutes
Marinating Time: 1–2 hours
Cooking Time: 6–8 minutes

Baking or broiling is the best cooking method for delicate fish such as this orange roughy. Also shown is Tossed Salad with Creamy Buttermilk Dressing (page 176).

6 (4-ounce) orange roughy fillets
2 tablespoons water
1 teaspoon peeled, minced gingerroot
½ teaspoon lemon juice
½ teaspoon low-sodium soy sauce
¼ teaspoon crushed red pepper
1 clove garlic, minced

2 tablespoons sesame seeds, toasted
   Vegetable cooking spray

¼ teaspoon paprika
   Lemon slices (optional)

1 Place fillets in a shallow baking dish. Combine water and next 5 ingredients in container of an electric blender; cover and process until smooth. Pour over fillets. Cover and marinate in refrigerator 1 to 2 hours.

2 Remove fillets from marinade; discard marinade. Coat both sides of each fillet with sesame seeds. Place fillets on rack of a broiler pan coated with cooking spray.

3 Broil 3½ inches from heat (with electric oven door partially opened) 6 to 8 minutes or until fish flakes easily when tested with a fork. Arrange fillets on a serving platter, and sprinkle evenly with paprika. Garnish with lemon slices, if desired. Yield: 6 servings.

Nutritional content per serving: Calories 92
Fat 2.1g (Sat Fat 0.2g) Carbohydrate 1.0g Fiber 0.2g
Protein 16.6g Cholesterol 22mg Sodium 81mg

Creole Red Snapper

Preparation Time: 15 minutes
Cooking Time: 15 minutes

1 tablespoon olive oil
¼ cup chopped onion
¼ cup chopped green pepper
1 clove garlic, minced

1 (14½-ounce) can no-salt-added whole tomatoes, undrained and chopped
2 teaspoons low-sodium Worcestershire sauce
2 teaspoons red wine vinegar
½ teaspoon dried basil
¼ teaspoon salt
¼ teaspoon freshly ground pepper
Dash of hot sauce

4 (4-ounce) red snapper fillets

Fresh basil sprigs (optional)

1 Heat oil in a large nonstick skillet over medium-high heat until hot. Add onion, green pepper, and garlic; sauté until tender.

2 Add tomato and next 6 ingredients. Bring to a boil; add fillets, spooning tomato mixture over fish. Reduce heat; cover and simmer 12 minutes or until fish flakes easily when tested with a fork. Garnish with basil sprigs, if desired. Yield: 4 servings.

Nutritional content per serving: Calories 173
Fat 5.0g (Sat Fat 0.8g) Carbohydrate 6.9g Fiber 0.8g
Protein 24.3g Cholesterol 42mg Sodium 243mg

Sweet-and-Sour Tuna Steaks

Preparation Time: 10 minutes
Marinating Time: 30 minutes
Cooking Time: 10–11 minutes

Tuna takes on an Oriental flavor here. Round out the meal with a crisp side dish of Snow Pea Stir-Fry (page 41).

¼ cup plus 2 tablespoons honey
¼ cup plus 2 tablespoons sherry vinegar
¼ cup low-sodium soy sauce
2 teaspoons peeled, minced gingerroot
4 cloves garlic, crushed

4 (4-ounce) yellowfin tuna steaks

1½ teaspoons olive oil
¼ teaspoon salt
⅛ teaspoon freshly ground pepper

1 Combine first 5 ingredients; pour half of mixture into a shallow dish, reserving remaining mixture to serve with tuna steaks.

2 Place tuna steaks in mixture in dish, turning to coat both sides of each steak. Cover and marinate in refrigerator 30 minutes, turning once. Remove tuna steaks from marinade, discarding marinade.

3 Heat oil in a large nonstick skillet over medium-high heat. Add tuna steaks, and cook 5 minutes on one side. Turn; sprinkle evenly with salt and pepper. Cook 5 to 6 minutes or until fish flakes easily when tested with a fork. Transfer tuna steaks to a serving platter, and spoon reserved honey mixture evenly over tuna steaks. Yield: 4 servings.

Nutritional content per serving: Calories 256
Fat 7.3g (Sat Fat 1.7g) Carbohydrate 16.7g Fiber 0g
Protein 26.7g Cholesterol 43mg Sodium 500mg

Grilling Directions: Follow directions for steps 1 and 2. Coat grill rack with cooking spray; place on grill over medium-hot coals (350° to 400°). Place fish on rack; grill, uncovered, 5 minutes on one side. Turn; sprinkle evenly with salt and pepper. Grill 4 to 5 minutes or until fish flakes easily when tested with a fork. Transfer to a serving platter, and spoon reserved honey mixture evenly over tuna steaks. Yield: 4 servings.

Nutritional content per serving: Calories 240
Fat 5.6g (Sat Fat 1.4g) Carbohydrate 16.7g Fiber 0g
Protein 26.7g Cholesterol 43mg Sodium 500mg

Creamy Lobster with Angel Hair Pasta

Preparation Time: 30 minutes
Cooking Time: 12 minutes

2 quarts water
2 (8-ounce) fresh or thawed lobster tails

8 ounces angel hair pasta, uncooked

¾ cup sliced fresh mushrooms
⅓ cup chopped green onions
⅓ cup Chablis or other dry white wine
1 large clove garlic, minced

2 tablespoons reduced-calorie stick margarine
2 tablespoons all-purpose flour

1 cup skim milk
⅓ cup nonfat sour cream alternative
2 tablespoons grated Parmesan cheese
½ teaspoon paprika
Fresh parsley sprigs (optional)

1 Bring water to a boil in a large saucepan; add lobster tails. Cover, reduce heat, and simmer 6 minutes. Drain; rinse with cold water. Split and clean tails; cut meat into bite-size pieces.

2 Cook pasta according to package directions, omitting salt and fat. Drain well. Set aside, and keep warm.

3 Combine mushrooms and next 3 ingredients in a large nonstick skillet. Bring to a boil. Reduce heat, and simmer, uncovered, until liquid evaporates.

4 Add margarine, stirring to melt. Add flour, and cook, stirring constantly, 1 minute. Gradually stir in milk. Cook over medium heat, stirring constantly, until mixture thickens and begins to boil. Stir in lobster and sour cream; cook an additional 1 minute or until thoroughly heated. Spoon over pasta; sprinkle with cheese and paprika. Garnish with parsley sprigs, if desired. Yield: 4 servings.

Nutritional content per serving: Calories 390
Fat 6.3g (Sat Fat 1.5g) Carbohydrate 52.8g Fiber 2.0g
Protein 28.8g Cholesterol 59mg Sodium 464mg

Variation:

Creamy Shrimp with Angel Hair Pasta: Substitute 1 pound unpeeled medium-size fresh shrimp for lobster. Bring 1 quart water to a boil in a Dutch oven. Add shrimp; cook for 3 to 5 minutes. Drain; rinse with cold water. Chill; peel and devein shrimp. Yield: 4 servings.

Nutritional content per serving: Calories 378
Fat 6.6g (Sat Fat 1.6g) Carbohydrate 51.8g Fiber 2.0g
Protein 26.5g Cholesterol 128mg Sodium 317mg

Scallops in Tarragon Sauce

Preparation Time: 20 minutes
Cooking Time: 8 minutes

The tarragon sauce
is deceiving—
this rich-tasting mixture
gets its creaminess
from nonfat
sour cream alternative.

4 ounces spinach fettuccine, uncooked

Vegetable cooking spray
1½ cups sliced fresh mushrooms
2 tablespoons sliced green onions
1 clove garlic, minced

1 pound bay scallops
⅓ cup Chablis or other dry white wine
1½ tablespoons lemon juice
1½ teaspoons chopped fresh tarragon or ½
    teaspoon dried tarragon

1 tablespoon reduced-calorie stick margarine
1½ tablespoons all-purpose flour
¼ teaspoon salt
⅓ cup nonfat sour cream alternative
Chopped fresh parsley (optional)

1 Cook pasta according to package directions, omitting salt and fat; drain well. Set aside, and keep warm.

2 Coat a large nonstick skillet with cooking spray; place over medium-high heat until hot. Add mushrooms, green onions, and garlic; sauté until tender.

3 Add scallops and next 3 ingredients to mushroom mixture. Cook over low heat 4 minutes or until scallops are opaque. Remove scallops and vegetables from skillet, using a slotted spoon; set aside.

4 Simmer wine mixture, uncovered, 5 to 6 minutes or until liquid is reduced to ¾ cup. Remove from heat, and set aside.

5 Melt margarine in a small heavy saucepan over medium heat; add flour and salt. Cook, stirring constantly with a wire whisk, 1 minute. Gradually add wine mixture, stirring constantly. Cook, stirring constantly, until thickened and bubbly. Remove from heat, and let cool 1 minute. Stir in scallop mixture and sour cream. Serve scallop mixture over fettuccine. Garnish with chopped parsley, if desired. Yield: 4 servings.

Nutritional content per serving: Calories 260
Fat 4.3g (Sat Fat 0.7g) Carbohydrate 28.7g Fiber 2.4g
Protein 25.6g Cholesterol 65mg Sodium 394mg

Lime-Marinated Shrimp Kabobs

Preparation Time: 20 minutes
Marinating Time: 30 minutes
Cooking Time: 6–8 minutes

Mesquite wood chips
impart a smoky,
slightly sweet flavor
to the grilled shrimp.

½ cup mesquite wood chips or other seasoned
　　wood chips

2 pounds unpeeled large fresh shrimp

¼ cup lime juice
3 tablespoons chopped fresh parsley
2 tablespoons low-sodium soy sauce
1 tablespoon olive oil
3 cloves garlic, minced

　　Vegetable cooking spray

　　Lime wedges (optional)
　　Orange curls (optional)

1 Soak wood chips in water 30 minutes; drain.

2 Peel and devein shrimp, leaving tails intact.

3 Combine lime juice and next 4 ingredients in a shallow dish; stir well. Add shrimp, tossing to coat. Cover and chill 30 minutes. Drain shrimp, reserving marinade. Thread shrimp on 6 (12-inch) skewers. Brush kabobs with reserved marinade.

4 Place wood chips on top of coals. Coat grill rack with cooking spray; place on grill over medium-hot coals (350° to 400°). Place kabobs on rack; grill, covered, 3 to 4 minutes. Turn kabobs, and brush with marinade. Grill, covered, an additional 3 to 4 minutes or until shrimp turn pink. (Do not overcook.) If desired, garnish with lime wedges and orange curls. Yield: 6 servings.

Nutritional content per serving: Calories 113
Fat 3.3g (Sat Fat 0.6g) Carbohydrate 1.5g Fiber 0.1g
Protein 18.0g Cholesterol 166mg Sodium 322mg

SALADS & SALAD DRESSINGS

~~~~~

page 167

page 180

page 186

Fruit Salads
Apple Salad with Honey-Yogurt Dressing   164
Mexican Fruit Salad   165
Fruit Salad with Curry Dressing   166
Mixed Melon Salad   167

Vegetable Salads
Hot Three-Bean Salad   168
Toasted Pita Triangles   168
Zesty Marinated Beans   169
Colorful Coleslaw   170
Minted Cucumber Salad   171
Hearts of Palm Salad with Fruit   172
Mushroom-Zucchini Salad   173
Spinach-Garbanzo Salad with
Guacamole Dressing   174
Three-Green Salad   175
Tossed Salad with
Creamy Buttermilk Dressing   176

Pasta and Rice Salads
Garden Pasta Salad   177
Confetti Rice Salad   178
Black Bean and Rice Salad   179

Main Dish Salads
Bacon, Lettuce, and Tomato Salad   180
Chicken and Fettuccine Salad   181
Beef and Fettuccine Salad   181
Pork and Fettuccine Salad   181
Chicken, Apple, and Pear Salad   182
Turkey Salad for Two   183

Salad Dressings
Creamy Coleslaw Dressing   184
Zesty Yogurt Dressing   185
Versatile Vinaigrette   186
Basil Vinaigrette   186
Garlic-Blue Cheese Vinaigrette   186

Apple Salad with Honey-Yogurt Dressing

Preparation Time: 25 minutes
Chilling Time: at least 30 minutes

Spoon this crunchy, slightly sweet salad onto raddichio leaves for a unique presentation.

1½ cups coarsely chopped Granny Smith apple
1½ cups coarsely chopped Golden Delicious apple
 1 cup thinly sliced celery
 ¾ cup coarsely chopped Red Delicious apple
 ½ cup seedless red grapes, halved
 ½ cup golden raisins
 ¼ cup coarsely chopped pecans

 ½ cup plain nonfat yogurt
 2 tablespoons honey
 1 tablespoon white wine vinegar
1½ teaspoons Dijon mustard

   Raddichio leaves (optional)

1 Combine first 7 ingredients in a large bowl; toss well.

2 Combine yogurt and next 3 ingredients in a bowl, stirring well with a wire whisk. Add yogurt mixture to apple mixture, tossing gently. Cover and chill 30 minutes.

3 Line 6 individual salad plates evenly with raddichio leaves, if desired. Place 1 cup salad on each plate. Yield: 6 (1-cup) servings.

Nutritional content per serving: Calories 160
Fat 3.8g (Sat Fat 0.4g) Carbohydrate 32.7g Fiber 3.9g
Protein 2.2g Cholesterol 0mg Sodium 72mg

Mexican Fruit Salad

Preparation Time: 25 minutes

Lime Dressing

1 small head romaine lettuce, shredded
3 large oranges, peeled and sliced crosswise
1 papaya, peeled, seeded, and thinly sliced
2 cups fresh pineapple chunks
1 cup fresh strawberries, hulled
⅓ cup flaked coconut
1 tablespoon pine nuts, toasted

1 Prepare Lime Dressing.

2 Place shredded lettuce on a large serving platter. Arrange orange slices, papaya slices, pineapple chunks, and strawberries over lettuce. Sprinkle with coconut and pine nuts. Drizzle Lime Dressing over salad. Serve immediately. Yield: 8 servings.

Lime Dressing

¾ cup sugar
3 tablespoons water
¾ teaspoon grated lime rind
Juice of 1 large lime

1 Combine sugar and water in a small saucepan; bring to a boil, stirring constantly until sugar dissolves. Remove from heat; stir in lime rind and juice. Cool; cover and chill thoroughly. Yield: ¾ cup.

Nutritional content per serving: Calories 175
Fat 2.3g (Sat Fat 1.3g) Carbohydrate 39.0g Fiber 4.2g
Protein 2.0g Cholesterol 0mg Sodium 15mg

Fruit Salad with Curry Dressing

Preparation Time: 25 minutes

2 cups coarsely chopped Red Delicious apple
2 cups coarsely chopped Anjou pear
3 tablespoons lime juice

1 cup fresh orange sections
¾ cup seedless red grape halves
½ cup sliced fresh strawberries
½ cup peeled, sliced kiwifruit
Curry Dressing

1 Combine first 3 ingredients in a large bowl; toss well.

2 Add orange sections and next 3 ingredients; toss gently. Spoon Curry Dressing over salad; toss gently to coat. Yield: 7 (1-cup) servings.

Curry Dressing

⅔ cup plain low-fat yogurt
1 tablespoon honey
1 teaspoon lime juice
¼ teaspoon curry powder

1 Combine all ingredients in a small bowl; stir well. Yield: ¾ cup.

Nutritional content per serving: Calories 108
Fat 0.9g (Sat Fat 0.3g) Carbohydrate 25.6g Fiber 4.5g
Protein 2.1g Cholesterol 1mg Sodium 16mg

Mixed Melon Salad

Preparation Time: 25 minutes
Chilling Time: at least
30 minutes

Burgundy Poppy Seed Dressing

1 small ripe pineapple (about 2 pounds)
3 cups ripe cantaloupe melon balls
2 cups watermelon balls
2 cups ripe honeydew melon balls

1 Prepare Burgundy Poppy Seed Dressing.

2 Peel and core pineapple; cut into 1-inch cubes (about 5 cups). Combine pineapple and remaining ingredients in a large bowl. Pour Burgundy Poppy Seed Dressing over fruit mixture, and toss to coat. Cover and chill before serving. Yield: 8 (1-cup) servings.

Burgundy Poppy Seed Dressing

¼ cup plus 2 tablespoons sugar
3 tablespoons minced onion
⅛ teaspoon salt
¼ cup plus 2 tablespoons water
⅓ cup Burgundy or other dry red wine

1 teaspoon unflavored gelatin
1½ tablespoons cold water
1½ teaspoons poppy seeds

1 Combine first 3 ingredients in a saucepan; add ¼ cup plus 2 tablespoons water and wine. Cook over medium heat until sugar dissolves, stirring frequently.

2 Sprinkle gelatin over cold water in a small bowl; let stand 1 minute. Add gelatin mixture to wine mixture, stirring until gelatin dissolves. Remove from heat; stir in poppy seeds. Cover and chill thoroughly. Yield: 1 cup.

Nutritional content per serving: Calories 155
Fat 1.1g (Sat Fat 0.3g) Carbohydrate 37.7g Fiber 3.1g
Protein 1.9g Cholesterol 0mg Sodium 58mg

Hot Three-Bean Salad

Preparation Time: 10 minutes
Cooking Time: 5 minutes

~~

Toasted Pita Triangles

Preparation Time: 5 minutes
Cooking Time: 8 minutes

Vegetable cooking spray
½ cup chopped carrot
½ cup chopped celery

¼ cup water
¼ cup red wine vinegar
2 teaspoons sugar
2 teaspoons Dijon mustard
1 teaspoon chicken bouillon granules
¼ teaspoon celery seeds
1 large clove garlic, minced

1 cup drained canned Great Northern beans
1 cup drained canned red kidney beans
½ cup drained canned black beans
¼ cup chopped fresh parsley

1 Coat a large skillet with cooking spray. Place over medium-high heat until hot. Add carrot and celery; sauté 3 minutes or until crisp-tender.

2 Add water and next 6 ingredients to carrot mixture; stir well. Bring to a boil, stirring frequently; cook 1 minute.

3 Add beans; cook until thoroughly heated, stirring frequently. Remove from heat; add parsley, stirring well. Yield: 6 (½-cup) servings.

Nutritional content per serving: Calories 119
Fat 0.8g (Sat Fat 0.2g) Carbohydrate 21.8g Fiber 3.6g
Protein 7.4g Cholesterol 0mg Sodium 395mg

Toasted Pita Triangles

3 (6-inch) pita bread rounds

¼ cup commercial oil-free Italian dressing
½ cup freshly grated Parmesan cheese

1 Split each pita round in half crosswise; cut each half into 8 triangles.

2 Place pita triangles on ungreased baking sheets. Brush triangles with dressing, and sprinkle evenly with Parmesan cheese. Bake at 425° for 5 to 8 minutes or until crisp and lightly browned. Yield: 4 dozen.

Nutritional content per triangle: Calories 18
Fat 0.4g (Sat Fat 0.2g) Carbohydrate 2.6g Fiber 0.5g
Protein 0.7g Cholesterol 1mg Sodium 32mg

Zesty Marinated Beans

Preparation Time: 10 minutes
Chilling Time: at least
30 minutes

Chilled bean salads are
a snap to prepare
and a refreshing opening
course or side dish.

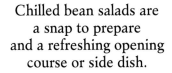

1 (17-ounce) can no-salt-added lima beans,
   drained
1 (16-ounce) can no-salt-added cut green beans,
   drained
1 (16-ounce) can cut wax beans, drained
1 (16-ounce) can red kidney beans, drained
1 cup chopped sweet red pepper
1 cup chopped onion

½ cup sugar
⅓ cup white vinegar
1 tablespoon vegetable oil
½ teaspoon ground red pepper

1 Combine first 6 ingredients in a large bowl; toss gently.

2 Combine sugar and remaining ingredients in a small saucepan. Cook over medium heat 1 to 2 minutes or until sugar dissolves, stirring frequently.

3 Pour hot vinegar mixture over beans; toss gently. Cover and chill thoroughly. Serve with a slotted spoon. Yield: 12 (¾-cup) servings.

Nutritional content per serving: Calories 93
Fat 1.4g (Sat Fat 0.3g) Carbohydrate 18.3g Fiber 1.9g
Protein 3.1g Cholesterol 0mg Sodium 64mg

Colorful Coleslaw

Preparation Time: 20 minutes
Chilling Time: at least
2 hours

Keep the preparation time
to a minimum by using a
food processor.

~~~~~~~~~~

    8 cups shredded cabbage
1½ cups frozen whole kernel corn, thawed
    1 cup shredded carrot
    1 cup chopped purple onion
    1 cup chopped sweet red pepper

½   cup sugar
½   cup white vinegar
    2 tablespoons water
    1 tablespoon vegetable oil
    1 teaspoon celery seeds
½   teaspoon salt
½   teaspoon chicken-flavored bouillon granules
¼   teaspoon ground white pepper
¼   teaspoon mustard seeds
    Dash of hot sauce

1 Combine first 5 ingredients in a large bowl; toss well.

2 Combine sugar and remaining ingredients in a small saucepan. Bring to a boil, stirring constantly until sugar dissolves. Pour over cabbage mixture; toss well.

3 Cover and chill at least 2 hours. Toss before serving. Serve with a slotted spoon. Yield: 10 (1-cup) servings.

Nutritional content per serving: Calories 106
Fat 1.8g (Sat Fat 0.3g) Carbohydrate 23.0g Fiber 3.2g
Protein 2.1g Cholesterol 0mg Sodium 178mg

Minted Cucumber Salad

Preparation Time: 10 minutes
Chilling Time: at least
30 minutes

½ cup vanilla low-fat yogurt
3 tablespoons chopped fresh mint
2 tablespoons white wine vinegar
2 teaspoons sugar
　Dash of hot sauce

3 medium cucumbers, peeled and thinly sliced
1 small purple onion, sliced and separated into
　rings

　Boston lettuce leaves (optional)

1 Combine first 5 ingredients in a small bowl; stir well.

2 Place cucumber and onion slices in a shallow dish. Spoon yogurt mixture over vegetables. Cover and chill at least 30 minutes. Serve over Boston lettuce leaves, if desired. Yield: 6 (1-cup) servings.

Nutritional content per serving: Calories 43
Fat 0.4g (Sat Fat 0.2g) Carbohydrate 8.8g Fiber 1.4g
Protein 1.7g Cholesterol 1mg Sodium 16mg

Hearts of Palm Salad with Fruit

Preparation Time: 20 minutes
Chilling Time: at least
30 minutes

This salad is
bursting with
color, texture, and
unexpected flavors.

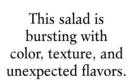

¼ cup evaporated skimmed milk
3 tablespoons nonfat mayonnaise
2½ tablespoons orange juice
2 tablespoons 25% less-fat creamy peanut butter
¾ teaspoon sugar
½ teaspoon ground ginger

2 heads Bibb lettuce, divided
1 (14.4-ounce) can hearts of palm, drained and
  sliced
1 (11-ounce) can mandarin orange segments in
  light syrup, drained
1 cup sliced fresh strawberries
¾ cup sliced celery

1 head radicchio

2 tablespoons coarsely chopped unsalted peanuts

1 Combine first 6 ingredients in container of an electric blender or food processor; cover and process until smooth. Transfer mayonnaise mixture to a small bowl; cover and chill at least 30 minutes.

2 Tear one head of Bibb lettuce into bite-size pieces. Combine torn lettuce and next 4 ingredients; toss gently.

3 Separate remaining head of Bibb lettuce and radicchio into leaves. Arrange leaves on 6 individual salad plates.

4 Spoon strawberry mixture evenly over lettuce leaves. Drizzle 2 tablespoons mayonnaise mixture over each salad. Sprinkle peanuts evenly over salads, and serve immediately. Yield: 6 (1-cup) servings.

Nutritional content per serving: Calories 161
Fat 4.7g (Sat Fat 0.7g) Carbohydrate 27.2g Fiber 2.4g
Protein 5.8g Cholesterol 0mg Sodium 259mg

Mushroom-Zucchini Salad

Preparation Time: 15 minutes
Chilling Time: at least
30 minutes

Chilling this salad
at least 30 minutes
allows the vegetables
to soak up the
tangy dressing.

1½ cups sliced fresh mushrooms
1 small zucchini, sliced
¼ cup sliced green onions
1 tablespoon diced pimiento

2 tablespoons commercial oil-free Italian dressing
2 tablespoons white wine vinegar
1 tablespoon grated Parmesan cheese
1 tablespoon water
¼ teaspoon freshly ground pepper

Fresh spinach leaves (optional)

1 Combine first 4 ingredients in a shallow dish, and toss gently.

2 Combine dressing and next 4 ingredients in a small bowl; stir well. Pour over mushroom mixture; toss gently. Cover and chill at least 30 minutes.

3 Line 4 individual salad plates with spinach leaves, if desired. Spoon mushroom mixture evenly over spinach leaves, using a slotted spoon. Yield: 4 (½-cup) servings.

Nutritional content per serving: Calories 26
Fat 0.6g (Sat Fat 0.3g) Carbohydrate 4.0g Fiber 0.7g
Protein 1.7g Cholesterol 1mg Sodium 108mg

Spinach-Garbanzo Salad with Guacamole Dressing

Preparation Time: 22 minutes
Chilling Time: at least
25 minutes

Guacamole Dressing

5½ cups shredded iceberg lettuce
3 cups tightly packed shredded fresh spinach
1 (15-ounce) can garbanzo beans, drained
1 (14.4-ounce) can hearts of palm, drained and
    cut into ¾-inch slices
¾ cup chopped sweet red pepper

2 ounces small fresh spinach leaves

1 Prepare Guacamole Dressing.

2 Combine lettuce and next 4 ingredients in a large bowl; toss well.

3 Arrange spinach leaves evenly on 8 individual salad plates. Spoon lettuce mixture evenly over spinach leaves. Spoon Guacamole Dressing evenly over salads. Serve immediately. Yield: 8 (1½-cup) servings.

Guacamole Dressing

¾ cup peeled, chopped avocado
¼ cup evaporated skimmed milk
1½ tablespoons lemon juice
1 tablespoon nonfat sour cream alternative
½ teaspoon chili powder
¼ teaspoon Worcestershire sauce
⅛ teaspoon ground cumin
1 large clove garlic, crushed

1 Combine all ingredients in container of an electric blender; cover and process until smooth, stopping once to scrape down sides. Cover; chill thoroughly. Yield: 1 cup.

Nutritional content per serving: Calories 143
Fat 4.1g (Sat Fat 0.6g) Carbohydrate 23.0g Fiber 4.4g
Protein 6.7g Cholesterol 0mg Sodium 190mg

Three-Green Salad

Preparation Time: **15 minutes**

Kiwifruit lends
a sweet-tart
flavor to
Three-Green Salad.

3 cups tightly packed torn fresh spinach
3 cups tightly packed torn Bibb lettuce
2 medium kiwifruit, peeled and sliced
1 small purple onion, thinly sliced and separated
    into rings

3 tablespoons lemon juice
2 tablespoons honey
2 teaspoons vegetable oil
¼ teaspoon freshly ground pepper

1 Combine first 4 ingredients in a large bowl; toss gently.

2 Combine lemon juice and remaining ingredients in a small jar; cover tightly, and shake vigorously to blend. Drizzle over spinach mixture, and toss gently. Serve immediately. Yield: 6 (1½-cup) servings.

Nutritional content per serving: Calories 65
Fat 1.8g (Sat Fat 0.2g) Carbohydrate 12.2g Fiber 2.1g
Protein 1.3g Cholesterol 0mg Sodium 15mg

Tossed Salad with Creamy Buttermilk Dressing

Preparation Time: **20 minutes**

Creamy Buttermilk Dressing tastes so fresh and is so simple to make you may abandon commercial brands.

2 cups tightly packed torn romaine lettuce
2 cups tightly packed torn leaf lettuce
1¼ cups halved cherry tomatoes
½ cup sliced purple onion
¼ cup chopped celery

     Creamy Buttermilk Dressing

1 Combine first 5 ingredients in a large bowl; toss well. Spoon Creamy Buttermilk Dressing evenly over salad; toss gently to coat. Serve immediately. Yield: 6 (½-cup) servings.

Creamy Buttermilk Dressing

½ cup nonfat buttermilk
¼ cup plus 2 tablespoons nonfat mayonnaise
1 tablespoon grated Parmesan cheese
1 teaspoon dried parsley flakes
¼ teaspoon cracked pepper
1 clove garlic, minced

1 Combine all ingredients in a small bowl; stir well. Yield: ¾ cup plus 2 tablespoons.

Nutritional content per serving: Calories 42
Fat 0.5g (Sat Fat 0.3g) Carbohydrate 7.8g Fiber 1.3g
Protein 2.1g Cholesterol 1mg Sodium 239mg

Garden Pasta Salad

Preparation Time: 30 minutes
Chilling Time: at least
30 minutes

6 ounces corkscrew macaroni, uncooked

3 cups peeled, seeded, and coarsely chopped
    tomato (about 4 medium)
1 cup peeled, seeded, and chopped cucumber
    (about 1 medium)
¼ cup chopped green pepper
¼ cup chopped fresh parsley
2 tablespoons sliced green onions

⅓ cup commercial oil-free Italian dressing
    Dash of hot sauce

¾ cup crumbled feta cheese
    Chopped fresh parsley (optional)

1 Cook pasta according to package directions, omitting salt and fat. Drain; set aside.

2 Combine tomato and next 4 ingredients in a large bowl. Combine dressing and hot sauce, stirring well.

3 Add pasta and dressing mixture to vegetable mixture, and toss gently. Cover and chill at least 30 minutes. Sprinkle cheese evenly over salad just before serving. Garnish with chopped parsley, if desired. Yield: 6 (1-cup) servings.

Nutritional content per serving: Calories 173
Fat 3.8g (Sat Fat 2.2g) Carbohydrate 28.5g Fiber 2.1g
Protein 6.7g Cholesterol 13mg Sodium 313mg

Confetti Rice Salad

Preparation Time: 12 minutes
Cooking Time: 20 minutes
Chilling Time: at least
25 minutes

1 (10½-ounce) can low-sodium chicken broth
1 cup plus 2 tablespoons water
1 cup long-grain rice, uncooked
½ cup diced carrot

¼ cup lemon juice
1 tablespoon olive oil

¾ cup seeded, chopped plum tomato (about 2 medium)
¾ cup diced cooked reduced-fat, low-salt ham
⅓ cup freshly grated Parmesan cheese
⅓ cup sliced green onions
⅓ cup chopped fresh parsley

1 Combine chicken broth and water in a large saucepan; bring to a boil. Add rice and carrot; stir well. Reduce heat to low; cover and simmer 20 minutes or until liquid is absorbed and rice is tender.

2 Add lemon juice and oil to rice mixture; stir well. Add tomato and remaining ingredients; toss gently. Transfer to a serving bowl. Cover; chill thoroughly. Yield: 5 (1-cup) servings.

Nutritional content per serving: Calories 244
Fat 6.6g (Sat Fat 2.5g) Carbohydrate 35.4g Fiber 1.5g
Protein 10.9g Cholesterol 17mg Sodium 339mg

Microwaving Directions: Combine first 4 ingredients in a 2-quart casserole. Cover with heavy-duty plastic wrap, and vent. Microwave at HIGH 5 minutes; stir well. Cover and microwave at MEDIUM (50% power) 11 to 12 minutes or until liquid is absorbed and rice is tender. Continue with step 2 as directed above.

Black Bean and Rice Salad

Preparation Time: 15 minutes
Cooking Time: 20–25 minutes
Chilling Time: at least
30 minutes

In this recipe, the rice and lentils cook in chicken broth, which infuses flavor but adds little fat or sodium.

~~~~~~~~

2 teaspoons olive oil
1 cup diced carrot
1 cup diced green pepper
⅓ cup minced onion

2 (10½-ounce) cans low-sodium chicken broth
¾ cup long-grain rice, uncooked
½ cup dried red lentils

1 (15-ounce) can black beans, drained
3 tablespoons chopped fresh cilantro
½ teaspoon ground cumin

1½ cups tightly packed shredded fresh spinach
2 tablespoons plus 2 teaspoons grated Parmesan cheese
Fresh cilantro sprigs (optional)

1 Place oil in a large nonstick skillet over medium-high heat until hot. Add carrot, green pepper, and onion; sauté until vegetables are crisp-tender.

2 Bring broth to a boil in a large saucepan. Add rice and lentils. Cover, reduce heat, and simmer 20 to 25 minutes or until rice and lentils are tender and liquid is absorbed. Remove from heat.

3 Stir carrot mixture, black beans, cilantro, and cumin into rice and lentil mixture. Cover and chill thoroughly.

4 Stir in spinach, and sprinkle evenly with cheese just before serving. Garnish with cilantro sprigs, if desired. Yield: 8 (¾-cup) servings.

Nutritional content per serving: Calories 175
Fat 2.7g (Sat Fat 0.7g) Carbohydrate 30.2g Fiber 3.6g
Protein 8.2g Cholesterol 1mg Sodium 154mg

Bacon, Lettuce, and Tomato Salad

Preparation Time: 30 minutes
Chilling Time: at least
30 minutes

Tangy French Dressing

8 cups tightly packed torn red leaf lettuce
4 small tomatoes, cut into wedges
6 ounces Canadian bacon, coarsely chopped

4 (1-ounce) slices French bread, cubed and
    toasted
¾ cup (3 ounces) shredded reduced-fat sharp
    Cheddar cheese
4 slices turkey bacon, cooked and coarsely
    crumbled

1 Prepare Tangy French Dressing.

2 Combine lettuce, tomato, and Canadian bacon in a large bowl; toss well. Place lettuce mixture evenly on 8 individual salad plates.

3 Top salads evenly with toasted bread cubes, and sprinkle evenly with cheese and turkey bacon. Serve each salad with 2 tablespoons Tangy French Dressing. Yield: 8 (1¼-cup) servings.

Tangy French Dressing

½ teaspoon unflavored gelatin
1 tablespoon cold water
¼ cup boiling water

½ cup spicy hot vegetable juice
1½ tablespoons sugar
2 tablespoons cider vinegar
1 tablespoon low-sodium Worcestershire sauce
¼ teaspoon salt
¼ teaspoon dry mustard
⅛ teaspoon garlic powder
    Dash of freshly ground pepper

1 Sprinkle gelatin over cold water; let stand 1 minute. Add boiling water; stir until gelatin dissolves. Set aside.

2 Combine vegetable juice and remaining ingredients in container of an electric blender; cover and process 30 seconds. Add gelatin mixture; process until well blended. Transfer mixture to a small bowl; cover and chill thoroughly. Stir well before serving. Yield: 1 cup.

Nutritional content per serving: Calories 163
Fat 5.4g (Sat Fat 2.1g) Carbohydrate 17.4g Fiber 1.5g
Protein 11.2g Cholesterol 24mg Sodium 667mg

Chicken and Fettuccine Salad

Preparation Time: 30 minutes

This salad is a great way to use leftover cooked chicken breast, pork tenderloin, or roast beef.

~~~~~~~~~~

6 ounces uncooked fettuccine, broken in half

2½ cups broccoli flowerets
1 cup diagonally sliced carrot
¾ cup diagonally sliced celery

⅓ cup commercial oil-free Italian dressing
⅓ cup reduced-calorie mayonnaise
2½ tablespoons prepared horseradish
½ teaspoon freshly ground pepper
12 cherry tomatoes, halved

4 (3-ounce) cooked, boned chicken breast halves (skinned before cooking and cooked without salt and fat)

1 Cook fettuccine according to package directions, omitting salt and fat. Drain and rinse under cold water; drain again. Set aside.

2 Cook broccoli, carrot, and celery in a small amount of boiling water 6 minutes or until crisp-tender. Drain; plunge into ice water, and drain again.

3 Combine cooked fettuccine and broccoli mixture in a large bowl. Combine Italian dressing and next 3 ingredients; stir well. Add to fettuccine mixture; toss gently. Gently stir in tomato.

4 Cut chicken into ½-inch-wide strips. Arrange evenly over salad. Yield: 8 (1-cup) servings.

Nutritional content per serving: Calories 196
Fat 4.7g (Sat Fat 0.9g) Carbohydrate 22.2g Fiber 3.7g
Protein 17.6g Cholesterol 39mg Sodium 238mg

Variations:

Beef and Fettuccine Salad: Substitute ½ pound sliced lean cooked roast beef for chicken. Yield: 8 (1-cup) servings.

Nutritional content per serving: Calories 170
Fat 5.5g (Sat Fat 0.9g) Carbohydrate 22.2g Fiber 3.7g
Protein 10.0g Cholesterol 27mg Sodium 379mg

Pork and Fettuccine Salad: Substitute ½ pound sliced cooked pork tenderloin for chicken. Yield: 8 (1-cup) servings.

Nutritional content per serving: Calories 194
Fat 7.1g (Sat Fat 1.4g) Carbohydrate 22.2g Fiber 3.7g
Protein 12.0g Cholesterol 28mg Sodium 226mg

Chicken, Apple, and Pear Salad

Preparation Time: 25 minutes
Chilling Time: at least
25 minutes

2½ cups chopped fresh pear (about 2 medium)
2 cups chopped apple (about 2 small)
2 tablespoons lemon juice
1 cup coarsely chopped celery

½ cup jellied whole-berry cranberry sauce
⅓ cup nonfat mayonnaise
1 teaspoon sugar
½ teaspoon ground ginger

2½ cups chopped cooked chicken breast (skinned
before cooking and cooked without salt)
2 tablespoons chopped pecans, toasted

1 Combine first 3 ingredients in a medium bowl; toss well. Stir in celery; set aside.

2 Combine cranberry sauce and next 3 ingredients in a bowl; stir well. Add to pear mixture, and toss gently.

3 Stir in chicken; cover and chill thoroughly. Sprinkle with pecans before serving. Yield: 6 (1½-cup) servings.

Nutritional content per serving: Calories 215
Fat 4.8g (Sat Fat 0.8g) Carbohydrate 26.7g Fiber 3.8g
Protein 17.7g Cholesterol 46mg Sodium 232mg

Turkey Salad for Two

Preparation Time: 20 minutes

2 cups tightly packed torn iceberg lettuce
1 cup chopped cooked turkey breast
½ cup unsweetened mandarin orange segments
⅓ cup seedless green grapes, halved
⅓ cup seedless red grapes, halved
⅓ cup diagonally sliced celery

Creamy Curry Dressing

4 leaves red leaf lettuce
Celery leaves (optional)
Orange rind curls (optional)

1 Combine first 6 ingredients in a medium bowl; toss gently. Spoon Creamy Curry Dressing evenly over lettuce mixture, and toss gently.

2 Spoon evenly onto individual serving plates lined with red leaf lettuce. If desired, garnish with celery leaves and orange rind curls. Yield: 2 (2¼-cup) servings.

Creamy Curry Dressing

¼ cup nonfat mayonnaise
2 tablespoons skim milk
1 teaspoon cracked pepper
½ teaspoon curry powder
¼ teaspoon dried tarragon

1 Combine all ingredients in a small bowl, stirring well. Yield: ¼ cup plus 2 tablespoons.

Nutritional content per serving: Calories 225
Fat 3.2g (Sat Fat 1.0g) Carbohydrate 23.3g Fiber 2.7g
Protein 25.5g Cholesterol 54mg Sodium 469mg

Make Ahead: Creamy Curry Dressing may be made up to one day ahead. You can also chop, measure, and prepare salad ingredients up to one day in advance and store in separate zip-top plastic bags. Chill dressing and other ingredients until ready to serve.

Creamy Coleslaw Dressing

Preparation Time: **8 minutes**
Chilling Time: **at least 30 minutes**

Enjoy Creamy Coleslaw Dressing without guilt; ours uses nonfat mayonnaise and nonfat sour cream.

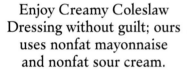

½ cup nonfat mayonnaise
½ cup nonfat sour cream
2 tablespoons sugar
2 tablespoons vinegar
½ teaspoon prepared mustard
¼ teaspoon salt
¼ teaspoon freshly ground pepper

1 Combine all ingredients in a small bowl; stir until well blended. Cover and chill at least 30 minutes. Toss with your favorite coleslaw ingredients. Yield: 1 cup plus 2 tablespoons.

Nutritional content per tablespoon: Calories 16 Fat 0.0g (Sat Fat 0g) Carbohydrate 3.3g Fiber 0g Protein 0.5g Cholesterol 0mg Sodium 123mg

Zesty Yogurt Dressing

Preparation Time: 6 minutes

~~~~~~~~~~

½ cup plain nonfat yogurt
1 tablespoon minced fresh parsley
1 tablespoon skim milk
1 tablespoon lemon juice
2 teaspoons sugar
1 teaspoon honey-mustard
   Dash of liquid red pepper seasoning

1 Combine all ingredients in a small bowl; stir well. Store in the refrigerator up to 3 days. Serve with salad greens. Yield: ¾ cup.

Nutritional content per tablespoon: Calories 10 Fat 0.0g (Sat Fat 0g) Carbohydrate 1.9g Fiber 0g Protein 0.6g Cholesterol 0mg Sodium 11mg

Versatile Vinaigrette

Preparation Time: **5 minutes**
Chilling Time: **30 minutes**

This vinaigrette takes just five minutes to prepare, but it should chill thoroughly to blend the flavors.

~~~~~~~~~~

¾ cup canned no-salt-added chicken broth, undiluted
¼ cup white wine vinegar
2 teaspoons minced garlic
1½ teaspoons olive oil
1 teaspoon Dijon mustard
⅛ teaspoon pepper

1 Combine all ingredients in a jar; cover tightly, and shake vigorously to blend. Chill thoroughly. Serve with salad greens. Yield: 1¼ cups.

Nutritional content per tablespoon: Calories 5
Fat 0.4g (Sat Fat 0.1g) Carbohydrate 0.1g Fiber 0g
Protein 0.1g Cholesterol 0mg Sodium 13mg

Variations:

Basil Vinaigrette: Omit garlic and mustard. Add 3 tablespoons finely chopped fresh basil and 1 green onion, finely chopped. Yield: 1¼ cups.

Nutritional content per tablespoon: Calories 5
Fat 0.4g (Sat Fat 0.1g) Carbohydrate 0.1g Fiber 0g
Protein 0.1g Cholesterol 0mg Sodium 5mg

Garlic-Blue Cheese Vinaigrette: Add ¼ cup crumbled blue cheese and 1 teaspoon sugar. Yield: 1¼ cups.

Nutritional content per tablespoon: Calories 12
Fat 0.9g (Sat Fat 0.4g) Carbohydrate 0.4g Fiber 0g
Protein 0.5g Cholesterol 1mg Sodium 38mg

SIDE DISHES

page 194

page 198

page 203

Grains

Confetti Rice   188
Broccoli-Rice Timbales   189
Fiesta Spanish Rice   190
Spanish Beef and Rice Casserole   190
Chilled Red Beans and Rice   191
Waldorf Rice   192
Turmeric Rice   193
Seasoned Couscous   194

Pasta

Cracked Pepper Linguine   195
New Orleans Pasta   196
Pizzeria Pasta   197
Spaghetti with Fontina and Greens   198
Tangy Dijon Pasta   199

Vegetables

Oriental Broccoli   200
French-Style Green Beans   201
German-Style Lima Beans   202
Lemon-Dill Carrots   203
Cauliflower with Cheese Sauce   204
Corn-Zucchini-Tomato Sauté   205
Okra-Tomato-Zucchini Medley   206
Cheesy Scalloped Onions   207
Snow Peas, Red Pepper, and Pineapple   208
Browned Basil New Potatoes   209
Fruit-Glazed Acorn Squash   210
Summer Squash Casserole   211
Spinach-Topped Tomatoes   212
Savory Creamed Turnips   213
Vegetable-Stuffed Zucchini   214

Confetti Rice

Preparation Time: 10 minutes
Cooking Time: 23 minutes

Confetti Rice
complements baked
chicken drumsticks
for a satisfying,
colorful meal.

2 tablespoons reduced-calorie stick margarine
1 cup sliced green onions
¾ cup long-grain rice, uncooked
1 medium-size green pepper, seeded and cut into
   ½-inch pieces
1 medium-size sweet red pepper, seeded and cut
   into ½-inch pieces
1 teaspoon ground cumin
½ teaspoon dried whole oregano
¼ teaspoon salt
2 cloves garlic, minced

¼ cup water
1 (10½-ounce) can low-sodium chicken broth

Fresh oregano sprigs (optional)

1 Melt margarine in a large nonstick skillet over medium heat. Add green onions and next 7 ingredients; sauté 3 minutes.

2 Add water and chicken broth; bring to a boil. Cover, reduce heat, and simmer 20 minutes or until rice is tender and liquid is absorbed. Garnish with oregano sprigs, if desired. Yield: 8 (½-cup) servings.

Nutritional content per serving: Calories 94
Fat 2.4g (Sat Fat 0.3g) Carbohydrate 16.5g Fiber 0.8g
Protein 2.1g Cholesterol 0mg Sodium 117mg

Broccoli-Rice Timbales

Preparation Time: 15 minutes
Cooking Time: 10 minutes

Create a perfect timbale by packing the broccoli-rice mixture into custard cups and inverting onto plates.

~~~~~~~~~~

1 (10-ounce) package frozen chopped broccoli

Vegetable cooking spray
½ cup chopped onion
1 clove garlic, minced

2 cups cooked short-grain rice (cooked without salt or fat)
½ teaspoon salt

Pimiento strips (optional)

1 Cook broccoli according to package directions, omitting salt. Drain well, and set aside.

2 Coat a large nonstick skillet with cooking spray; place over medium-high heat until hot. Add onion and garlic; sauté until tender. Stir in broccoli, rice, and salt. Cook until mixture is thoroughly heated, stirring frequently.

3 Pack broccoli mixture evenly into 6 (6-ounce) custard cups coated with cooking spray. Invert onto serving plates; garnish with pimiento strips, if desired. Serve immediately. Yield: 6 servings.

Nutritional content per serving: Calories 94
Fat 0.5g (Sat Fat 0.1g) Carbohydrate 19.8g Fiber 1.8g
Protein 3.0g Cholesterol 0mg Sodium 207mg

Fiesta Spanish Rice

Preparation Time: 15 minutes
Cooking Time: 20–25 minutes

Fiesta Spanish Rice is a traditional accompaniment to tacos, fajitas, and other Mexican fare.

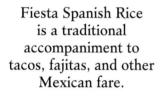

Vegetable cooking spray
¼ cup chopped onion
2 cloves garlic, minced

1 (14½-ounce) can no-salt-added whole tomatoes, undrained and chopped
1 (13¾-ounce) can no-salt-added beef broth
1 (4-ounce) can chopped green chiles, undrained
1½ teaspoons chili powder
⅛ teaspoon salt
Dash of hot sauce

1 cup long-grain rice, uncooked

1 Coat a large saucepan with cooking spray; place over medium-high heat until hot. Add onion and garlic; sauté until crisp-tender.

2 Stir in tomato and next 5 ingredients; bring to a boil.

3 Stir in rice. Cover, reduce heat, and simmer 20 to 25 minutes or until rice is tender and liquid is absorbed. Yield: 6 (½-cup) servings.

Nutritional content per serving: Calories 145
Fat 0.5g (Sat Fat 0.1g) Carbohydrate 31.1g Fiber 2.0g
Protein 3.5g Cholesterol 0mg Sodium 143mg

Variation:

Spanish Beef and Rice Casserole: Stir 1 (16-ounce) can drained pinto beans and 1 pound cooked, drained ground chuck into cooked rice mixture in step 3 above. Spoon into a 2-quart baking dish coated with cooking spray. Cover; bake at 350° for 20 minutes or until thoroughly heated. Sprinkle with ½ cup (2 ounces) shredded reduced-fat Cheddar cheese; bake, uncovered, an additional 5 minutes or until cheese melts. Yield: 8 (1-cup) servings.

Nutritional content per serving: Calories 242
Fat 3.9g (Sat Fat 1.3g) Carbohydrate 32.8g Fiber 2.2g
Protein 17.7g Cholesterol 35mg Sodium 143mg

Chilled Red Beans and Rice

Preparation Time: 15 minutes
Chilling Time: at least
20 minutes

You can make this
dish 24 hours
before serving.

~~~~~~~~~~~~

¼ cup commercial reduced-calorie Italian dressing
3 tablespoons water
2 tablespoons white vinegar
½ teaspoon dried oregano
¼ teaspoon ground red pepper
¼ teaspoon dried thyme
⅛ teaspoon freshly ground black pepper

1 (15-ounce) can red kidney beans, drained
1 cup cooked long-grain rice (cooked without salt
   or fat), chilled
1 cup sliced celery
¾ cup chopped onion
¾ cup chopped tomato

Celery leaves (optional)

1 Combine first 7 ingredients in a jar. Cover tightly, and shake vigorously. Chill.

2 Combine dressing mixture, kidney beans, and next 4 ingredients in a medium bowl; toss well. Cover and chill. Garnish with celery leaves, if desired. Yield: 5 (1-cup) servings.

Nutritional content per serving: Calories 138
Fat 0.7g (Sat Fat 0.1g) Carbohydrate 27.5g Fiber 3.3g
Protein 6.4g Cholesterol 0mg Sodium 300mg

Waldorf Rice

Preparation Time: 10 minutes
Cooking Time: 25 minutes

1 cup chopped cooking apple
1 tablespoon lemon juice

Vegetable cooking spray
¾ cup long-grain rice, uncooked
1½ cups unsweetened apple juice

¾ cup chopped celery
¼ cup chopped pecans, toasted
8 pecan halves
Celery leaves (optional)

1 Combine apple and lemon juice in a small bowl; toss gently to coat. Set aside.

2 Coat a large nonstick skillet with cooking spray; place over medium-high heat until hot. Add rice; sauté until rice is lightly browned. Stir in apple juice. Bring to a boil; cover, reduce heat, and simmer 15 minutes.

3 Stir in chopped celery; cover and cook an additional 10 minutes or until rice is tender and liquid is absorbed. Stir in apple and chopped pecans. Transfer rice mixture to a serving bowl. Garnish with pecan halves and celery leaves, if desired. Yield: 4 (1-cup) servings.

Nutritional content per serving: Calories 265
Fat 7.8g (Sat Fat 0.7g) Carbohydrate 46.2g Fiber 2.5g
Protein 3.6g Cholesterol 0mg Sodium 28mg

Turmeric Rice

Preparation Time: 8 minutes
Cooking Time: 12–15 minutes

1 cup water
1 teaspoon chicken-flavored bouillon granules
1 teaspoon lemon juice
⅛ teaspoon ground turmeric

1 cup instant brown rice, uncooked
3 tablespoons currants

Lemon peels (optional)
Currants (optional)

1 Combine first 4 ingredients in a medium saucepan; bring to a boil.

2 Stir in rice; cover, reduce heat, and simmer 12 to 15 minutes or until rice is tender and liquid is absorbed. Remove from heat, and stir in 3 tablespoons currants. If desired, garnish with lemon peels and currants. Serve immediately. Yield: 4 (½-cup) servings.

Nutritional content per serving: Calories 82
Fat 1.0g (Sat Fat 0.1g) Carbohydrate 17.9g Fiber 1.1g
Protein 1.9g Cholesterol 0mg Sodium 210mg

Seasoned Couscous

Preparation Time: 12 minutes
Cooking Time: 5 minutes

Couscous, a tiny grain milled from wheat, becomes tender and fluffy after soaking just five minutes in hot liquid.

Vegetable cooking spray
½ teaspoon peanut oil
¼ cup sliced green onions

¾ cup water
1 teaspoon chicken-flavored bouillon granules

½ cup uncooked couscous
2 teaspoons low-sodium soy sauce
⅓ cup peeled, seeded, and chopped tomato
1 tablespoon chopped fresh parsley
⅓ teaspoon freshly ground pepper

1 Roma tomato (optional)
½ teaspoon whole peppercorns (optional)

1 Coat a saucepan with cooking spray; add oil. Place over medium-high heat until hot. Add green onions, and sauté until tender.

2 Add water and bouillon granules; bring to a boil. Remove from heat.

3 Add couscous and soy sauce; cover and let stand 5 minutes. Stir in chopped tomato, parsley, and pepper.

4 If garnish is desired, cut top third from Roma tomato; discard. Use a paring knife to make decorative cuts around edge of tomato; place peppercorns in center. Yield: 4 (½-cup) servings.

Nutritional content per serving: Calories 97
Fat 1.0g (Sat Fat 0.2g) Carbohydrate 18.5g Fiber 0.7g
Protein 3.3g Cholesterol 0mg Sodium 275mg

Cracked Pepper Linguine

Preparation Time: 20 minutes
Cooking Time: 5 minutes

Nonfat sour cream is
the secret to this creamy,
low-fat linguine.

〰〰〰〰〰

8 ounces linguine, uncooked

¼ cup minced onion
2 cloves garlic, minced
1 tablespoon reduced-calorie stick margarine,
   melted

1 (8-ounce) carton nonfat sour cream alternative
1 tablespoon skim milk
1 tablespoon cracked pepper

2 tablespoons freshly grated Parmesan cheese
1½ tablespoons chopped fresh parsley

1 Cook linguine according to package directions, omitting salt and fat. Drain. Set aside, and keep warm.

2 Sauté onion and garlic in margarine in a small skillet over medium heat until onion is crisp-tender.

3 Combine sour cream, milk, and pepper in a small bowl; stir well.

4 Combine linguine, onion mixture, and sour cream mixture; toss well. Sprinkle with Parmesan cheese and parsley. Serve immediately. Yield: 6 (¾-cup) servings.

Nutritional content per serving: Calories 193
Fat 2.4g (Sat Fat 0.6g) Carbohydrate 32.8g Fiber 1.4g
Protein 8.6g Cholesterol 1mg Sodium 82mg

New Orleans Pasta

Preparation Time: 15 minutes
Cooking Time: 5 minutes

8 ounces farfalle (bow tie) pasta, uncooked

½ (8-ounce) package Neufchâtel cheese, softened

¼ cup no-salt-added tomato juice
2 tablespoons chopped onion
2 tablespoons chopped celery
2 tablespoons chopped green pepper
¼ teaspoon ground white pepper
¼ teaspoon ground red pepper
⅛ teaspoon black pepper

1 Cook pasta according to package directions, omitting salt and fat; drain well. Set aside, and keep warm.

2 Beat cheese in a medium bowl at medium speed of an electric mixer until fluffy.

3 Cook tomato juice in a small saucepan over medium heat until thoroughly heated. Slowly add warm tomato juice to cheese, and beat at low speed until smooth. Stir in onion and remaining ingredients.

4 Add pasta to cheese mixture, tossing gently. Serve immediately. Yield: 8 (½-cup) servings.

Nutritional content per serving: Calories 146
Fat 3.8g (Sat Fat 2.2g) Carbohydrate 22.5g Fiber 0.8g
Protein 5.2g Cholesterol 11mg Sodium 61mg

Pizzeria Pasta

Preparation Time: 10 minutes
Cooking Time: 5 minutes

Pizzeria Pasta is
a real family-pleaser that's
easy on the cook.
It uses fresh cheese
tortellini, which cooks in
just five minutes.

1 (9-ounce) package fresh cheese tortellini

Vegetable cooking spray
½ cup chopped green pepper
⅓ cup chopped onion

1 (8-ounce) can no-salt-added tomato sauce
¼ cup sliced ripe olives
1 teaspoon dried Italian seasoning
⅛ teaspoon garlic powder

1 Cook tortellini according to package directions, omitting salt and fat; drain well. Place in a serving bowl.

2 Coat a medium nonstick skillet with cooking spray. Place over medium-high heat until hot. Add green pepper and onion; sauté until tender.

3 Stir in tomato sauce and remaining ingredients. Cook over medium-low heat until thoroughly heated, stirring occasionally. Add tomato mixture to tortellini; toss gently. Serve immediately. Yield: 6 (½-cup) servings.

Nutritional content per serving: Calories 168
Fat 4.2g (Sat Fat 1.2g) Carbohydrate 24.9g Fiber 2.0g
Protein 7.2g Cholesterol 20mg Sodium 246mg

Spaghetti with Fontina and Greens

Preparation Time: 20 minutes
Cooking Time: 12 minutes

Fontina cheese has a mild, nutty flavor, and it melts smoothly, making it ideal for this distinctive pasta dish.

1 pound Swiss chard
Vegetable cooking spray

8 ounces spaghetti, uncooked

2 tablespoons all-purpose flour
2½ cups skim milk, divided
¼ cup Marsala or other cooking wine

½ cup (2 ounces) shredded fontina cheese
¼ teaspoon ground red pepper

2 tablespoons pine nuts, toasted

1 Rinse Swiss chard; remove and discard stalks. Cut leaves into ½-inch wide strips, and place in a Dutch oven coated with cooking spray. Cover and cook over medium-high heat 5 minutes, stirring occasionally. Drain and set aside.

2 Cook pasta according to package directions, omitting salt and fat. Drain and set aside.

3 Combine flour and ½ cup milk in a glass jar; cover and shake vigorously until smooth. Pour into a medium saucepan; gradually stir in remaining 2 cups milk and wine. Cook over medium heat, stirring constantly, until thickened and bubbly.

4 Add Swiss chard, cheese, and red pepper. Reduce heat, and cook until mixture is thoroughly heated and cheese is melted. Add cheese mixture to pasta, and toss gently to coat. Sprinkle with pine nuts. Serve immediately. Yield: 12 (½-cup) servings.

Nutritional content per serving: Calories 168
Fat 3.4g (Sat Fat 1.2g) Carbohydrate 19.7g Fiber 0.9g
Protein 6.4g Cholesterol 7mg Sodium 135mg

Tangy Dijon Pasta

Preparation Time: 20 minutes
Cooking Time: 4–6 minutes

〜〜〜〜〜〜〜〜

2 cups fresh snow pea pods

¼ cup plus 2 tablespoons low-fat sour cream
3 tablespoons Chablis or other dry white wine
2 tablespoons Dijon mustard

4 ounces capellini (angel hair pasta), uncooked

Vegetable cooking spray
½ cup diced purple onion
1 (2-ounce) jar sliced pimiento, drained

1 Wash peas; trim ends, and remove strings. Cook, uncovered, in a small amount of boiling water 3 minutes. Drain; set aside, and keep warm.

2 Combine sour cream, wine, and mustard in a small bowl; stir well using a wire whisk, and set aside.

3 Cook pasta according to package directions, omitting salt and fat. Drain and set aside.

4 Coat a large skillet with cooking spray; place over medium-high heat until hot. Add onion, and sauté 2 to 3 minutes or until tender. Add snow peas, sour cream mixture, pasta, and pimiento. Cook, stirring constantly, 2 to 3 minutes or until thoroughly heated. Serve immediately. Yield: 7 (½-cup) servings.

Nutritional content per serving: Calories 102
Fat 2.3g (Sat Fat 1.0g) Carbohydrate 16.5g Fiber 1.3g
Protein 3.4g Cholesterol 5mg Sodium 137mg

Oriental Broccoli

Preparation Time: **15 minutes**
Cooking Time: **10 minutes**

A touch of
strong, nutty-flavored
dark sesame oil
accents this
Oriental side dish.

1½ **pounds fresh broccoli**

  3 **tablespoons low-sodium soy sauce**
  2 **teaspoons dark sesame oil**
  1 **teaspoon honey**
 ½ **teaspoon peeled, grated gingerroot or** ¼
     teaspoon ground ginger
 ¼ **teaspoon dry mustard**

  8 **small cherry tomatoes, halved**
 ½ **cup sliced water chestnuts**
  2 **green onions, diagonally sliced**

1 Trim off large leaves of broccoli, and remove tough ends of lower stalks. Wash broccoli thoroughly, and coarsely chop. Arrange in a vegetable steamer over boiling water. Cover and steam 5 to 8 minutes or until crisp-tender. Drain; transfer to a serving bowl, and keep warm.

2 Combine soy sauce and next 4 ingredients in a small saucepan; stir well. Bring to a boil over medium heat. Pour over broccoli. Add remaining ingredients; toss gently. Serve immediately. Yield: 6 (1-cup) servings.

Nutritional content per serving: Calories 56
Fat 1.9g (Sat Fat 0.3g) Carbohydrate 8.2g Fiber 3.2g
Protein 3.1g Cholesterol 0mg Sodium 223mg

French-Style Green Beans

Preparation Time: 15 minutes
Cooking Time: 15 minutes

One (16-ounce) package frozen French-style green beans can be substituted for fresh green beans, if desired. Sauté frozen beans as directed below, and decrease simmering time to ten minutes.

~~~~~~~~~~~~

¾ **pound fresh green beans, ends trimmed and strings removed**
1 **tablespoon nonfat margarine**

¾ **cup low-sodium chicken broth**
¼ **teaspoon freshly ground pepper**
⅛ **teaspoon salt**

1½ **teaspoons cornstarch**
1 **tablespoon water**
2 **teaspoons lemon juice**

2 **tablespoons sliced almonds, toasted**

1 Slice beans in half lengthwise. Melt margarine in a large skillet. Add beans, and sauté 5 minutes.

2 Add chicken broth, pepper, and salt. Bring to a boil. Cover, reduce heat, and simmer 15 minutes.

3 Combine cornstarch and water; pour over beans. Cook, stirring constantly, 1 minute. Stir in lemon juice. Just before serving, sprinkle with toasted almonds. Yield: 4 (½-cup) servings.

Nutritional content per serving: Calories 49
Fat 1.3g (Sat Fat 0.2g) Carbohydrate 8.1 g Fiber 2.0g
Protein 2.4g Cholesterol 0mg Sodium 113mg

Microwaving Directions: Slice beans in half lengthwise. Place margarine in a microwave-safe 2-quart baking dish; cover with heavy-duty plastic wrap. Microwave at HIGH 30 seconds or until margarine melts. Add beans; cover and vent. Microwave at HIGH 4 minutes. Add chicken broth, pepper, and salt. Cover and vent. Microwave at HIGH 6 to 8 minutes. Combine cornstarch and water; stir into beans. Cover and microwave at HIGH 1 minute. Uncover and stir. Cover and let stand 5 minutes. Stir in lemon juice. Just before serving, sprinkle with toasted almonds.

German-Style Lima Beans

Preparation Time: 20 minutes
Cooking Time: 5 minutes

1 (16-ounce) package frozen lima beans

½ cup water
⅓ cup cider vinegar
2 tablespoons sugar
2 tablespoons all-purpose flour
½ teaspoon chicken-flavored bouillon granules
¼ teaspoon freshly ground black pepper

¾ cup chopped celery
½ cup chopped sweet red pepper
¼ cup sliced green onions

1 Cook lima beans in boiling water to cover 15 minutes or until tender; drain. Set aside, and keep warm.

2 Combine ½ cup water and next 5 ingredients in a saucepan, stirring well. Cook over medium heat, stirring constantly, 5 minutes or until mixture thickens.

3 Combine lima beans, celery, red pepper, green onions, and cider vinegar mixture, tossing well. Serve warm. Yield: 7 (½-cup) servings.

Nutritional content per serving: Calories 108
Fat 0.3g (Sat Fat 0g) Carbohydrate 22.0g Fiber 1.7g
Protein 5.4g Cholesterol 0mg Sodium 166mg

Lemon-Dill Carrots

Preparation Time: 15 minutes
Cooking Time: 8 minutes

Season carrots with lemon juice and dillweed to enhance their flavor.

~~~~~~~~~~~~~~~~~~

8 medium-size carrots, scraped and diagonally sliced

1 teaspoon cornstarch
1 tablespoon lemon juice
⅓ cup water

1 teaspoon margarine
½ teaspoon dried dillweed
¼ teaspoon grated lemon rind
⅛ teaspoon salt

Fresh dillweed sprigs (optional)

1 Arrange carrot in a vegetable steamer over boiling water. Cover; steam 2 to 3 minutes or until crisp-tender. Transfer carrot to a serving bowl, and keep warm.

2 Combine cornstarch and lemon juice in a small saucepan, stirring until smooth. Add water; cook over medium heat, stirring constantly, until thickened.

3 Stir in margarine and next 3 ingredients. Cook, stirring constantly, until margarine melts.

4 Pour lemon juice mixture over carrots, and toss gently. Garnish with dillweed sprigs, if desired. Yield: 8 (½-cup) servings.

Nutritional content per serving: Calories 41
Fat 0.6g (Sat Fat 0.1g) Carbohydrate 8.8g Fiber 2.6g
Protein 0.9g Cholesterol 0mg Sodium 71mg

Cauliflower with Cheese Sauce

Preparation Time: 15 minutes
Cooking Time: 5 minutes

1 medium cauliflower, broken into flowerets

1 tablespoon all-purpose flour
¾ cup skim milk, divided
⅛ teaspoon salt
⅛ teaspoon dry mustard

½ cup (2 ounces) shredded 50% less-fat sharp
    Cheddar cheese
2 tablespoons nonfat sour cream alternative
2 tablespoons (½ ounce) shredded 50% less-fat
    sharp Cheddar cheese

1 Cook cauliflower, covered, in a small amount of boiling water 8 to 10 minutes or until tender; drain. Place cauliflower in a serving dish; set aside, and keep warm.

2 Combine flour and ¼ cup milk; stir until smooth. Combine flour mixture, remaining ½ cup milk, salt, and dry mustard in a small saucepan; stir well. Cook over medium heat, stirring constantly, until mixture is thickened and bubbly.

3 Add ½ cup cheese; cook over low heat, stirring until cheese melts. Remove from heat, and stir in sour cream. Pour cheese sauce over cauliflower; sprinkle with 2 tablespoons cheese. Yield: 6 (1-cup) servings.

Nutritional content per serving: Calories 93
Fat 2.1g (Sat Fat 0.9g) Carbohydrate 12.5g Fiber 4.6g
Protein 8.6g Cholesterol 6.8mg Sodium 188mg

Corn-Zucchini-Tomato Sauté

Preparation Time: 10 minutes
Cooking Time: 8 minutes

Bursting with just-picked flavor, Corn-Zucchini-Tomato Sauté goes great with burgers, steaks, or grilled chicken.

1½ tablespoons reduced-calorie stick margarine
  2 cups fresh corn cut from cob (about 3 ears)
  1 medium-size zucchini, trimmed and thinly sliced
½ cup sliced green onions
¼ cup chopped green pepper

  1 cup peeled and chopped tomato
  2 teaspoons chopped fresh basil
  2 teaspoons chopped fresh oregano
  1 teaspoon sugar
¼ teaspoon salt
¼ teaspoon salt-free lemon-pepper seasoning

1 Melt margarine in a large skillet over medium-high heat. Add corn and next 3 ingredients; sauté vegetables 5 minutes or until crisp-tender.

2 Add tomato and remaining ingredients. Cook over medium heat until vegetables are tender, stirring frequently. Yield: 8 (½-cup) servings.

Nutritional content per serving: Calories 60
Fat 2.0g (Sat Fat 0.3g) Carbohydrate 10.8g Fiber 2.0g
Protein 1.9g Cholesterol 0mg Sodium 104mg

Okra-Tomato-Zucchini Medley

Preparation Time: 10 minutes
Cooking Time: 9 minutes

1 small zucchini

Vegetable cooking spray
1½ cups sliced fresh okra
2 tablespoons chopped onion

1 cup chopped fresh tomato
⅛ teaspoon dried basil
⅛ teaspoon dried thyme
Dash of freshly ground pepper

1 Cut zucchini in half lengthwise; cut into ¼-inch-thick slices.

2 Coat a nonstick skillet with cooking spray; place over medium-high heat until hot. Add zucchini, okra, and onion; sauté 4 minutes.

3 Stir in tomato and remaining ingredients. Cover and cook over low heat 5 minutes or until thoroughly heated, stirring frequently. Yield: 4 (½-cup) servings.

Nutritional content per serving: Calories 31
Fat 0.4g (Sat Fat 0g) Carbohydrate 6.3g Fiber 1.3g
Protein 1.5g Cholesterol 0mg Sodium 8mg

Cheesy Scalloped Onions

Preparation Time: 15 minutes
Cooking Time: 20 minutes

4 large Vidalia or other sweet onions, thinly sliced

2 tablespoons reduced-calorie stick margarine
2 tablespoons all-purpose flour
1½ cups skim milk

½ cup (2 ounces) shredded 50% less-fat sharp
    Cheddar cheese
1 tablespoon plus 1 teaspoon chopped fresh
    parsley
½ teaspoon dry mustard
¼ teaspoon salt
¼ teaspoon freshly ground pepper

Vegetable cooking spray
1½ tablespoons soft breadcrumbs, toasted

Chopped fresh parsley (optional)

1 Separate onion into rings. Cook onion in boiling water to cover 5 minutes or until tender. Drain well.

2 Melt margarine in a medium saucepan over medium heat; add flour. Cook 1 minute, stirring constantly with a wire whisk. Gradually add milk, stirring constantly. Cook, stirring constantly, an additional 10 minutes or until thickened and bubbly.

3 Add onion, cheese, and next 4 ingredients; stir well.

4 Spoon mixture into a shallow 1½-quart casserole coated with cooking spray; sprinkle with breadcrumbs. Bake, uncovered, at 375° for 20 minutes or until bubbly. Sprinkle with parsley, if desired. Yield: 6 servings.

Nutritional content per serving: Calories 145
Fat 4.8g (Sat Fat 1.2g) Carbohydrate 19.7g Fiber 3.1g
Protein 7.2g Cholesterol 7mg Sodium 247mg

Microwaving Directions: Separate onion into rings. Arrange onion in a shallow 1½-quart casserole; add 3 tablespoons water. Cover with heavy-duty plastic wrap, and vent. Microwave at HIGH 6 to 8 minutes or until onion is tender; drain. Place margarine in a medium-size microwave-safe bowl. Microwave, uncovered, at HIGH 30 seconds or until margarine melts. Add flour; stir until smooth. Gradually add milk, stirring well. Microwave, uncovered, at HIGH 3 to 4 minutes or until mixture is thickened, stirring after every minute. Stir in onion, cheese, and next 4 ingredients. Spoon onion mixture into a shallow 1½-quart casserole coated with cooking spray; sprinkle with breadcrumbs. Microwave at HIGH 4 to 5 minutes or until bubbly, rotating a half-turn after 2 minutes. Sprinkle with parsley, if desired.

Snow Peas, Red Pepper, and Pineapple

Preparation Time: 15 minutes
Cooking Time: 5 minutes

Cider vinegar blends with pineapple juice and soy sauce to give this side dish a sweet-and-sour twist.

1 (15¼-ounce) can unsweetened pineapple tidbits in juice

10 ounces fresh snow pea pods (about 2¼ cups)

1 tablespoon plus 1 teaspoon cider vinegar
1 tablespoon reduced-sodium soy sauce
2½ teaspoons cornstarch
2 teaspoons sugar

1 small sweet red pepper, seeded and cut into ¼-inch-wide strips

1 Drain pineapple, reserving ½ cup juice.

2 Wash snow peas; trim ends, and remove strings. Set aside.

3 Combine reserved pineapple juice, vinegar, and next 3 ingredients in a large nonstick skillet. Cook over medium heat, stirring constantly, until thickened and bubbly.

4 Add snow peas, pineapple, and red pepper; toss gently. Cook over medium heat 5 minutes or until thoroughly heated. Serve immediately. Yield: 8 (½-cup) servings.

Nutritional content per serving: Calories 51
Fat 0.2g (Sat Fat 0g) Carbohydrate 12.0g Fiber 1.1g
Protein 1.0g Cholesterol 0mg Sodium 63mg

Browned Basil New Potatoes

Preparation Time:
18–20 minutes
Cooking Time: **5–10 minutes**

2½ **pounds round red potatoes**

 2 **tablespoons vegetable oil**
1½ **tablespoons minced fresh garlic**

 ⅓ **cup shredded fresh basil**
 1 **teaspoon freshly ground pepper**
 ½ **teaspoon salt**

1 Cook potatoes in boiling water to cover 15 to 18 minutes or until tender. Let cool to touch; quarter potatoes. Set aside.

2 Heat oil in a large nonstick skillet over medium-high heat. Add potato and garlic; sauté 5 to 10 minutes or until potato is browned.

3 Sprinkle with basil, pepper, and salt; toss gently. Serve warm. Yield: 10 (½-cup) servings.

Nutritional content per serving: Calories 111
Fat 2.9g (Sat Fat 0.4g) Carbohydrate 19.5g Fiber 2.1g
Protein 2.6g Cholesterol 0mg Sodium 125mg

Fruit-Glazed Acorn Squash

Preparation Time: 12 minutes
Cooking Time: 35 minutes

Acorn squash are
very firm, so microwave
them for a few minutes
before slicing.
This also shortens the
baking time for
this recipe.

2 small acorn squash (about 2 pounds)

¾ cup unsweetened pineapple juice
¾ cup unsweetened orange juice
¼ cup currants
1½ tablespoons brown sugar
1 tablespoon cornstarch
¼ teaspoon ground cloves

1 Prick squash several times with a fork. Place squash on two layers of paper towels. Microwave, uncovered, at HIGH 5 to 6 minutes or until slightly tender. Let cool. Cut ends off squash and discard seeds; slice into 1-inch-thick slices. Arrange squash slices in a 13- x 9- x 2- inch baking dish.

2 Combine pineapple juice and remaining ingredients; stir well. Pour over squash slices.

3 Bake, uncovered, at 350° for 35 minutes or until squash is tender, brushing frequently with glaze. Yield: 4 servings.

Nutritional content per serving: Calories 164
Fat 0.6g (Sat Fat 0g) Carbohydrate 41.1g Fiber 2.2g
Protein 2.2g Cholesterol 0mg Sodium 12mg

Summer Squash Casserole

Preparation Time: 20 minutes
Cooking Time: 25–30 minutes

1¾ pounds yellow squash, sliced
1 cup chopped onion

½ cup canned one-third-less-salt cream of chicken
    soup, undiluted
½ cup soft whole-wheat breadcrumbs
½ cup nonfat sour cream alternative
1 (4-ounce) jar diced pimiento, drained
½ teaspoon salt
¼ teaspoon freshly ground pepper
¼ teaspoon garlic powder
¼ teaspoon dried basil
    Vegetable cooking spray

1 cup soft whole-wheat breadcrumbs
⅓ cup (1.3 ounces) shredded reduced-fat sharp
    Cheddar cheese
2 tablespoons reduced-calorie stick margarine,
    melted
½ teaspoon paprika

1 Cook squash and onion in a small amount of boiling water in a large saucepan 12 to 15 minutes or until tender. Drain well. Mash squash mixture with a potato masher.

2 Combine squash mixture, soup, and next 7 ingredients; stir well. Spoon into a 1½-quart casserole coated with cooking spray.

3 Combine 1 cup breadcrumbs and remaining ingredients in a small bowl; stir well. Sprinkle over squash mixture. Bake, uncovered, at 350° for 25 to 30 minutes or until thoroughly heated. Yield: 8 servings.

Nutritional content per serving: Calories 105
Fat 3.6g (Sat Fat 0.9g) Carbohydrate 14.5g Fiber 2.3g
Protein 5.3g Cholesterol 5mg Sodium 344mg

Spinach-Topped Tomatoes

Preparation Time: 15 minutes
Cooking Time: 10–12 minutes

You'll get plenty of compliments when you serve these tasty tomatoes with Honey-Sesame Grilled Pork Tenderloin (page 140).

12 (½-inch-thick) tomato slices
   Vegetable cooking spray

1 (10-ounce) package frozen chopped spinach

⅓ cup grated Parmesan cheese, divided
⅔ cup Italian-seasoned breadcrumbs
½ cup thinly sliced green onions
½ cup frozen egg substitute, thawed
1 tablespoon skim milk

12 pimiento strips (about 1 tablespoon)
¼ teaspoon freshly ground pepper

1 Arrange tomato slices in a 13- x 9- x 2-inch baking dish coated with cooking spray; set aside.

2 Cook spinach according to package directions, omitting salt; drain well. Press spinach between paper towels until barely moist. Combine spinach, ¼ cup Parmesan cheese, and next 4 ingredients; stir well.

3 Spoon 2 tablespoons spinach mixture over each tomato slice; sprinkle slices evenly with remaining Parmesan cheese. Top each tomato slice with a pimiento strip, and sprinkle slices with pepper. Bake at 375° for 10 to 12 minutes or until thoroughly heated and lightly browned. Yield: 6 servings.

Nutritional content per serving: Calories 86
Fat 1.2g (Sat Fat 0.4g) Carbohydrate 14.3g Fiber 2.9g
Protein 6.2g Cholesterol 1mg Sodium 360mg

Savory Creamed Turnips

Preparation Time: 5 minutes
Cooking Time: 10–12 minutes

The delicious combination of Savory Creamed Turnips and Crispy Herbed Chicken (page 148) is hard to beat.

1½ **pounds turnips, diced**
 ½ **cup chopped onion**
  2 **cloves garlic, minced**

  1 **tablespoon reduced-calorie stick margarine**
  1 **tablespoon plus 1 teaspoon all-purpose flour**
  1 **cup skim milk**

  1 **teaspoon minced fresh thyme**
 ¼ **teaspoon ground white pepper**
 ⅛ **teaspoon salt**

1 Combine first 3 ingredients in a medium saucepan; add water to cover. Bring to a boil; cover, reduce heat, and simmer 10 to 12 minutes or until turnips are tender. Drain well, and set aside.

2 Melt margarine in a large heavy saucepan over medium heat. Add flour; cook, stirring constantly, 1 minute. Gradually add milk; cook, stirring constantly, until mixture is thickened and bubbly.

3 Remove from heat; stir in thyme, pepper, and salt. Add turnip mixture, tossing gently to combine. Serve immediately. Yield: 5 (¾-cup) servings.

Nutritional content per serving: Calories 81
Fat 1.7g (Sat Fat 0.3g) Carbohydrate 14.2g Fiber 2.8g
Protein 3.2g Cholesterol 1mg Sodium 195mg

Vegetable-Stuffed Zucchini

Preparation Time: 18 minutes
Cooking Time: 20 minutes

4 medium-size zucchini (about 1½ pounds)

¾ cup finely chopped tomato
⅓ cup chopped green pepper
¼ cup chopped onion
¼ teaspoon salt
¼ teaspoon dried basil
¼ teaspoon dried oregano

⅓ cup (1.3 ounces) shredded one-third-less-fat
    Cheddar cheese

1 Place zucchini in a large saucepan with water to cover. Bring to a boil; cover, reduce heat, and simmer 4 to 6 minutes or until crisp-tender. Drain and let cool.

2 Cut zucchini in half lengthwise. Scoop out pulp, leaving ¼-inch-thick shells. Chop pulp; reserve shells.

3 Combine zucchini pulp, tomato, and next 5 ingredients; stir well. Spoon into zucchini shells. Place shells in a 13- x 9- x 2-inch baking dish. Bake, uncovered, at 400° for 15 minutes. Sprinkle with cheese. Bake an additional 5 minutes or until cheese melts. Yield: 8 servings.

Nutritional content per serving: Calories 34
Fat 1.1g (Sat Fat 0.6g) Carbohydrate 4.3g Fiber 0.9g
Protein 2.6g Cholesterol 3mg Sodium 112mg

SOUPS & SANDWICHES

page 224

page 231

page 233

Soups

Fresh Blueberry Soup   216

Tropical Soup   217

Cream of Mushroom Soup   218

Creamy Spinach Soup   219

Light Beer-Cheese Soup   220

Curried Lentil Soup   221

Chunky Chicken-Potato Soup   222

White Chili with Tomatillo Salsa   223

Harvest Stew   224

Hearty Pork Stew   225

Sandwiches

Mediterranean Pitas   226

Spicy Chicken Pockets   227

Marinated Chicken Sandwiches   228

Fish Sandwich with Onion Relish   229

Spicy Joes   230

Triple Treat Burgers   231

Italian Meatball Sandwich   232

Turkey Reubens   233

Shrimp Calzones   234

Fresh Blueberry Soup

Preparation Time: 18 minutes
Chilling Time: at least
30 minutes

Fresh Blueberry Soup
is equally
impressive as either
a first course or a dessert.

〜〜〜〜〜〜〜

2 cups fresh blueberries
2½ cups unsweetened grape juice
¼ cup sugar
1 (3-inch) stick cinnamon

1 tablespoon plus 2 teaspoons cornstarch
2 tablespoons water
¼ teaspoon ground cardamom

3 tablespoons crème de cassis

1 teaspoon vanilla low-fat yogurt

1 Combine first 4 ingredients in a medium saucepan. Bring mixture to a boil; cover, reduce heat, and simmer 5 minutes.

2 Combine cornstarch and water; stir well. Add cornstarch mixture and cardamom to blueberry mixture, stirring well. Cook, stirring constantly, until mixture is thickened and bubbly. Remove from heat, and let cool.

3 Stir in crème de cassis. Cover and chill thoroughly. Remove and discard cinnamon stick before serving. Ladle soup into individual bowls; drizzle yogurt in 3 small circles over each serving. Pull a wooden pick or the tip of a knife through each circle, forming hearts. Yield: 4 (1-cup) servings.

Nutritional content per serving: Calories 226
Fat 0.3g (Sat Fat 0g) Carbohydrate 54.6g Fiber 3.7g
Protein 0.6g Cholesterol 0mg Sodium 13mg

Tropical Soup

Preparation Time: 15 minutes
Chilling Time: at least
30 minutes

4 cups chopped mango
¾ cup unsweetened apple juice
2 teaspoons honey
1 teaspoon vanilla extract
¼ teaspoon ground allspice
⅛ teaspoon ground cinnamon

¾ cup evaporated skimmed milk
¼ cup plus 2 tablespoons vanilla low-fat yogurt
  Strawberry halves (optional)
  Fresh mint sprigs (optional)

1 Combine first 6 ingredients in container of an electric blender; cover and process until smooth, stopping once to scrape down sides.

2 Transfer mango mixture to a large bowl. Stir in milk and yogurt. Cover and chill at least 30 minutes. Ladle soup into individual bowls. If desired, garnish with strawberry halves and mint sprigs. Yield: 5 (1-cup) servings.

Nutritional content per serving: Calories 184
Fat 0.8g (Sat Fat 0.3g) Carbohydrate 43g Fiber 2.7g
Protein 4.6g Cholesterol 2mg Sodium 60mg

Cream of Mushroom Soup

Preparation Time: 15 minutes
Cooking Time: 10 minutes

Skim milk and nonfat
sour cream combine for a
rich and creamy but
low-fat soup base.

Vegetable cooking spray
¾ pound sliced fresh mushrooms
¼ cup sliced green onions
2 tablespoons dry sherry

2 tablespoons reduced-calorie stick margarine
3 tablespoons all-purpose flour
2½ cups skim milk

1¼ teaspoons chicken-flavored bouillon granules
¼ teaspoon freshly ground pepper
⅔ cup nonfat sour cream alternative

Green onion strips (optional)

1 Coat a large saucepan with cooking spray; place over medium-high heat until hot. Add mushrooms, ¼ cup green onions, and sherry; sauté until vegetables are tender. Set aside.

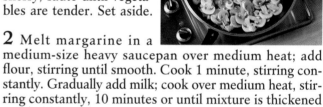

2 Melt margarine in a medium-size heavy saucepan over medium heat; add flour, stirring until smooth. Cook 1 minute, stirring constantly. Gradually add milk; cook over medium heat, stirring constantly, 10 minutes or until mixture is thickened and bubbly.

3 Stir in mushroom mixture, bouillon granules, and pepper. Cook until thoroughly heated. Remove from heat, and stir in sour cream. Ladle soup into individual bowls. Garnish with onion strips, if desired. Yield: 4 (1-cup) servings.

Nutritional content per serving: Calories 161
Fat 4.8g (Sat Fat 0.8g) Carbohydrate 19.4g Fiber 1.4g
Protein 10.5g Cholesterol 3mg Sodium 423mg

Creamy Spinach Soup

Preparation Time: 18 minutes
Cooking Time: 30 minutes

3 (1-ounce) slices white bread

½ pound fresh spinach

2 teaspoons margarine
1 cup chopped onion
1 clove garlic, minced

1 cup water
2 teaspoons beef-flavored bouillon granules
2 medium baking potatoes, peeled and cubed
1 bay leaf

3½ cups skim milk
¼ cup instant nonfat dry milk powder
4 ounces Neufchâtel cheese, cut into cubes
¼ teaspoon pepper

1 Trim crust from bread slices; reserve crust for another use. Cut bread into ¾-inch cubes; arrange in a single layer in a 15- x 10- x 1-inch jellyroll pan. Bake at 350° for 12 minutes or until golden, stirring twice. Set croutons aside.

2 Remove stems from spinach; wash leaves, and pat dry with paper towels. Set spinach aside.

3 Melt margarine in a large Dutch oven over medium-high heat. Add onion and garlic; sauté until tender. Combine water and bouillon granules; add to onion mixture. Stir in spinach, potato, and bay leaf. Bring to a boil; cover, reduce heat, and simmer 15 to 20 minutes or until potato is tender, stirring occasionally. Remove and discard bay leaf.

4 Pour spinach mixture into container of an electric blender; cover and process until smooth, stopping once to scrape down sides. Return puree to Dutch oven.

5 Combine milk and milk powder; stir well. Add to spinach mixture; stir well. Stir in cheese and pepper. Cook over medium heat until cheese melts and mixture is thoroughly heated, stirring frequently. Ladle soup into individual bowls. Top evenly with croutons. Yield: 7 (1-cup) servings.

Nutritional content per serving: Calories 198
Fat 5.8g (Sat Fat 3.0g) Carbohydrate 26.7g Fiber 2.7g
Protein 10.4g Cholesterol 16mg Sodium 502mg

Light Beer-Cheese Soup

Preparation Time: 26 minutes
Cooking Time: 20 minutes

3½ **cups skim milk, divided**
¼ **cup cornstarch**

1 **(10½-ounce) can low-sodium chicken broth**
1 **tablespoon white wine Worcestershire sauce**
¼ **to ½ teaspoon ground red pepper**
¼ **teaspoon garlic powder**

1½ **cups (6 ounces) finely shredded reduced-fat Cheddar cheese**
½ **cup flat light beer**
⅓ **cup nonfat sour cream alternative**

Toast Triangles
1 **tablespoon finely shredded reduced-fat Cheddar cheese**

1 Combine ½ cup milk and cornstarch; stir well. Set cornstarch mixture aside.

2 Combine remaining 3 cups milk, chicken broth, and next 3 ingredients in a large saucepan. Cook over medium heat until thoroughly heated. Gradually add cornstarch mixture, stirring well. Cook over low heat, stirring constantly, until thickened and bubbly.

3 Add 1½ cups cheese; cook, stirring constantly, until cheese melts and mixture is smooth. Stir in beer and sour cream. Cook just until thoroughly heated, stirring occasionally. Ladle soup into individual bowls. Top each serving with 3 Toast Triangles, and sprinkle with ½ teaspoon cheese. Yield: 6 (1-cup) servings.

Toast Triangles

3 **(¾-ounce) slices reduced-calorie white bread**
Butter-flavored vegetable cooking spray

1 Trim crust from bread slices; reserve for another use. Cut each slice into 4 squares; cut each square into 2 triangles. Place 18 triangles on an ungreased baking sheet; reserve remaining triangles for another use. Spray both sides of each triangle with cooking spray. Bake at 350° for 10 to 12 minutes or until triangles are dry and lightly browned. Yield: 18 triangles.

Nutritional content per serving: Calories 186
Fat 5.8g (Sat Fat 3.3g) Carbohydrate 16.0g Fiber 0.5g
Protein 14.9g Cholesterol 21mg Sodium 344mg

Curried Lentil Soup

Preparation Time: 12 minutes
Cooking Time: 25–35 minutes

Lentils are legumes
and an excellent
source of protein.

~~~~~~~~~

Vegetable cooking spray
2 teaspoons vegetable oil
2 cups chopped onion (about 2 medium)
6 cloves garlic, minced

¾ cup dry lentils, uncooked
1 (19-ounce) can garbanzo beans, drained
3½ cups canned low-sodium chicken broth,
    undiluted
2 cups water
1 tablespoon peeled, grated gingerroot
1 teaspoon ground cumin
1 teaspoon ground coriander
½ teaspoon dried crushed red pepper
½ teaspoon curry powder

1 cup seeded, chopped fresh tomato
½ teaspoon salt
½ cup nonfat sour cream alternative

1 Coat a Dutch oven with cooking spray; add oil, and place over medium-high heat until hot. Add onion and garlic; sauté 5 minutes or until tender.

2 Add lentils and next 8 ingredients; stir well. Bring to a boil; cover, reduce heat, and simmer 25 to 35 minutes or until lentils are tender.

3 Stir in tomato and salt. Ladle soup into individual bowls. Top each serving with 1 tablespoon sour cream. Yield: 8 (1-cup) servings.

Nutritional content per serving: Calories 195
Fat 3.4g (Sat Fat 0.6g) Carbohydrate 31.1g Fiber 4.7g
Protein 11.5g Cholesterol 0mg Sodium 281mg

Chunky Chicken-Potato Soup

Preparation Time: 15 minutes
Cooking Time: 40 minutes

Pureeing part of the vegetable mixture helps to thicken the soup.

4 cups canned no-salt-added chicken broth, undiluted
3 cups peeled, cubed baking potato
2 cups chopped onion
1 cup chopped carrot
½ teaspoon salt
⅛ teaspoon ground red pepper
⅛ teaspoon ground black pepper

2 cups chopped cooked chicken breast (skinned before cooking and cooked without salt)
¼ cup skim milk
1 (2-ounce) jar diced pimiento, drained

½ cup nonfat sour cream alternative
½ cup (2 ounces) shredded reduced-fat sharp Cheddar cheese
Chives, cut into 1-inch pieces (optional)

1 Combine first 7 ingredients in a Dutch oven; bring to a boil. Cover, reduce heat, and simmer 35 minutes or until vegetables are tender.

2 Place half of vegetable mixture in container of an electric blender or food processor; cover and process until smooth. Add pureed mixture, chicken, and milk to mixture in Dutch oven. Cook over medium heat until thoroughly heated, stirring occasionally. Stir in pimiento.

3 Ladle soup into individual bowls; top evenly with sour cream and cheese. Garnish with chives, if desired. Yield: 8 (1-cup) servings.

Nutritional content per serving: Calories 193
Fat 3.1g (Sat Fat 1.3g) Carbohydrate 19.7g Fiber 2.5g
Protein 19.3g Cholesterol 43mg Sodium 262mg

White Chili with Tomatillo Salsa

Preparation Time: 20 minutes
Cooking Time: 30 minutes

A tomatillo is
a small green fruit
covered with a papery
brown husk.
Its acidic flavor
contains hints
of apple and lemon.

Tomatillo Salsa

3 (10½-ounce) cans low-sodium chicken broth, divided
1 (19-ounce) can cannellini beans, drained and divided
1 (16-ounce) can navy beans, drained and divided

4 cups chopped cooked chicken breast (skinned before cooking and cooked without salt)
1 cup chopped onion
1 (16-ounce) package frozen white corn
1 (4-ounce) can chopped green chiles
1 teaspoon ground cumin
¾ teaspoon dried oregano
¼ teaspoon ground red pepper

1 Prepare Tomatillo Salsa.

2 Place 1 cup broth, ½ cup cannellini beans, and ½ cup navy beans in container of an electric blender or food processor; cover and process until smooth.

3 Place bean mixture, remaining broth, remaining cannellini beans, remaining navy beans, chicken, and remaining ingredients in a Dutch oven. Bring to a boil; cover, reduce heat, and simmer 30 minutes. Ladle chili into individual bowls. Top servings evenly with Tomatillo Salsa. Yield: 10 (1-cup) servings.

Tomatillo Salsa

½ pound husked, diced tomatillos or diced green tomatoes
¼ cup diced red onion
¼ cup chopped sweet yellow or green pepper
⅛ cup chopped fresh cilantro
1 tablespoon orange juice
½ small jalapeño pepper, seeded and chopped
½ clove garlic, minced
1 teaspoon sugar
Dash of salt

1 Combine all ingredients in a medium bowl. Cover and chill at least 30 minutes. Yield: 2 cups.

Nutritional content per serving: Calories 249
Fat 3.5g (Sat Fat 0.8g) Carbohydrate 25.9g Fiber 3.5g
Protein 26.8g Cholesterol 58mg Sodium 292 mg

Harvest Stew

Preparation Time: 15 minutes
Cooking Time: 30 minutes

Stews needn't contain a lot of meat to be hearty. This one is thick with tomatoes, sweet potatoes, and acorn squash.

Vegetable cooking spray
1 pound ultra-lean ground beef
¾ cup chopped onion
½ teaspoon pepper
2 cloves garlic, minced

3½ cups water
1 (14½-ounce) can no-salt-added tomatoes, undrained and chopped
2¼ cups peeled, chopped sweet potato
1 cup coarsely chopped unpeeled round red potato
1 cup peeled, chopped acorn squash
2 teaspoons vegetable-flavored bouillon granules
½ teaspoon chili powder
¼ teaspoon ground allspice
¼ teaspoon ground cloves
2 bay leaves

1 Coat a Dutch oven with cooking spray; place over medium-high heat until hot. Add ground beef and next 3 ingredients. Cook until beef is browned, stirring until it crumbles. Drain and pat dry with paper towels. Wipe drippings from Dutch oven with a paper towel.

2 Combine beef mixture, water, and remaining ingredients in Dutch oven; bring to a boil. Cover, reduce heat, and simmer 30 minutes or until vegetables are tender. Remove and discard bay leaves. Ladle into individual bowls. Yield: 8 (1¼-cup) servings.

Nutritional content per serving: Calories 156 Fat 3.9g (Sat Fat 1.4g) Carbohydrate 19.6g Fiber 2.3g Protein 12.4g Cholesterol 36mg Sodium 163mg

Hearty Pork Stew

Preparation Time: **15 minutes**
Cooking Time: **45 minutes**

1 pound lean boneless pork loin
  Vegetable cooking spray
1 cup chopped onion

1 (14½-ounce) can no-salt-added whole tomatoes,
    undrained and chopped
2 cups canned low-sodium chicken broth,
    undiluted
1 (10-ounce) package frozen baby lima beans
1 (10-ounce) package frozen whole kernel corn
1 (4-ounce) can chopped green chiles, undrained
½ teaspoon salt
½ teaspoon hot sauce
¼ teaspoon garlic powder
¼ teaspoon onion powder
¼ teaspoon freshly ground pepper

2 tablespoons all-purpose flour
2 tablespoons water

1 Trim fat from pork; cut pork into ½-inch cubes. Coat a Dutch oven with cooking spray; place over medium-high heat until hot. Add pork and onion; cook 5 minutes or until pork is browned and onion is tender, stirring frequently. Drain and pat dry with paper towels. Wipe drippings from Dutch oven with a paper towel.

2 Return pork mixture to Dutch oven; add tomato and next 9 ingredients. Bring to a boil; cover, reduce heat, and simmer 40 minutes or until pork and vegetables are tender.

3 Combine flour and water; stir until smooth. Add flour mixture to soup. Cook, stirring constantly, until mixture is thickened. Yield: 8 (1-cup) servings.

Nutritional content per serving: Calories 211
Fat 6.6g (Sat Fat 2.2g) Carbohydrate 22.7g Fiber 2.4g
Protein 16.5g Cholesterol 37mg Sodium 258mg

Mediterranean Pitas

Preparation Time: **20 minutes**

Mediterranean Pitas
are a natural for picnics.
Make the bean
mixture ahead, and
add the toppings
right before eating.

~~~~~~~~~~~~

1 (19-ounce) can garbanzo beans, undrained
2 tablespoons sliced green onions
2 tablespoons sesame seeds, toasted
1½ tablespoons lemon juice
⅛ teaspoon salt
⅛ teaspoon hot sauce
1 clove garlic, minced

8 (8-inch) pita bread rounds
8 green leaf lettuce leaves
2 cups alfalfa sprouts
1 medium cucumber, thinly sliced
½ cup plain nonfat yogurt

1 Drain beans, reserving 2 tablespoons liquid. Position knife blade in food processor bowl; add beans, reserved liquid, green onions, and next 5 ingredients. Process until smooth, scraping sides of processor bowl once.

2 Spread bean mixture evenly on top of pitas. Place 1 lettuce leaf on each pita. Divide alfalfa sprouts and cucumber evenly among pitas. Drizzle 1 tablespoon yogurt over cucumbers on each pita. Roll each pita toward center at bottom. Wrap bottom of each pita in wax paper for decorative tissue paper. Serve immedi-at1ely. Yield: 8 servings.

Nutritional content per serving: Calories 298
Fat 3.7g (Sat Fat 0.5g) Carbohydrate 53.5g Fiber 9.4g
Protein 9.6g Cholesterol 0mg Sodium 586mg

Spicy Chicken Pockets

Preparation Time: **15 minutes**
Chilling Time: **30 minutes**
Cooking Time: **12 minutes**

Spicy Creole Seasoning Blend
6 (4-ounce) skinned, boned chicken breast halves

1 tablespoon vegetable oil
  Vegetable cooking spray

8 lettuce leaves
4 (6-inch) whole wheat pita bread rounds, cut in
  half crosswise
1 small purple onion, thinly sliced and separated
  into rings
1 cup alfalfa sprouts
¾ cup diced cucumber
¾ cup chopped tomato

1 Prepare Spicy Creole Seasoning Blend.

2 Rub chicken breasts with Spicy Creole Seasoning Blend, and place in a large shallow dish. Cover and chill at least 30 minutes.

3 Brush both sides of each chicken breast with oil. Coat grill rack with cooking spray; place on grill over medium-hot coals (350° to 400°). Place chicken on rack; grill, covered, 6 minutes on each side or until chicken is done.

4 Place 1 lettuce leaf in each pita half. Layer onion and remaining ingredients evenly into pita halves.

5 Cut chicken into strips, and arrange evenly over vegetables. Yield: 8 servings.

Spicy Creole Seasoning Blend

1 tablespoon paprika
2 teaspoons dried thyme, crushed
2 teaspoons garlic powder
2 teaspoons onion powder
1 teaspoon ground red pepper
½ teaspoon salt
½ teaspoon dry mustard
¼ teaspoon freshly ground black pepper

1 Combine all ingredients; stir well. Yield: 3½ tablespoons.

Nutritional content per serving: Calories 231
Fat 5.1g (Sat Fat 1.1g) Carbohydrate 21.4g Fiber 4.4g
Protein 22.6g Cholesterol 54mg Sodium 391mg

Broiling Directions: Follow directions in steps 1 and 2. Brush each side of chicken breasts with oil. Place on rack of a broiler pan coated with cooking spray. Broil 5½ inches from heat (with electric oven door partially opened) 8 minutes on each side or until chicken is done. Continue with step 4 as directed above.

Marinated Chicken Sandwiches

Preparation Time: 12 minutes
Marinating Time: 30 minutes
Cooking Time: 8–10 minutes

You can substitute
four 4-ounce skinned,
boned chicken breast
halves for the
chicken tenderloins.

⅓ cup low-sodium soy sauce
¼ cup honey
¼ cup unsweetened orange juice
¼ teaspoon garlic powder
¼ teaspoon ground ginger
1 pound chicken tenderloins

3 tablespoons plain nonfat yogurt
1 tablespoon reduced-calorie mayonnaise
1 tablespoon honey
1½ teaspoons Dijon mustard
1½ teaspoons coarse-grained mustard

Vegetable cooking spray

4 green leaf lettuce leaves
4 (¼-inch-thick) tomato slices
4 (¼-inch-thick) purple onion slices
4 (1½-ounce) sandwich rolls with sesame seeds,
   split and toasted

1 Combine first 5 ingredients in a small bowl, stirring with a wire whisk. Place chicken in a shallow dish; pour soy sauce mixture over chicken, turning to coat. Cover and marinate in refrigerator 30 minutes.

2 Combine yogurt and next 4 ingredients in a small bowl, stirring well; set aside.

3 Remove chicken from marinade, reserving marinade. Place chicken on rack of a broiler pan coated with cooking spray. Broil 5½ inches from heat (with electric oven door partially opened) 8 minutes or until done, turning and basting frequently with reserved marinade.

4 Arrange lettuce, tomato, and onion evenly on bottom halves of rolls. Arrange chicken evenly over onion. Spread yogurt mixture evenly over chicken. Top with remaining halves of rolls. Serve warm. Yield: 4 servings.

Nutritional content per serving: Calories 364
Fat 7.2g (Sat Fat 1.5g) Carbohydrate 40.9g Fiber 1.1g
Protein 32.2g Cholesterol 74mg Sodium 704mg

Fish Sandwich with Onion Relish

Preparation Time: 10 minutes
Marinating Time: 30 minutes
Cooking Time: 6 minutes

This healthy
fish sandwich is
dressed with a savory
onion relish instead
of tartar sauce.

4 (4-ounce) amberjack fillets
½ cup Chablis or other dry white wine
2 tablespoons low-sodium soy sauce
1 teaspoon peeled, grated gingerroot
1 clove garlic, minced

Vegetable cooking spray
2 teaspoons olive oil
1 large onion, thinly sliced and separated into
   rings
2 teaspoons honey
2 teaspoons low-sodium soy sauce

¼ cup nonfat mayonnaise
½ teaspoon peeled, grated gingerroot
4 (2-ounce) French bread rolls, split and toasted
4 green leaf lettuce leaves

1 Place fish in a shallow dish. Combine wine and next 3 ingredients in a small bowl, stirring well; set aside ¼ cup mixture. Pour remaining mixture over fish. Cover and marinate in refrigerator 30 minutes.

2 Coat a large nonstick skillet with cooking spray; add olive oil. Place over medium-high heat until hot. Add onion; sauté 5 minutes or until tender. Stir in honey and 2 teaspoons soy sauce; set aside, and keep warm.

3 Remove fish from marinade, discarding marinade in dish. Place fish on rack of a broiler pan coated with cooking spray. Broil 5½ inches from heat (with electric oven door partially opened) 3 minutes. Turn fillets, and broil an additional 3 minutes or until fish flakes easily when tested with a fork, basting occasionally with ¼ cup reserved wine mixture.

4 Combine mayonnaise and ½ teaspoon gingerroot; spread evenly on bottom halves of rolls. Top with lettuce and fillets; spoon onion mixture evenly over fillets and top with remaining bun halves. Serve immediately. Yield: 4 servings.

Nutritional content per serving: Calories 336
Fat 4.7g (Sat Fat 1.0g) Carbohydrate 41.3g Fiber 2.2g
Protein 27.8g Cholesterol 44mg Sodium 686mg

Spicy Joes

Preparation Time: 18 minutes
Cooking Time: 10 minutes

Enhance the flavor
of these spicy sloppy
joes with Colorful
Coleslaw (page 170).

Vegetable cooking spray
½ cup chopped green pepper
¼ cup minced onion

1½ pounds ground round

1¼ cups no-salt-added tomato sauce
1 (6-ounce) can no-salt-added tomato paste
1 (4-ounce) can chopped green chiles, drained
¼ cup water
¼ cup reduced-calorie chili sauce
1 tablespoon chili power
½ teaspoon salt
¼ teaspoon freshly ground black pepper
¼ teaspoon ground red pepper

8 reduced-calorie whole wheat hamburger buns

1 Coat a large nonstick skillet with cooking spray; place over medium-high heat until hot. Add green pepper and onion; sauté until crisp-tender. Remove pepper mixture from skillet.

2 Add ground round to skillet; cook over medium heat until meat is browned, stirring until it crumbles. Drain and pat dry with paper towels. Wipe drippings from skillet with a paper towel.

3 Return meat mixture and pepper mixture to skillet. Add tomato sauce and next 8 ingredients; stir well. Cook over medium heat 10 minutes or until thoroughly heated, stirring occasionally. Spoon evenly over bottom halves of buns. Top with remaining bun halves. Serve immediately. Yield: 8 servings.

Nutritional content per serving: Calories 253
Fat 6.6g (Sat Fat 2.2g) Carbohydrate 25.3g Fiber 3.2g
Protein 22.2g Cholesterol 69mg Sodium 479mg

Triple Treat Burgers

Preparation Time: 20 minutes
Cooking Time: 4–6 minutes

One bite will reveal the treat in these burgers—a center filled with Dijon mustard, melted Swiss cheese, and lean ham.

1 pound ground round
2 tablespoons minced green pepper
1 tablespoon instant minced onion
2 teaspoons low-sodium Worcestershire sauce
¼ teaspoon black pepper

1 teaspoon Dijon mustard
2 (¾-ounce) slices low-fat process Swiss cheese, quartered
2 (¾-ounce) slices lean cooked ham, quartered

Vegetable cooking spray

4 (2-ounce) onion-flavored buns
4 green leaf lettuce leaves
4 (¼-inch-thick) tomato slices

1 Combine first 5 ingredients in a large bowl; stir well. Shape mixture into 8 (5-inch) patties. Spread each of 4 patties with ¼ teaspoon mustard; top each with 2 cheese pieces and 2 ham pieces. Top filled patties with remaining 4 patties, pressing edges to seal.

2 Coat grill rack with cooking spray; place on grill over medium-hot coals (350° to 400°). Place patties on rack; grill, covered, 2 to 3 minutes on each side or to desired degree of doneness. Place 1 cooked patty on bottom half of each bun. Top each patty with 1 lettuce leaf, 1 tomato slice, and top half of bun. Yield: 4 servings.

Nutritional content per serving: Calories 380
Fat 10.4g (Sat Fat 3.4g) Carbohydrate 35.2g Fiber 1.0g
Protein 34.6g Cholesterol 77mg Sodium 563mg

Italian Meatball Sandwich

Preparation Time: 18 minutes
Cooking Time: 20–25 minutes

Use a 1-tablespoon ice cream scoop to make just-the-right-size meatballs for these sandwiches.

6 (2-ounce) whole wheat submarine loaves

1 pound ground round
¼ cup finely chopped onion
3 tablespoons Italian-seasoned breadcrumbs
2 tablespoons water
¼ teaspoon pepper
1 egg white, lightly beaten

Vegetable cooking spray

1½ cups low-fat, reduced-sodium pasta sauce

¾ cup (3 ounces) shredded part-skim mozzarella cheese
Fresh basil sprigs (optional)

1 Slanting knife at an angle, cut an oval piece out of top of each loaf; set loaves aside, reserving top pieces of loaves for another use.

2 Combine ground round and next 5 ingredients in a bowl; stir well. Shape mixture into 36 (1-inch) balls.

3 Coat a large nonstick skillet with cooking spray; place over medium heat until hot. Add meatballs, and cook 8 to 10 minutes or until browned on all sides, turning frequently. Remove from heat, and pat dry with paper towels. Wipe drippings from skillet with a paper towel.

4 Return meatballs to skillet; add pasta sauce, and cook over medium-low heat 10 minutes or until thoroughly heated. Set aside, and keep warm.

5 Place submarine loaves on an ungreased baking sheet; top each with 6 meatballs. Spoon sauce evenly over meatballs. Sprinkle evenly with cheese. Bake at 400° for 5 minutes or until cheese melts. Garnish with basil sprigs, if desired. Serve immediately. Yield: 6 servings.

Nutritional content per serving: Calories 269
Fat 7.6g (Sat Fat 2.4g) Carbohydrate 23.4g Fiber 1.2g
Protein 25.8g Cholesterol 60mg Sodium 621mg

Turkey Reubens

Preparation Time: 12 minutes
Cooking Time: 8 minutes

1½ cups finely shredded cabbage
1½ tablespoons commercial nonfat Thousand Island
    dressing
1 tablespoon reduced-calorie mayonnaise

1 tablespoon Dijon mustard
12 (1-ounce) slices rye bread
6 ounces thinly sliced cooked turkey breast
6 (¾-ounce) slices reduced-fat Swiss cheese

    Butter-flavored vegetable cooking spray

1 Combine first 3 ingredients in a medium bowl; toss well, and set aside.

2 Spread mustard evenly over 6 bread slices, and top with turkey. Top each with 1 cheese slice and ¼ cup cabbage mixture. Top with remaining bread slices.

3 Spray both sides of each sandwich with cooking spray; place on a hot griddle or skillet coated with cooking spray. Cook 2 minutes on each side or until bread is lightly browned and cheese melts. Serve immediately. Yield: 6 servings.

Nutritional content per serving: Calories 274
Fat 7.1g (Sat Fat 2.7g) Carbohydrate 32.4g Fiber 3.9g
Protein 21.0g Cholesterol 34mg Sodium 497mg

Shrimp Calzones

Preparation Time: 16 minutes
Cooking Time: 18 minutes

Refrigerated pizza crust and frozen cooked shrimp keep preparation time to a minimum for Shrimp Calzones, a healthy answer to fast food.

1 (10-ounce) package refrigerated pizza crust

⅓ cup Italian-style tomato paste
1 tablespoon water
¼ teaspoon dried Italian seasoning

1 (8-ounce) package frozen cooked salad shrimp,
    thawed and drained
    Butter-flavored vegetable cooking spray
1 tablespoon grated Parmesan cheese

1 Roll pizza crust into an 18- x 10-inch rectangle. Cut into 6 (6- x 5- inch) rectangles.

2 Combine tomato paste, water, and Italian seasoning. Spread evenly over rectangles, leaving a ½-inch border.

3 Arrange shrimp evenly over half of each rectangle. Brush edges of rectangles with water. Fold rectangles in half crosswise over shrimp; press edges together with a fork. Place on a large baking sheet coated with cooking spray. Coat tops with cooking spray, and sprinkle evenly with Parmesan cheese. Bake at 400° for 18 minutes or until lightly brown. Yield: 6 servings.

Nutritional content per serving: Calories 182
Fat 2.7g (Sat Fat 0.6g) Carbohydrate 24.8g Fiber 1.0g
Protein 12.8g Cholesterol 74mg Sodium 370mg

INDEX

Over 250 time-saving recipes cross-referenced for easy retrieval *plus* photos for key kitchen organization.

~~~~~~

Ambrosia Parfaits, 99
Appetizers
  Antipasto Kabobs, 50
  Banana-Chocolate Chip Pops, 56
  Black Bean Empanaditas, 53
  Chicken Tostadas, Miniature, 55
  Dips
    Artichoke and Green Chile Dip, 48
    Orange-Poppy Seed Dip, 47
    Pineapple Dip, Creamy, 46
  Fruit Kabobs, Broiled, 51
  Ground Beef and Cheese Snacks, 52
  Honey-Banana Pops, 56
  Mix, Spicy Snack, 49
  Pita Triangles, Toasted, 168
  Potato Skins, Chicken-Chile, 54
Apples
  Cider, Spiked Cranberry-Apple, 39
  Pancakes with Apple Topping,
    Whole Wheat-Apple, 67
  Punch, Apple-Grape, 59
  Rice, Waldorf, 192
  Salad, Chicken, Apple, and Pear, 182
  Salad with Honey-Yogurt Dressing,
    Apple, 164
  Topping, Apple, 67
  Turnovers, Apple-Cinnamon, 101
Applesauce Spice Cupcakes, 82
Apricot-Pear Crisp, 17
Apricot Sauce, Jalapeño 139
Artichoke and Green Chile Dip, 48
Avocados
  Guacamole Dressing, 174

spice drawer

Bacon, Lettuce, and Tomato
    Salad, 180
Bananas
  Foster, Bananas, 25
  Loaf, Whole Wheat-Banana, 72
  Melba, Bananas, 90
  Muffins, Whole Wheat-Banana, 72

Pops, Banana-Chocolate Chip, 56
Pops, Honey-Banana, 56
Pudding, Banana, 105
Beans
  Burritos, Bean, 116
  Chili, Jamaican, 115
  Chili with Tomatillo Salsa,
    White, 223
  Empanaditas, Black Bean, 53
  Green Beans, French-Style, 201
  Green Beans in Tomato Sauce 21
  Lima Beans, German-Style, 202
  Peppers, Bean- and Rice-
    Stuffed, 120
  Pinto
    Casserole, Spanish Beef and
      Rice, 190
    Tostadas, Chili Vegetable, 119
  Pitas, Mediterranean, 226
  Red Beans and Rice, 153
  Red Beans and Rice, Chilled, 191
  Rellenos, Pastry-Wrapped
    Chiles, 118
  Rice and Beans, Caribbean, 22
  Salads
    Black Bean and Rice Salad, 179
    Garbanzo Salad with Guacamole
      Dressing, Spinach-, 174
    Marinated Beans, Zesty, 169
    Three-Bean Salad, Hot, 168
  Soup, Italian Pasta and Bean, 32
  Tacos, Bean and Vegetable Soft, 117
  Wontons with Pepper Cheese Sauce,
    Black Bean and Corn, 114
Beef
  Kabobs, Marinated Beef, 134
  Rolls, Chicken Reuben, 145
  Salad, Beef and Fettuccine, 181
  Steaks
    Flank Steak, Broiled, 133
    Spicy Skillet Steaks, 135
    Tenderloin Steaks, Calypso
      Beef, 42
Beef, Ground
  Bake, Ground Beef and
    Noodle, 26
  Burgers, Triple Treat, 231
  Casserole, Spanish Beef and
    Rice, 190
  Meatballs over Rice, Greek, 132
  Sandwich, Italian Meatball, 232
  Sloppy Joes, 28
  Snacks, Ground Beef and Cheese, 52
  Spicy Joes, 230
  Stew, Harvest, 224

Beverages
  Alcoholic
    Amaretto Velvet Frosty, 33
    Cider, Spiked Cranberry-Apple, 39
    Daiquiris, Raspberry Frozen, 58
    Daiquiris, Strawberry Frozen, 58
    Zippy Red-Eye, 61
  Berry Slush, Very, 60
  Cocoa Mix, Hot, 62
  Cocoa Mix, Minted Hot, 62
  Cocoa Mix, Mocha-, 62
  Milkshake, Creamy Vanilla, 57
  Milkshake, Strawberry, 57
  Milkshake, Tropical, 57
  Orange Frost, Creamy 30
  Orange-Pineapple Slush, 60
  Orange Twist, 39
  Punch, Apple-Grape, 59
  Raspberry Frost, Creamy, 30
  Strawberry Frost, Creamy 30
  Tomato Sipper, Spicy, 61
  Tropical Cooler, 23

pull-out
pantry shelves

Biscuits
  Buttermilk Biscuits, 64
  Red Pepper-Rosemary
    Pinwheels, 65
  Sage and Cheese Biscuits, 33
Blackberry Frozen Yogurt, 91
Blueberries
  Cobbler, Blueberry-Pineapple, 102
  Muffins, Blueberry, 70
  Muffins, Miniature Blueberry, 70
  Soup, Fresh Blueberry, 216
Bran Muffins, Oat, 17
Bran Muffins, Overnight, 71
Breads. *See also* specific types.
  Cinnamon Breadsticks, 66
  Cumin Mini-Loaf, 77
  Garlic Bread, Herbed, 80
  Orange-Glazed Breadsticks, 66

Breads (continued)

Parmesan Breadsticks, 66
Popovers, Triple Herb, 76
Pumpkin Bread with Pineapple
  Spread, Spiced, 79
Strawberry Bread, 78
Toast Triangles, 220
Whole Wheat-Banana Loaf, 72
Broccoli, Oriental, 200
Broccoli-Rice Timbales, 189
Bulgur
Pilaf, Lamb and Spinach, 138
Burritos, Bean, 116
Butterscotch Brownies, 87

Cabbage
Coleslaw, Colorful, 170
Cakes. See also Breads, Cookies.
Carrot-Raisin Snack Cake, 83
Cheesecake Tartlets with Strawberry
  Glaze, 104
Coffee Cake, Moist Cranberry, 85
Coffee Crunch Cake, 84
Cupcakes, Applesauce Spice, 82
Cupcakes, Chocolate, 29
Torte, Frozen Rainbow, 97
Cantaloupe. See Melons.
Carrots
Cake, Carrot-Raisin Snack, 83
Coconut Baby Carrots, 43
Lemon-Dill Carrots, 203
Salad, Tangy Carrot-Jicama, 37
Casseroles
Green Chile-Rice Casserole, 121
Macaroni and Cheese, Baked, 130
Meat
  Beef and Rice Casserole,
    Spanish, 190
  Ground Beef and Noodle Bake, 26
Onions, Cheesy Scalloped, 207
Potatoes, Basil Scalloped, 43
Squash Casserole, Summer, 211
Cauliflower with Cheese Sauce, 204
Cheese
Breads
  Biscuits, Sage and Cheese, 33
  Cornbread, Chile-Cheese, 75
  Parmesan Breadsticks, 66
Fontina and Greens, Spaghetti
  with, 198
Macaroni and Cheese, Baked, 130
Onions, Cheesy Scalloped, 207
Sauces
  Caraway Cheese Sauce, 145
  Cheese Sauce, Cauliflower
    with, 204
  Pepper Cheese Sauce, Black Bean
    and Corn Wontons with, 114
Snacks, Ground Beef and Cheese, 52
Soup, Light Beer-Cheese, 220
Turkey Romano, 151
Vinaigrette, Garlic-Blue Cheese, 186
Chicken
Cajun-Spiced Chicken, 14
Citrus-Ginger Chicken, 146

Greek-Seasoned Chicken with
  Orzo, 147
Herbed Chicken, Crispy, 148
Herbed Chicken with Sour Cream-
  Wine Sauce, 149
Molasses-Sauced Chicken, 18
Pockets, Spicy Chicken, 227
Potato Skins, Chicken-Chile, 54
Rolls, Chicken Reuben, 145
Salads
  Apple, and Pear Salad,
    Chicken, 182
  Fettuccine Salad, Chicken
    and, 181
Sandwiches, Marinated
  Chicken, 228
Smoked Chicken, Pasta, and Sun-
  Dried Tomatoes, 142
Soup, Chunky Chicken-Potato, 222
Stir-Fry, Chicken and Snow Pea, 143
Sweet Curry Chicken, 38
Tomato-Vegetable Sauce,
  Chicken in, 144
Tostadas, Miniature Chicken, 55

recycling
storage areas

Chili
Jamaican Chili, 115
Tostadas, Chili Vegetable, 119
White Chili with Tomatillo Salsa, 223
Chocolate
Beverages
  Cocoa Mix, Mocha-, 62
  Hot Cocoa Mix, 62
  Hot Cocoa Mix, Minted, 62
Brownies, Peanut Butter
  Swirl, 88
Cupcakes, Chocolate, 29
Pops, Banana-Chocolate Chip, 56
Pudding, Double Chocolate, 106
Sauce, Chocolate-Mint, 93
Soufflés with Custard Sauce, Warm
  Chocolate, 108
Sundae, Hot Fudge, 27
Coconut Baby Carrots, 43
Coffee Crunch Cake, 84
Coleslaw, Colorful, 170
Cookies
Brownies, Butterscotch, 87
Brownies, Peanut Butter
  Swirl, 88
Lemon Soufflé Bars, 89
Orange Soufflé Bars, 89
Strawberry-Oat Squares, 86

Corn-Zucchini-Tomato Sauté, 205
Corn Wontons with Pepper Cheese
  Sauce, Black Bean and, 114
Cornbreads
Chile-Cheese Cornbread, 75
Sticks, Buttermilk Corn, 73
Sticks, Mexican Corn, 74
Cornish Hens with Raspberry-Currant
  Glaze, 150
Couscous, Seasoned, 194
Crab, Deviled, 34
Cranberries
Cake, Moist Cranberry
  Coffee, 85
Cider, Spiked Cranberry-Apple, 39
Slush, Very Berry, 60
Cucumber Salad, Minted, 171
Curry
Chicken, Sweet Curry, 38
Dressing, Creamy Curry, 183
Dressing, Curry, 166
Soup, Curried Lentil, 221
Custard with Chocolate-Mint Sauce,
  Frozen Vanilla, 93

Desserts. See also specific types.
Apricot-Pear Crisp, 17
Bananas Foster, 25
Cakes, Lemon-Sauced, 44
Cakes, Lime-Sauced, 44
Frozen
  Bananas Melba, 90
  Blackberry Frozen Yogurt, 91
  Mandarin Phyllo Baskets, 95
  Peanutty Dessert, Frozen, 96
  Raspberry Frozen Yogurt, 92
Fruit Compote, Champagne, 98
Parfaits, Ambrosia, 99
Peaches en Papillote with Raspberry
  Sauce, 37
Sauces
  Brandied Fruit Sauce, 109
  Chocolate-Mint Sauce, 93
  Custard Sauce, Warm Chocolate
    Soufflés with, 108
  Pineapple Sauce, Chunky, 111
  Praline-Pecan Sauce, 110
  Raspberry Sauce, 37
  Strawberry Sauce, Luscious, 112
Peach Trifle, 100

Fettuccine
Salad, Beef and Fettuccine, 181
Salad, Chicken and Fettuccine, 181
Salad, Pork and Fettuccine, 181
Fillings. See Frostings, Fillings, and
  Toppings.
Fish. See also specific types.
Amberjack au Poivre,
  Grilled, 36
Catfish Fillets, Baked, 154
Flounder, Garlic, 155
Grouper Fingers with Lemon-Pepper
  Mayonnaise, 20
Grouper, Spicy Grilled, 156

Orange Roughy, Sesame-
    Baked, 157
Red Snapper, Creole, 158
Sandwich with Onion Relish,
    Fish, 229
Frostings, Fillings, and Toppings
    Apple Topping, 67
    Maple Topping, Creamy, 69
    Raspberry-Currant Glaze, Cornish
        Hens with, 150
    Strawberry Glaze, Cheesecake
        Tartlets with, 104
Fruit. See also specific types.
    Compote, Champagne
        Fruit, 98
    Kabobs, Broiled Fruit, 51
    Milkshake, Tropical, 57
    Parfaits, Ambrosia, 99
    Salads
        Curry Dressing, Fruit Salad
            with, 166
        Hearts of Palm Salad with
            Fruit, 172
        Mexican Fruit Salad, 165
    Sauce, Brandied Fruit, 109

Grape Punch, Apple-, 59

Ham. See also Pork.
    Burgers, Triple Treat, 231
    Kabobs, Mustard-Honey Glazed
        Ham, 141
Honey
    Ham Kabobs, Mustard-Honey
        Glazed, 141
    Pops, Honey-Banana, 56
    Pork Tenderloin, Honey-Sesame
        Grilled, 140
Honeydew. See Melons.
Hors d'Oeuvres. See Appetizers.

Ice Milks and Sherbets
    Orange Frost, Creamy, 30
    Raspberry Frost, Creamy, 30
    Strawberry Frost,
        Creamy, 30
    Sundae, Hot Fudge, 27

Jicama Salad, Tangy Carrot-, 37

swing-out shelves

Kabobs
    Antipasto Kabobs, 50
    Beef Kabobs, Marinated, 134
    Fruit Kabobs, Broiled, 51
    Ham Kabobs, Mustard-Honey
        Glazed, 141
    Shrimp Kabobs, Lime-
        Marinated, 162
Kiwifruit
    Salad, Three-Green, 175

Lamb
    Pilaf, Lamb and Spinach, 138
    Steaks with Jalapeño-Apricot
        Sauce, Lamb, 139
Lemon
    Bars, Lemon Soufflé, 89
    Cakes, Lemon-Sauced, 44
    Mayonnaise, Lemon-Pepper, 20
Lentils and Rice, Sweet-and-
    Tangy, 122
Lentil Soup, Curried, 221
Lime
    Cakes, Lime-Sauced, 44
    Dressing, Lime, 165
    Shrimp Kabobs, Lime-
        Marinated, 162
Linguine, Cracked Pepper, 195
Lobster with Angel Hair Pasta,
    Creamy, 160

Macaroni and Cheese,
    Baked, 130
Mangoes
    Soup, Tropical, 217
Marinades. See Sauces.
Mayonnaise, Lemon-Pepper, 20
Meatballs
    Greek Meatballs over Rice, 132
    Sandwich, Italian Meatball, 232
Melon Salad, Mixed, 167
Muffins
    Blueberry Muffins, 70
    Blueberry Muffins, Miniature, 70
    Bran Muffins, Overnight, 71
    Cumin Muffins, 77
    Oat Bran Muffins, 17
    Whole Wheat-Banana
        Muffins, 72
Mushrooms
    Rice with Mushrooms, Seasoned
        Browned, 41
    Salad, Mushroom-Zucchini, 173
    Soup, Cream of Mushroom, 218
    Vermicelli with Mushrooms and
        Pine Nuts, 128
Mustard
    Dressing, Dijon, 27
    Ham Kabobs, Mustard-Honey
        Glazed, 141
    Tomatoes, Mustard-Glazed
        Broiled, 23

Noodle Bake, Ground Beef and, 26

space-saving glass rack

Oatmeal
    Muffins, Oat Bran, 17
    Squares, Strawberry-Oat, 86
Okra-Tomato-Zucchini Medley, 206
Onions
    Relish, Fish Sandwich with
        Onion, 229
    Rice, Green Onion, 39
    Scalloped Onions, Cheesy, 207
Oranges
    Breadsticks, Orange-Glazed, 66
    Citrus-Ginger Chicken, 146
    Desserts
        Bars, Orange Soufflé, 89
        Mandarin Phyllo Baskets, 95
    Dip, Orange-Poppy Seed, 47
    Sauce, Orange, 146
    Slush, Orange-Pineapple, 60
    Twist, Orange, 39
Orzo, Greek-Seasoned Chicken
    with, 147

Pancakes with Apple Topping, Whole
    Wheat-Apple, 67
Pastas. See also specific types.
    Bow Ties, Spicy, 15
    Dijon Pasta, Tangy, 199
    Italian Pasta and Bean Soup, 32
    Lobster with Angel Hair Pasta,
        Creamy, 160
    New Orleans Pasta, 196
    Penne Pasta with Tomato
        Cream, 24
    Pepper Pasta, Fresh, 129
    Pizzeria Pasta, 197
    Salad, Garden Pasta, 177
    Shrimp with Angel Hair Pasta,
        Creamy, 160
    Smoked Chicken, Pasta, and Sun-
        Dried Tomatoes, 142
    Vermicelli with Mushrooms and Pine
        Nuts, 128
Peaches
    Cobbler, Peach, 103
    en Papillote with Raspberry Sauce,
        Peaches, 37
    Trifle, Peach, 100
Peanut Butter
    Brownies, Peanut Butter
        Swirl, 88
    Dessert, Frozen Peanutty, 96

Peanuts
    Mix, Spicy Snack, 49
Pear Crisp, Apricot-, 17
Pear Salad, Chicken, Apple, and, 182
Peas
    Fancy Peas, 19
    Pie, Shepherd's, 126
    Snow
        Red Pepper, and Pineapple, Snow
            Peas, 208
        Stir-Fry, Chicken and Snow
            Pea, 143
        Stir-Fry, Snow Pea, 41
Pecan Sauce, Praline-, 110

easy-access pantry

Peppers
    Chile
        Casserole, Green Chile-
            Rice, 121
        Cornbread, Chile-Cheese, 75
        Dip, Artichoke and Green
            Chile, 48
        Potato Skins, Chicken-Chile, 54
        Rellenos, Pastry-Wrapped
            Chiles, 118
    Jalapeño-Apricot Sauce, 139
    Lentils and Rice, Sweet-and-
        Tangy, 122
    Pasta, Fresh Pepper, 129
    Red Pepper, and Pineapple, Snow
        Peas, 208
    Red Pepper-Rosemary
        Pinwheels, 65
    Relish, Tricolored Pepper, 154
    Sauce, Black Bean and Corn Wontons
        with Pepper Cheese, 114
    Stuffed Peppers, Bean- and
        Rice-, 120
    Sweet-and-Sour Peppers and
        Tofu, 123
Phyllo
    Baskets, Mandarin Phyllo, 95
    Rellenos, Pastry-Wrapped
        Chiles, 118
    Turnovers, Apple-Cinnamon, 101
Pies and Pastries
    Apple-Cinnamon Turnovers, 101
    Cobblers
        Blueberry-Pineapple
            Cobbler, 102
        Peach Cobbler, 103
    Shepherd's Pie, 126

Yogurt Pie with Raspberry-Graham
    Crust, Frozen, 94
Yogurt Pie with Strawberry-Graham
    Crust, Frozen, 94
Pineapple
    Cobbler, Blueberry-Pineapple, 102
    Dip, Creamy Pineapple, 46
    Sauce, Chunky Pineapple, 111
    Slush, Orange-Pineapple, 60
    Snow Peas, Red Pepper, and
        Pineapple, 208
    Spread, Pineapple, 79
Pizza, Niçoise, 125
Pork. See also Bacon, Ham, Sausage.
    Salad, Grilled Pork and Rice, 16
    Stew, Hearty Pork, 225
    Tenderloin
        Grilled Pork Tenderloin, Honey-
            Sesame, 140
        Salad, Pork and Fettuccine, 181
Potatoes
    Garlic Potatoes, Creamy, 19
    New Potatoes, Browned
        Basil, 209
    Pie, Shepherd's, 126
    Scalloped Potatoes, Basil, 43
    Skins, Chicken-Chile Potato, 54
    Soup, Chunky Chicken-Potato, 222
Potatoes, Sweet
    Sticks, Sweet Potato, 29
Praline-Pecan Sauce, 110
Pretzels
    Mix, Spicy Snack, 49
Puddings. See also Custards.
    Banana Pudding, 105
    Brown Sugar Pudding, 106
    Chocolate Pudding, Double, 106
    Vanilla Pudding, 15
Pumpkin Bread with Pineapple Spread,
    Spiced, 79

Raisin Snack Cake, Carrot-, 83
Raspberries
    Bananas Melba, 90
    Crust, Frozen Yogurt Pie with
        Raspberry-Graham, 94
    Daiquiris, Raspberry Frozen, 58
    Frost, Creamy Raspberry, 30
    Sauce, Raspberry, 37
    Slush, Very Berry, 60
    Yogurt, Raspberry Frozen, 92
Relish
    Onion Relish, Fish Sandwich
        with, 229
    Pepper Relish, Tricolored, 154
Rice
    Beans and Rice, Chilled Red, 191
    Beans and Rice, Red, 153
    Beans, Caribbean Rice and, 22
    Browned Rice with Mushrooms,
        Seasoned, 41
    Casserole, Green Chile-Rice, 121
    Casserole, Spanish Beef and
        Rice, 190
    Confetti Rice, 188
    Green Onion Rice, 39

Lentils and Rice, Sweet-and-
    Tangy, 122
Meatballs over Rice, Greek, 132
Peppers and Tofu, Sweet-and-
    Sour, 123
Peppers, Bean- and Rice-
    Stuffed, 120
Risotto Primavera, Quick, 124
Salad, Black Bean and Rice, 179
Salad, Confetti Rice, 178
Salad, Grilled Pork and Rice, 16
Savory Rice, 21
Spanish Rice, Fiesta, 190
Timbales, Broccoli-Rice, 189
Turmeric Rice, 193
Waldorf Rice, 192
Wild Rice Salad, 35

Salad Dressings
    Burgundy Poppy Seed Dressing, 167
    Buttermilk Dressing, Creamy, 176
    Coleslaw Dressing, Creamy, 184
    Curry Dressing, 166
    Curry Dressing, Creamy, 183
    Dijon Dressing, 27
    French Dressing, Tangy, 180
    Guacamole Dressing, 174
    Honey-Yogurt Dressing, Apple Salad
        with, 164
    Italian Dressing, Creamy, 25
    Lime Dressing, 165
    Vinaigrette, Basil, 186
    Vinaigrette, Garlic-Blue
        Cheese, 186
    Vinaigrette, Versatile, 186
    Yogurt Dressing, Zesty, 185
Salads
    Bacon, Lettuce, and Tomato
        Salad, 180
    Bean
        Black Bean and Rice Salad, 179
        Marinated Beans, Zesty, 169
        Three-Bean Salad, Hot, 168
    Beef and Fettuccine Salad, 181
    Carrot-Jicama Salad, Tangy, 37
    Chicken and Fettuccine Salad, 181
    Chicken, Apple, and Pear Salad, 182
    Coleslaw, Colorful, 170
    Cucumber Salad, Minted, 171
    Fruit
        Apple Salad with Honey-Yogurt
            Dressing, 164
        Curry Dressing, Fruit Salad
            with, 166
        Melon Salad, Mixed, 167
        Mexican Fruit Salad, 165
    Green
        Mixed Green Salad with Dijon
            Dressing, 27
        Three-Green Salad, 175
        Tossed Salad with Creamy
            Buttermilk Dressing, 176
    Hearts of Palm Salad with Fruit, 172
    Mushroom-Zucchini Salad, 173
    Pasta Salad, Garden, 177
    Pork and Fettuccine Salad, 181

Pork and Rice Salad, Grilled, 16
Rice Salad, Confetti, 178
Spinach-Garbanzo Salad with
    Guacamole Dressing, 174
Spinach Salad with Creamy Italian
    Dressing, 25
Turkey Salad for Two, 183
Wild Rice Salad, 35
Sandwiches
    Burgers, Triple Treat, 231
    Chicken Pockets, Spicy, 227
    Chicken Sandwiches,
        Marinated, 228
    Fish Sandwich with Onion
        Relish, 229
    Meatball Sandwich, Italian, 232
    Pitas, Mediterranean, 226
    Shrimp Calzones, 234
    Sloppy Joes, 28
    Spicy Joes, 230
    Turkey Reubens, 233
Sauces. See also Desserts/Sauces.
    Caper Sauce, Veal Steaks with, 137
    Cheese
        Caraway Cheese Sauce, 145
        Cauliflower with Cheese
            Sauce, 204
        Pepper Cheese Sauce, Black Bean
            and Corn Wontons with, 114
    Jalapeño-Apricot Sauce, 139
    Orange Sauce, 146
    Salsa, Tomatillo, 223
    Sour Cream-Wine Sauce, Herbed
        Chicken with, 149
    Tarragon Sauce, Scallops in, 161
    Tomato-Vegetable Sauce,
        Chicken in, 144
Sausage
    Red Beans and Rice, 153
Scallops in Tarragon Sauce, 161
Sherbets. See Ice Milks and Sherbets.
Shrimp
    Calzones, Shrimp, 234
    Creamy Shrimp with Angel Hair
        Pasta, 160
    Kabobs, Lime-Marinated
        Shrimp, 162
Soufflés with Custard Sauce, Warm
    Chocolate, 108
Soups. See also Chili, Stews.
    Beer-Cheese Soup, Light, 220
    Blueberry Soup, Fresh, 216
    Chicken-Potato Soup, Chunky, 222
    Lentil Soup, Curried, 221
    Mushroom Soup, Cream of, 218
    Pasta and Bean Soup, Italian, 32
    Spinach Soup, Creamy, 219
    Tropical Soup, 217
Spaghetti, Fresh Tomato, 127
Spaghetti with Fontina and Greens, 198
Spice
    Creole Seasoning Blend, Spicy, 227
    Cupcakes, Applesauce Spice, 82
Spinach
    Pilaf, Lamb and Spinach, 138
    Salad with Creamy Italian Dressing,
        Spinach, 25

Salad with Guacamole Dressing,
    Spinach-Garbanzo, 174
Soup, Creamy Spinach, 219
Tomatoes, Spinach-Topped, 212
Spread, Pineapple, 79
Squash. See also Zucchini.
    Acorn Squash, Fruit-Glazed, 210
    Casserole, Summer Squash, 211
Stews. See also Chili, Soups.
    Harvest Stew, 224
    Pork Stew, Hearty, 225
Strawberries
    Bread, Strawberry, 78
    Crust, Frozen Yogurt Pie with
        Strawberry-Graham, 94
    Daiquiris, Strawberry
        Frozen, 58
    Glaze, Cheesecake Tartlets with
        Strawberry, 104
    Milkshake, Strawberry, 57
    Mousse, Fresh Strawberry, 107
    Sauce, Luscious Strawberry, 112
    Squares, Strawberry-Oat, 86
    Syrup, Strawberry, 68
Stroganoff, Turkey, 152
Swiss Chard
    Spaghetti with Fontina and
        Greens, 198
Syrup, Strawberry, 68

Tacos, Bean and Vegetable
    Soft, 117
Timbales, Broccoli-Rice, 189
Tofu, Sweet-and-Sour Peppers
    and, 123
Tomatillo Salsa, 223
Tomatoes
    Broiled Tomatoes, Mustard-
        Glazed, 23
    Cream, Penne Pasta with
        Tomato, 24
    Creole Red Snapper, 158
    Medley, Okra-Tomato-Zucchini, 206
    Salad, Bacon, Lettuce, and
        Tomato, 180
    Sauce, Chicken in Tomato-
        Vegetable, 144
    Sauté, Corn-Zucchini-Tomato, 205
    Sipper, Spicy Tomato, 61
    Smoked Chicken, Pasta, and Sun-
        Dried Tomatoes, 142
    Spaghetti, Fresh Tomato, 127
    Spanish Rice, Fiesta, 190
    Spinach-Topped Tomatoes, 212
    Zippy Red-Eye, 61
Tortillas. See also Burritos, Tacos.
    Tostadas, Chili Vegetable, 119
    Tostadas, Miniature Chicken, 55
Tuna Steaks, Sweet-and-Sour, 159
Turkey
    Jalapeño, Turkey, 40
    Reubens, Turkey, 233
    Romano, Turkey, 151
    Salad for Two, Turkey, 183
    Stroganoff, Turkey, 152
Turnips, Savory Creamed, 213

Vanilla
    Custard with Chocolate-Mint Sauce,
        Frozen Vanilla, 93
    Milkshake, Creamy Vanilla, 57
    Pudding, Vanilla, 15
    Sauce, Warm Chocolate Soufflés with
        Vanilla Custard, 108
Veal Cordon Bleu, 136
Veal Steaks with Caper Sauce, 137
Vegetables. See also specific types.
    Kabobs, Antipasto, 50
    Pizza, Niçoise, 125
    Primavera, Quick Risotto, 124
    Sauce, Chicken in Tomato-
        Vegetable, 144
    Stew, Harvest, 224
    Stew, Hearty Pork, 225
    Stir-Fry, Vegetable, 35
    Tacos, Bean and Vegetable
        Soft, 117
    Tostadas, Chili Vegetable, 119
    Zucchini, Vegetable-
        Stuffed, 214

Waffles
    Gingerbread Waffles with Creamy
        Maple Topping, 69
    Strawberry Syrup, Waffles
        with, 68
Watermelon. See Melons.
Wild Rice Salad, 35
Wontons with Pepper Cheese Sauce,
    Black Bean and Corn, 114

Yogurt
    Blackberry Frozen Yogurt, 91
    Dressing, Apple Salad with Honey-
        Yogurt, 164
    Dressing, Zesty Yogurt, 185
    Pie with Raspberry-Graham Crust,
        Frozen Yogurt, 94
    Pie with Strawberry-Graham Crust,
        Frozen Yogurt, 94
    Raspberry Frozen Yogurt, 92

Zucchini
    Medley, Okra-Tomato-Zucchini, 206
    Salad, Mushroom-Zucchini, 173
    Sauté, Corn-Zucchini-Tomato, 205
    Vegetable-Stuffed Zucchini, 214

island work center

ACKNOWLEDGMENTS & CREDITS

Oxmoor House wishes to thank the following merchants and individuals:

Anichini, Tunbridge, VT
Annieglass, Santa Cruz, CA
Archipelago, New York, NY
Barbara Eigen Arts, Jersey City, NJ
Cindy M. Barr, Birmingham, AL
Biot, New York, NY
Bridges Antiques, Birmingham, AL
Bromberg's, Birmingham, AL
Bridgewater/Boston International, Newton, MA
Cassis & Co., New York, NY
Cyclamen Studio, Berkeley, CA
Dande-Lion, Birmingham, AL
Dansk International Designs Ltd., Mount Kisco, NY
Deruta of Italy, New York, NY
Fioriware, Zanesville, OH
Fitz and Floyd, Dallas, TX
Gien, New York, NY
Goldsmith/Corot, Inc., New York, NY
Rebecca Hazuda, Birmingham, AL
The Holly Tree, Birmingham, AL
Howard Humber, Trimm-R. N. Builders,
   Birmingham, AL
Iden Pottery, c/o Edward Russell, Valhalla, NY
Izabel Lam, Long Island City, NY
Los Angeles Pottery, Los Angeles, CA
Maralyn Wilson Gallery, Birmingham, AL
Mesa International, Elkins, NH
Noritake Co., Inc., Secaucus, NJ
N.S. Gustin, Atlanta, GA
Old World Pewter, Gainesville, GA
Pillivuyt, Salinas, CA
Rina Peleg Ceramics, Brooklyn, NY
Sasaki, Secaucus, NJ
Swid Powell, New York, NY
Tom Stoenner, Rhinebeck, NY
Barbara Turpen, Birmingham, AL
Union Street Glass, Oakland, CA
Vietri, Hillsborough, NC
Waring Products, New Hartford, CT

Photography and photo styling by Oxmoor House Staff:

Photographers: Ralph Anderson and Jim Bathie
Photo Stylists: Kay E. Clarke and Virginia R. Cravens

Additional photography:

Cheryl Sales Dalton: pages 8, 235 (right), 237 (right),
   239 (right)
Colleen Duffley: pages 8, 235 (left), 237 (left)
Tina Evans: cover, pages 56, 145, 146, 151
Art Meripol: page 236
Charles Walton IV: page 12

Additional photo styling:

Katie Baker: pages 137, 166, 176
Angie Neskaug Sinclair: pages 74, 222, 228, 229